JESUS *FOR A* NEW GENERATION

Putting the Gospel in the Language of Xers

KEVIN GRAHAM FORD
WITH JIM DENNEY
FOREWORD BY GEORGE GALLUP JR.

InterVarsity Press
Downers Grove, Illinois

InterVarsity Press® is the book-publishing division of InterVarsity Christian Fellowship®, a student movement active on campus at hundreds of universities, colleges and schools of nursing in the United States of America, and a member movement of the International Fellowship of Evangelical Students. For information about local and regional activities, write Public Relations Dept., InterVarsity Christian Fellowship, 6400 Schroeder Rd., P.O. Box 7895, Madison, WI 53707-7895.

All Scripture quotations in this publication, unless otherwise indicated, are from THE MESSAGE. Copyright © 1993. Used by permission of NavPress Publishing Group.

Cover photograph: Michael Goss

ISBN 0-8308-1615-1

Printed in the United States of America ♾

Library of Congress Cataloging-in-Publication Data

Ford, Kevin Graham, 1965-
   Jesus for a new generation: putting the gospel in the language of
Xers/Kevin Graham Ford with Jim Denney; foreword by George Gallup, Jr.
     p.   cm.
   ISBN 0-8308-1615-1 (pbk.: alk. paper)
   1. Church work with young adults.   2. Generation X—Religious
life.   3. Generation X—Conduct of life.   4. Evangelistic work.
   I. Denney, Jim.
   BV4446.F67   1995
   259'.2—dc20   95-38606
                                                CIP

19	18	17	16	15	14	13	12	11	10	9	8	7	6	5	4	3	2	1
11	10	09	08	07	06	05	04	03	02	01	00	99	98	97	96	95		

*To my beautiful wife Carly, who lives out the message
of this book through a life of Christlike compassion
and by leveling the shallow misconceptions of what it really
means to follow Christ. Thanks for loving me,
for encouraging my ideas and for walking with me every step
of the way. And thanks to Edna, our child—
actually she's our cat, but Carly thinks she's our child.
Edna is really not a "she," she's a "he"—
or used to be a "he." You get the picture.*

Foreword

Through careful study and in-depth interviews, Kevin Ford sheds new light on a generation that has been misunderstood and maligned. He does so with keen understanding and sympathy not only because he is a member of this generation and well aware of its agonies, joys and frustrations but also because he is a follower of Jesus Christ and has discovered a way to deal with the pains and uncertainties of life.

This book tells the unchanging story of Jesus Christ in ways that can reach the hearts and minds of this generation, and thus it can help redeem a generation that in many respects has lost its way. The book describes seventeen practical steps that can be taken—steps that are loving and nonjudgmental but nevertheless powerful and compelling.

Ford and Denney write that a profound generational and cultural shift has taken place. It behooves churches (which tend to lag behind the times) and all other organizations and individuals that are concerned about the eternal destiny of young adults to pay full attention to this generation, to seek to understand it and to reach them in their deep needs with the gospel of Jesus Christ.

Ford encourages us to believe that this generation may come to be labeled not the bland, nihilistic, no-name generation but "the Generation of Christ." It is indeed thrilling to think of the lives that could be turned around by a careful reading and application of this book, not to mention the positive effect on society as a whole. To fail to give this generation full attention at its time of profound spiritual need would be to store up problems for all generations in the years to come.

George Gallup Jr.
Chairman
The George H. Gallup International Institute

Acknowledgments

How do I begin to thank all the people who have helped me see this project come to life? This book is the culmination of three years' worth of research, reflection, practice and, finally, writing. More significantly, it is the sum total of insight, advice, correction and encouragement from a diverse group of people. I want to thank God for putting in my heart a burning desire to share his story with a new generation. My prayer is that this book will bring him glory and will do nothing other than help to advance his kingdom.

I want to express my deepest gratitude to Carly for listening to my constant ramblings about these ideas and for supporting me throughout this entire process. I also thank Mom and Dad for their encouragement, input and ideas. I am deeply indebted to Jim Denney for sharpening my ideas, making them flow together, adding his own insights and being a model of godly humility. I am grateful for Jimmy Long, who has been an encourager, a channel of grace, a researcher and the first person to connect the philosophical framework of postmodernism with my generation. I want to express my gratitude to John Zimmerman for starting me down the road of understanding my generation. Also, Rodney Clapp and the staff of InterVarsity Press provided helpful suggestions, for which I am grateful.

The bulk of the research for this book came from a number of people, including George Gallup, Win Manning, Stan Grenz, Dick Peace, Jim Osterhaus, Dieter Zander, Tim Conder, Dan Webster, Dave Grigg, Todd Hahn, Tom Dunkerton, Stewart Ruch, Kris Potts, Rick Richardson, Virginia West, Kim Haley and Scott Wilson. I am indebted to them for grounding this book in reality rather than in the media hype surrounding "Generation X."

Scott and Susie Edlein, our close friends, read the manuscript from a non-Christian perspective and gave me helpful insights into their perspectives on Christians and Christianity. I am grateful to them for providing this important perspective and for even allowing me to write about our friendship in the process.

I want to thank all the people whose testimonies were the basis of the characters in this book's fictional narrative sections. I can't even begin to mention the specific names of my friends who have helped me reflect on the themes and strategies of this book. Finally, I am indebted to the InterVarsity Christian Fellowship staff who have given me specific evangelism strategies and constructive criticism—in particular Doug Schaupp and Una Lucey in California, who went the extra mile for me, and the IVCF staff team in Virginia, who read the manuscript in its early stages.

To God be the glory!

Kevin Ford

• • • • • • • • • • •

README.DOC
(It's, Like, an Introduction, Dude)

Every time you install a new program on your computer, you find one of those README.DOC files on the diskette, right? But do you ever actually read the file? No way!

Well, do us both a favor and check out *this* README file, okay? See, we're doing some different stuff in this book, and I want to make sure you and I are tracking together.

First, you should know that the ideas and insights in this book come from a variety of sources and experiences, including the following:

☐ Focus groups, in which I gathered about a dozen or so people—mostly nonbelievers, mostly in their twenties—to talk openly about their feelings, their issues, their hopes and their view of Christians and Christianity.

☐ An October 1993 consultation on evangelizing Generation X, held in Charlotte, North Carolina, cosponsored by Leighton Ford Ministries and InterVarsity Christian Fellowship. That consultation brought together experts from various fields, including pastoral ministry, youth work, evangelism, psychology, sociology and demographic analysis. Papers were presented, panel discussions were held, and much of the insight that came from that consultation has been distilled into this book.

☐ My experience as an evangelism specialist, first with InterVarsity Christian Fellowship in Virginia and later as a ministry consultant in Colorado to Leighton Ford Ministries.

☐ My everyday experience as a believer who tries to share the Christian hope with the people around me.

I also want to mention a term that is used in this book to refer to people we usually think of as "non-Christian." I prefer to call them *pre-Christian*—not because I believe that every pre-Christian will eventually become a Christian. The sad fact is that most will not.

But changing the words we use often changes the way we think. I'm convinced that if we would think of all the nonbelieving people we meet as *pre-*Christian rather than *non*-Christian, we would be more conscious of how we can be a part of helping those people to find their destiny in Jesus Christ. We have no way of knowing which of the people we are now befriending, witnessing to and praying for will one day commit themselves to Christ—and we have no way of knowing which ones won't. So why not just think of them all as pre-Christians, then do everything we can to love them into the kingdom of God— with the actual work of redemption left up to God?

Finally, I should tell you a story line runs through this book—a fictional story with a cast of fictional characters. But the fact that they're fictional doesn't mean they're not real. These people—Grant, Josie, Barry, Michael, Lindsey, Perry and the rest—have become like real people to me, because in a sense they *are* real people. They're composites of actual people I've talked to, prayed for, made friends with and in some cases introduced to the Lord. Their stories are woven throughout this book to illustrate the ideas and principles in the nonfiction sections of the book.

The first of these people I want you to meet is a woman with a lot of pain stored up inside her. She's typical of so many people in my generation. Her name is Josie.

An Accelerated Culture

It was, like, the ultimate act of

revenge," said Josie, wringing her hands as she talked. We sat at a small sidewalk table in front of La Boulangerie. I had the dregs of a nearly finished café latte in front of me. A raspberry-filled croissant sat in front of her, completely untouched. It was a warm morning in late September, just a few weeks before the fall colors begin to appear. All around us people were strolling and enjoying the sunshine. The mood that clung to Josie as she talked, however, was cold and wintry.

Josie's eyes refused to meet mine. Instead they seemed to focus somewhere in the distant reaches of a painful memory. Her voice, too, sounded distant, as if she had to depersonalize herself in order to talk about her memories. Josie was blond and short-haired, dressed in an old black T shirt, faded jeans with holes in them, and a red plaid flannel shirt tied around her waist. Three earrings adorned each ear, and a tiny nose ring pierced her right nostril. A discreet tattoo—a daisy—graced her bare ankle. The painful memory she recalled was of her brother, Rex.

"He had moved out for a couple years to go to college," Josie reflected. "Then, during my senior year in high school, he moved home again. I never understood why he came back. Rex was kind of sullen and withdrawn, and he and my parents were always arguing. I think he was depressed because life wasn't working out for him. I think he was devastated over having to live at home instead of making it on his own.

"Even when he was in his twenties, Mom would treat Rex like a kid, yelling at him to clean his room, tuck in his shirt or comb his hair. And Daddy used to tell him to go out and make something of himself. Daddy was, like, very aggressive in business, very successful, and he thought Rex was a bum just because he didn't share Daddy's values. That's what he called Rex—'the Bum.' He'd say, 'Josie, go call the Bum to dinner.' Or, 'Hey, you! The Bum! Move your melon! I can't see the TV!'

"You hear people talk about dysfunctional families, and I guess ours was pretty dysfunctional—although at the time I just thought it was normal. Course, there are so many screwed-up families nowadays, I guess 'dysfunctional' is becoming 'normal.' The thing is, my parents were both on him all the time, always making him miserable, you know? Like, no wonder he was so angry and depressed! He was their son. They brought him into the world. Why did they have to treat him like that?

"One day, about three years ago, my mom and I went out to the mall. It was Christmastime, and we were shopping. I remember we were having this big argument all the way home. It was about Rex. She had really been bitching at him that morning about what a slob he was. I tried to tell her that you don't treat someone like that when they're depressed. It just makes them feel worse. She wouldn't listen. She never listened.

"We got home from the mall, and I remember my mother and I carrying our packages into the living room, not talking to each other. She went into the back of the house, and I put my packages down and went into the kitchen to fix a sandwich. I walked past the Christmas tree and wanted to tear it down and stomp on it. I thought, *What a stupid, phony thing to have in our house!* I mean, here we were, four people living under the same roof—four people who couldn't stand each other, yet we were celebrating 'peace on earth, goodwill toward men' just as if it really meant something.

"All of a sudden, I heard this scream. I never heard a scream like that in my life! Not even in a horror flick! At first I just froze. It was my mother screaming, and the scream just went on and on. It was so scary! I was too scared to go see what happened. I just stood there with this half-made sandwich in my hand. Finally my mother came out and her face was all white, and she sat down on the couch and screamed at me, 'Call somebody, Josie! Please call somebody!' So I dialed 911 and gave the phone to Mom. She could just barely talk to the dispatcher.

"I knew something had happened to Rex, but I couldn't go into his room and look. I just sat down and waited for the police to come. I later found out that Rex had taken Daddy's shotgun into his bedroom, sat down on the bed, put the barrel under his chin and pushed down on the trigger with both thumbs. I think he deliberately tried to make as big a mess as possible.

"I moved out that night and went to stay with a friend. I never went back to that house again. I couldn't. And I could never forgive my parents for what they did to Rex. I haven't seen my parents in a long time. I think they're divorced now. They should have gotten a divorce a long time ago.

"I think Rex did it to get even with them. It was a revenge thing—an anger thing more than a depression thing. He left a note, and like, it was a real twist of the knife. He said,

"Mom, sorry I left the room in such a mess. Left my shirt untucked, too. And Dad, remember how you were always telling me to move my melon? Well, I blew my melon away, ha-ha! Have a nice life.

"Your son, The Bum"

My Generation

People who are currently in their teens, twenties and early thirties represent a different generation from generations past. Born in the decades of the 1960s and 1970s, this is an angry generation. An alienated generation. A depressed generation. A generation that is rapidly moving into the future, yet despairing of any hope of even having a future.

It is a generation in crisis. "Youth have always been subject to crises," observes Tim Conder, youth pastor at the Chapel Hill Bible Church in North Carolina. "But it seems that the severity and the frequency of youth crises is increasing in this generation. The kids I work with are becoming more sophisticated at an earlier age, so they are dealing with more sophisticated and complex problems. Their crises are dramatic—and often fatal. In my ministry I continually confront crises of teen depression, preoccupation with death, suicidal impulses and families in which a teen suicide has occurred."

Where did this angry, depressed, discouraged generation come from? Who are these people, and what do they want?

At the outset I want to make it clear that this generation is *my* generation. I was born in 1965, right at the forefront of this generation.

We've been called "Baby Busters"—a play on the "Baby Boomers" tag that was hung on the previous generation. When the post-World War II baby boom went bust in the 1960s (due to increased use of contraception and abortion), the generation that followed the Boomer generation became known as the Busters. Personally, I think "Buster" is a rather ugly-sounding demographic category. So do a lot of other people in my generation. For many, in fact, the term is a reminder that the Baby Busters were the remnants and survivors of a largely unwanted generation. We are the ones who were not aborted or contracepted out of existence. We are the ones who came late to the party, who arrived just as the world was "going bust." Who wants to be reminded of that fact? Who wants to be identified as the generation that "went bust"?

Then there's "Generation X," the tag that was affixed to my age bracket by Douglas Coupland in his 1991 novel *Generation X: Tales for an Accelerated Culture.* Thanks, but no thanks, Doug. Sounds too much like "Brand X." There is a blankness, a lack of identity, even a sense of negation in that big letter X that is disturbing to our self-image.

A couple of Boomer historians figured out that my generation is the thirteenth to be born since the American Constitution, so we've also been dubbed "13th Gen." Bummer. Thirteen is the floor where the elevator never stops. Thirteen is the row of seats that doesn't exist on the airplane. Thirteen is the universal symbol of bad luck. Being called "Thirteeners" makes us feel like we have a bull's-eye painted on our foreheads and a "Kick Me" sign hung on our backsides. No way. We reject that label too.

We've been called "baby bummers," "twenty-nothings," "slackers," "the Repair Generation," "the Marginalized Generation," "the Recovering Generation," "the Surviving Generation" and "the Generation After." We've been defined by demographics, time frames, societal trends, behavior, attitudes and the price of our sneakers. We've been called selfish, lazy, shallow, image-conscious, indifferent, unmotivated, apathetic, nihilistic, disenfranchised, angry and angst-ridden.

Labels are inevitable, I suppose. Yet if there is one characteristic I see again and again in the members of my generation, it is a near-universal disgust with labels! "Don't label us!" is the attitude—no, the demand—I've encountered again and again in my personal witnessing, my interviewing and my research. We all have a sense that when someone else sticks a name or a label on us, that person has assumed a power position over us—and we don't like to be in the "one down" position. So it's not hard to understand why my peers hate to be called "Busters" or "Xers" or "Thirteeners."

Yet in order to have any kind of meaningful discussion about this angry, wary, label-rejecting generation, we have to affix some sort of label, however distasteful. Terms like "Marginalized Generation" and "Recovering Generation" are more accurate and less offensive, but they have not yet come into common usage. So in this book I will (sparingly) use such terms as "Baby Buster" and "Generation X." But please remember, as you read this book, that in order to reach people of my generation with the story of Jesus Christ, we need to move past labels and stereotypes and get down to their social, attitudinal and behavioral realities. We must learn to understand my peers as they truly are, collectively and individually, so that the story of Jesus Christ can intersect with and have an impact on their inner reality.

There are different schools of thought as to what actually constitutes an Xer. The boundaries of this generation are variously described as "those born between 1961 and 1981," or "1965 to 1976," or "1965 to 1981." Mindset and worldview are important, not arbitrary dates. You might have a Boomer who was born in '65 and a Buster who was born in '61. In fact, those transitional years of the early sixties undoubtedly produced a few hybrid varieties of thirtysomethings who show characteristics of both generations.

I should make clear at this point that I don't share all of the attitudes and feelings I'm about to ascribe to my generation. When I say, "We are this," or "We feel that way," I am not necessarily identifying myself with every description or attitude that follows. Rather, I am making generalizations and describing trends. There are probably very few (if any) Baby Busters who fit all of these descriptions in every detail. In fact, I have yet to meet a single person of my generation who neatly fits all the categories I describe in this book.

But *all* of these trends can be found in a general sense throughout various strata of what we can identify as "the Generation X subculture"—the twentysomethings and early-thirtysomethings who have a toehold in the work force, the high-school and college students who are nervously anticipating their entrance into the work force, second- and third-generation ethnic groups, the inner-city gangs and the grunge culture.

What, then, is my generation like? Who are we? How do we feel? What makes us unique? And why are we collectively so full of angst and anger?

As a group, we feel shut out of the American dream, and we blame the generations of our parents and grandparents—the Boomers and the Silent Generation—for leaving us a social, economic and environmental mess to fix (hence "the Repair Generation"). We've grown up in an age of social malaise, urban decline, inept government, corrupt government, ineffective school systems, soaring national debt, increasing environmental concern, racial polarization, high divorce rates and declining values.

We are white and middle-class. But we are also urban and black. We are Hispanic and Asian-American and Native American. And we are, more than any preceding generation, racially colorblind. Interracial relationships—a hot controversy in previous decades—are nothing unusual to my peers.

The people of my generation are likely to offend the sensibilities of preceding generations, because we are generally a less civil lot.

Some of us routinely use foul language to shock, or merely because it's part of the vocabulary. Many of us equate the profane, the outrageous and the tasteless with everything that is "awesome" and "cool."

Like our Woodstock Generation parents, we have little respect for authority, whether at school, at church, on the job, in government or at home. But there is a big difference between us and our parents: whereas the Boomers of the sixties protested and attacked the system with their "Question Authority" and "Up the Establishment" slogans, my generation prefers to ignore or ridicule the system. We are the Beavis and Butthead generation. We don't like the establishment, but we don't like confrontation either. So we tend not to attack authority. It's easier to just avoid it—and, if possible, laugh at it.

"We've Heard It All Before"

From somewhere behind him came the steady *thunketta-thunketta* of the presses in the pressroom. From somewhere in front of him came the laughter and bantering voices of people in the lunchroom at the end of the hall. But as Perry walked through the doorway of the lunchroom, the laughter and voices died down. From a corner table by the Pepsi machine, five people—all in their twenties—looked him up and down, then looked away. An uncomfortable silence settled over the lunchroom.

"Hey, don't stop talking on my account," said Perry.

"Don't worry 'bout it, my man," one of them answered on behalf of the group. "We were just leaving." T.J., the one who spoke, leaned way back in his chair so that it balanced precariously on two legs. He was a lanky, athletic-looking African-American, wearing baggy black pants, a "Nunna Yo Bizness!" T-shirt and an L.A. Raiders cap perched backwards over his head. He brought the chair back on all fours with a clunk and started to get up.

"Hey, take it easy!" said Perry, smiling, raising both hands. "Lunch break's not over till one o'clock. I wanna talk to you guys. We're getting some people together at our place for a party, and I wanted you all to come."

"Is this another one of your church things, Perry?" asked Josie. The question was practically a sneer, but then almost everything Josie said sounded like a sneer. She was blond and short-haired, with makeup as flawless as any supermodel's, and dressed in her favorite color: black. A single tattoo, a daisy, adorned her ankle. Perry didn't know Josie very well—she was hard to get to know—but someone once told him she had been extremely bitter since her brother's suicide three years earlier.

"Well, no," Perry responded hesitantly. "It's not a church thing, exactly. I mean, there'll be some friends there from my church, sure. There'll be a lot of kids—I mean, you know, people your own age. We're gonna have a barbecue and music and games—"

"Like Truth or Dare?" asked Barry. He was lean, sandy-haired and athletic-looking, with a carefully cultivated three-days' growth of beard covering his square jaw. Except for a smug twinkle in his eye, his face and voice were deadpan. Perry never knew if the guy was serious or putting him on.

"What's Truth or Dare?" asked Perry, a question that evoked snickers.

"Never mind, Perry," said Lindsey, the dark-haired woman he always thought of as the "nice girl" of the bunch. She was the one who seemed the most "normal" to Perry among all the weird-dressing, weird-talking twentysomethings who worked in the shipping department of the print shop. "When is this party?"

"Tonight," Perry replied. "Six o'clock. I know it's short notice, but I thought maybe you guys wouldn't have anything planned for a Tuesday night. Maybe—"

"We got other plans, man," T.J. interrupted.

"Oh?"

"Yeah," added Lindsey, almost apologetically. "We were going to take Michael out for pizza tonight. Sort of a farewell thing."

Perry turned to Michael, the only one of the five who hadn't spoken yet. Michael worked in the camera department. He was leaning over the lunch table, his chin resting on his folded arms. "A farewell, you say? Michael, are you leaving us?"

Michael glanced up at Perry, shrugged and looked away.

"Mr. Hooper fired him," said T.J.

"He didn't fire me," Michael rasped. "I'm quitting. Old man Hoop told me he would fire me if I didn't cut off the ponytail and take the gold ring out of my nose. I won't do that for anyone—especially not to keep this lousy job."

Perry winced inwardly at the "old man Hoop" remark. Tom Hooper, the owner of the company and Perry's boss, was forty-five years old—just two years older than Perry himself. He reached out, as if to place one hand on Michael's shoulder, but Michael leaned away from him. Perry pulled his hand back and shoved it in his pocket. "What will you do if you leave here?" he asked.

Michael stared up at Perry, his eyes half-lidded. "The sky's the limit, man," he said with thick sarcasm. "There are all kinds of McJobs out there for a college-educated guy like me. I hear there's more money in tips doin' Pizza Hut deliveries than Donald Trump ever dreamed of. And my last boss said my shelf-stockin' job at the Wal-Mart was always there if I wanted it. Then again, I may just go into business for myself. Like, maybe I'll start a bicycle messenger service. I'm just sorting through my options." He settled his chin back onto his folded arms, end of discussion.

"Yeah, well, I hope everything works out for you, Michael."

Michael shrugged wordlessly.

There was a long, awkward silence—mercifully broken when a bell rang, signaling the end of the lunch hour. "That's it, boys and girls," said Barry, standing and running one hand through his thick brown hair. "Back to work."

As they all filed out of the lunchroom, Perry dug in his pocket for some change and eyed the Pepsi machine dispiritedly. Diet Pepsi or Diet Dew? He shoved the coins into the slot and punched the select button. With a *rattle-thumpity-klunk* sound, a cold can of Diet Pepsi fell into the tray. He took the can and popped the top.

"Perry," said a voice behind him.

Perry turned. It was Lindsey.

"I know you mean well, Perry," she continued, standing in the doorway. "Trying to be a friend to us and stuff. It's not that we don't appreciate the invitation. I can tell you really care—inviting us to your church, giving us those tracts to read, even if they were kind of dorky."

Perry grimaced. "Were they that bad?"

"Yeah, Perry," she replied, tossing her head and grinning. "They were pretty lame. Look, Perry, you have your religion and that's fine for you. But going to church and living by a bunch of rules in a big black book doesn't mean much to people like us."

Perry started to protest. "But that's not what Christianity is—"

"It's okay, Perry. Really. But we've heard it all before, you know? 'God loves you and has a wonderful plan for your life.' Well, I have wonderful plans for my own life. My weekends are the only time I have to go snowboarding or mountain biking. I'm not going to give that up just to hear a bunch of sermons about what a sinner I am."

"Lindsey—"

"Hey, I've gotta get back to work." A smile and a wave, and she was gone.

Just like that.

Perry took a sip of Diet Pepsi, thinking black thoughts. *Why don't I relate to these people? Since when did I end up on the wrong side of the generation gap? It was only yesterday that "Baby Boomer" was synonymous with "youth." What happened to those summers when I lived on the beach and hitchhiked to Grateful Dead concerts? When did I become 'old'?*

Suddenly Perry wasn't thirsty anymore. He poured the rest of the Diet Pepsi into the sink, crumpled the can and trudged back to work.

An Emerging Culture

Many Christians are like Perry—people who want to share their faith, who want to reach out to the people around them, but who don't understand that the new generation is not just a younger version of themselves. My "Baby Buster" peers are not just a new crop of Baby Boomers. They are a new and emerging culture with their own values, their own perception of reality, their own approach to truth and to faith.

When I interviewed James Davison Hunter, author of *Culture Wars*, he offered one reason there is such a cultural difference between Baby Boomers and Baby Busters. Boomers, he said, could be viewed as a separate sociological category because they had so many defining events in their formative history: the JFK, RFK and King assassinations, the Vietnam War, Woodstock and the Watergate scandal. Boomers actually felt themselves to be a part of a generation with a common heritage. People born during the sixties and seventies don't seem to have the same affinity for their generation that the Boomers did. Hunter suggests that my generation may actually be more of an "anticulture" than a culture, and he dismisses the notion that there is an identifiable "Baby Buster generation" with its own outlook and values.

I agree with Hunter to the extent that we need to be careful about making generalizations about my generation. It's important to understand that this entire concept of a single generation with a single mindset is really only a convenient shorthand grouping of a number of complex sociological phenomena. We truly are a diverse age group—diverse in our goals, worldviews, attitudes, politics and spirituality. Yet having acknowledged this diversity, we have to recognize that there are clear trends in the general culture that have strongly shaped and influenced the subculture we have (however reluctantly) dubbed "Generation X." In fact, it may well be that our lack of a collective consciousness is one of the unifying themes of my generation. Following are some of the identifying cultural features that can be observed in Generation X:

As a culture, we are less gender-specific than past generations. Young twentysomething businessmen go to work in three-piece suits, carrying briefcases and wearing earrings and ponytails. Young twentysomething women are competing aggressively for the top careers. They're also playing contact sports and doing their own car and motorcycle repairs.

My generation is an emotional basket case. As a class, our self-esteem is low. The prevalence of body art (tattoos) on both young men and young women suggests a lack of self-respect and self-esteem. To Xers the body is no longer a temple. It is just another bare wall upon which to scrawl our graffiti.

Fear and anger are a large part of our emotional makeup. We are fearful of our increasingly violent society. We are distrustful of big business marketing interests that seek to exploit us and manipulate our buying habits. We are resentful toward older generations and what we see as their economic oppression of us, their racist and homophobic attitudes, their yuppie greed and their rape of the environment. Many of us are bitter and calloused over having been neglected or abused in dysfunctional families. We are confused, sad, angry and clinically depressed.

We are scheduled to death—an entire culture of obsessive-compulsives. It's not uncommon to see teenagers on college and even high-school campuses carrying Day-Timers and driving around with cellular phones in their cars. More students are working these days, but they are also scheduling their leisure time very tightly—a behavioral pattern they have probably acquired from their driven, workaholic Boomer parents. Downtime is diminished, and teenagers spend less time relaxing or even sharing meals with their families. These tendencies produce increasing emotional fragmentation and relational dysfunction—and they make it hard for today's younger generation to be evangelized and mentored by Christian youth workers.

It may seem paradoxical that this generation is obsessed with leisure and yet is scheduled to death. Many Xer characteristics seem contradictory when in fact they are flip sides of the same coin. Overscheduling and workaholism are forms of escapism; so is an obsession with entertainment. Xers hate to be alone with time to reflect. Loneliness scares us more than anything else, so we go flat-out, living life at full throttle, dreading the day we run out of gas.

"Teenagers today have a very short attention span," says Tim Conder. "They live at a frenetic pace. As a result, the art of youth ministry has changed. Many churches and parachurch groups now focus on junior high because the junior highers are available, whereas high schoolers have more to do: jobs, sports and other activities. The only time I have to see high schoolers is when I visit them on their breaks at school."

Whereas Baby Boomers were, on balance, a comparatively serious, contemplative, philosophical generation, Baby Busters tend to be entertainment-conscious, playful, emotional and irreverent. My generation lives in the now and practices a philosophy of "just do it!" There is no core of absolute truth—no "true truth," as Francis Schaeffer used to say. Baby Busters pick and choose whatever philosophies they want to believe in, selecting from a smorgasbord of religions and worldviews that all seem equally valid to them.

There is no such thing as a set of Baby Buster values. My generation demands a modern lifestyle, a dismantling of tired and outmoded rules and structures. And yet at the same time there is a wistful longing for a simpler time (before we were born) when rules and values and family life seemed to make sense—which explains why many of my peers are addicted to reruns of old TV shows like *The Brady Bunch* and

The Dick Van Dyke Show.

For Generation X, the past is forever beyond reach, the present is black and bleak, and the future is a brick wall.

"No Way Out"

The cup of espresso was too hot to sip yet, so Lindsey held it under her nose, inhaling the aroma. I had met Lindsey at the printing company, where she works in shipping. I was picking up some flyers I had gotten printed there, and we got to talking about different things. She asked about my work, and I mentioned the book I was writing. One thing led to another, and I asked if Lindsey would mind being interviewed. "Bring a friend, if you want," I had said. So she had brought her boyfriend, Grant.

Grant leaned back in the booth with his fingers laced behind his head. It was clear that Lindsey and Grant were extremely image-conscious. She was sleekly dressed in an all-black outfit and Doc Marten's shoes. He was athletic-looking and square-jawed, dressed in faded Gap jeans with a gray sweatshirt.

"So," Grant said, "Lindsey says you're, like, writing a book or something?"

"That's right," I said, raising my voice to be heard above the babble in a restaurant. It was finals week, and Starbuck's—a favorite haunt of the university crowd—was packed with students studying together and consuming latte, mocha, espresso, capuccino and ordinary hot coffee by the gallon. I was enjoying a cup of my favorite, Gold Coast Blend. "I'm doing research, gathering quotes and stories. It'll all go into a book about our generation. From the things you tell me today, I'm going to select the most important statements and pass them along to the people who read the book. In effect, when you talk to me you'll be talking to thousands of people who want to understand how our generation thinks."

"Cool!" said Lindsey. "Are you gonna use our names in the book?"

"No. I'll change the names and situations, and I'll put some of your words together with the things other people tell me. That way I won't be invading anyone's privacy. I'll be telling some true stories, but most of the stories in the book will be fictionalized. But even the fictional stories will be true in a very real sense, because there will be real people and real feelings behind those stories."

"Okay," said Lindsey. "So what do you want to know?"

"First," I said, poising my pen over my notepad, "I want to know what you think about Christians, about the Christian faith."

Grant's demeanor was cool and detached, but Lindsey seemed eager to share her views. "I think of myself as a spiritual person," she said, leaning forward and speaking with animation, "but I don't like religion. I think you can be spiritual without being religious, you know?"

"What do you mean by 'religion'?"

"I mean going to church and trying to get everyone else to believe like you do."

"Yeah," Grant added. "That's the thing that always gripes me about these born-againers. Always trying to convert you, man. Why do they do that? You either believe in religion or you don't. It's not like you can prove religion either way. If you want to believe you're going to heaven after you die because some guy was tortured to death on a cross two thousand years ago, hey, that's fine—for you. But I don't have to believe it if I don't want to. Personally I just avoid religion. I don't need it. I don't think about it."

"Yeah," said Lindsey, nodding vigorously. "That's it exactly. I think Christians mean well. Most of them do, anyway. But why can't they just believe what they want to and leave the rest of us alone? Like, there's this guy where I work who's real religious. His name is Perry, and he's an older guy—fortysomething. He's nice, but he's always trying to push his religion on people. He wants the rest of us to believe the way he does. I mean, that's fine for him, but I just think religion is private. You can't prove a religion is true, so why try to convince everyone else? It's your truth, but it's not mine. I don't try to force my truth down your throat, so don't try to impose your truth on me, okay?"

"Well, Lindsey," I said, "you say you believe in spirituality. If you don't like religion, what kind of spirituality do you believe in?"

"To me," she replied, thinking carefully about her answer, "spirituality means being in touch with nature—like mountain biking on a cool fall morning. Spirituality means being in touch with other people, helping others, spending time with your friends. Spirituality can even be working out and getting in closer touch with your body. Most of all, spirituality is about love—about caring for another human being."

As Lindsey spoke, Grant took a pack of cigarettes from his pocket and lit up a smoke—one of those unfiltered, maximum tar, maximum nicotine brands, the kind favored by maximum risk-takers.

"Do you think Christians practice that kind of spirituality?" I asked. "Do you think Christians care about other people, that they are loving?"

Lindsey was about to answer when Grant spoke up. "Born-againers talk about love," he replied, "but they're all full of hate. They blow up abortion clinics and they tell homosexuals they're going to hell. Those born-againers act like they know it all, and they preach at you like you're a piece of garbage. Always telling you how you're going to hell if you don't believe what they believe." Grant's eyes turned hard and defiant. "Does that sound like love to you?"

"No," I said. "It doesn't. But then, many of the Christians I know aren't like that."

"The ones I know are," said Grant.

"I think some Christians are okay," Lindsey interjected. "Perry, for example. Like I said, he means well."

To be candid, this indictment of "well-meaning" Christians made me a little uncomfortable. I wasn't sure how to respond—so I changed the subject. "Tell me, do either of you ever think about the future?"

"What future?" Grant responded. "The afterlife? Or the next ten minutes?"

"Let's say the next ten years."

"I don't think there *is* a future. There aren't any good jobs left. No good houses left. The planet's turning into a sewer, the rain forests are disappearing, the cities are falling apart, nuclear weapons are spreading through the Third World, and if the nukes don't get us, the ozone hole or the next race riot will."

"Now *I'm* getting depressed," said Lindsey.

"It's just reality," Grant replied with a shrug. "I didn't invent it. It is what it is. And there's no way out."

Beneath the Radar

I can trace the origin of this book to a class I took on church planting at Regent College, on the campus of the University of British Columbia. My professor, John Zimmerman, was talking about strategies for reaching Baby Boomers, and I thought, *What is he talking about? I don't relate to any of this stuff!* At that moment, I had a revelation: *I'm not a Baby Boomer.* I didn't know yet what I was (and I'm still not really sure!), but I was certain I wasn't a Boomer. When I approached Zimmerman with my feelings about the course, he was very helpful in guiding me in my early research on Baby Busters.

By this time the Baby Boom generation had been analyzed and studied from every demographic and sociological angle possible—but my generation, the post-Boomer generation, was still beneath the radar, not even a blip on sociologists' scopes. In both secular circles and church growth circles, the Boomers were everywhere, my generation was nowhere.

After graduating from Regent, I accepted a position as an evangelism specialist with InterVarsity Christian Fellowship, an interdenominational campus ministry to college students. My wife, Carly, and I left Vancouver and arrived on the scene with InterVarsity in Virginia. I was immediately surprised to find that IVCF still employed the same evangelistic approaches in the 1990s that it had used in previous decades—*but with ever-decreasing effectiveness.* I went to the Bible and looked at the ways both Jesus and Paul approached their culture and the individuals within it. I saw how the same story took on different shadings and hues depending on whether it was being told to a Samaritan woman beside a well, or to a ruler of the Jews named Nicodemus, or to a crowd of pagan philosophers on Mars Hill in Athens. And I began to wonder if this same story couldn't be reshaped and recontextualized and retold to reach my own generation.

I'm not talking so much about "technique" here. I'm wary of our modern tendency to rely too heavily on techniques and approaches while ignoring the empowering and guiding presence of God's Spirit. But there is a difference between techniques and strategies, between manipulation and contextualization. In order to reach my generation, we have to find ways to

☐ understand my generation

☐ eliminate the barriers to the story of Jesus Christ and

☐ identify and take advantage of existing ports of entry in the culture of my peers so that the story of Jesus Christ can be injected and infused throughout that culture without being cheapened or compromised

The church was late in coming to grips with the culture of the Baby Boomers. Then, in many ways, it overcompensated by compromising with and accommodating itself to the Boomer culture. Will we also be late in understanding the Baby Busters? My goal in this book is to help Christians get up to speed with my generation so that we can meet the challenges of today's generation *today*.

Old approaches and strategies aren't effective anymore. This book will examine the reasons why. It will look at how and why my generation differs from the generation of my parents. It will look at the intellectual forces (such as postmodernism) and the emotional forces (such as dysfunctional families) that have shaped my generation. It will examine this generation from a variety of viewpoints and through a number of lenses: family systems, developmental stages, gender, socioeconomics, media influence, technological influence, philosophical influence and ethnicity. We will examine new ways of telling the story of Jesus Christ (such as narrative evangelism). We will explore and discover within a biblical framework what works, what doesn't work and why.

As you read this book you may wonder, is this generation really all that unique? Aren't the characteristics of Generation X really just markers of a certain stage of development that is common to all generations? Certainly some of the traits seen in my generation are common to a given age bracket—but not all of them. And even where this is the case, we are seeing that these developmental stages are being prolonged, so that rebelliousness and inability to make commitments—common traits of teenagers and early-twentysomethings—are being extended into the early thirties. Some of the traits we see in Generation X may be due to the fact that commitment-shy Xers start families later in life and thus are living out an extended adolescence—but even this developmental factor is a cultural innovation that needs to be acknowledged and understood.

The more closely we study the distinguishing characteristics of my peers, the clearer it becomes that a profound generational and cultural shift has already taken place. Those who wish to reach this generation for Christ—pastors, youth workers, evangelists and ordinary lay Christians with a heart for pre-Christian people—need to understand the meaning of this generational shift in order to be effective.

The gospel story never changes. But the world has changed—radically. And that means that the way we tell the story must also change.

2

The World Through Our RayBans

Tom Hooper sat in his oak-paneled office behind his big oak desk, a huge stylized painting of a Gutenberg printing press at his back. "Perry," he said with a troubled expression, "you know I've tried to run this business as a Christian business. I try to honor God by the excellence of our service and by the way I treat my employees."

"Absolutely," Perry agreed, sitting in one of the plush-upholstered chairs opposite the desk. "I can name at least half a dozen people who have come to know the Lord at least in part because you run this printing company as a distinctly Christian business."

"That's why I wanted to talk to you about a problem I'm having," said Hooper. "I need someone with your spiritual perspective on our business. Perry, since I took this company over from my dad, it's grown from a small six-man print shop to a company that employs eighty people and grosses almost fifty million dollars a year. Despite our size, we've always tried to treat our employees like family."

"I think you do that well."

"I'm not so sure. I just lost a man in the pre-press department—"

"Michael?"

"You heard about him."

"I talked to him the other day," said Perry, recalling his conversation in the lunchroom. "He said he was quitting. He was a camera operator, wasn't he?"

"Right."

"Was he good at his job?"

"Competent enough," Hooper sighed. "A fairly good worker, I guess. I could never get him to come in on weekends when I needed him, but other than that—"

Hooper was interrupted by a knock at his office door. "Come in," he called.

The door opened, and Wade Gardner stuck his head in. He was head of the pre-press department. "Sorry to interrupt," he said. "I was just checking to see if you had a replacement for Michael's job yet. I'm really running short-handed over there."

"Come in and close the door," said Hooper. "I was just talking to Perry about this problem."

"Oh?" said Wade, closing the door and taking the chair next to Perry's. Wade was young (mid to late twenties), bearded, balding and a bit overweight.

"Maybe you two fellas can help me sort this thing out," said Hooper. "Fact is, I don't have a candidate for that job yet."

Wade blinked. "I thought you interviewed—"

"I did, I did!" said Hooper with a trace of annoyance. "I've interviewed a dozen people, and I wouldn't hire any of them. Fact is, I felt like they were interviewing me! Do you know the kinds of questions they asked me? 'Will I be valued as a person?' And 'How much vacation time do I get?' Five of 'em told me, 'I've gotta have my weekends free.' I mean, whatever happened to drive and ambition and wanting to get ahead?"

Perry shrugged. "I guess young adults today aren't as career-obsessed as you and I are."

"Perry's right," said Wade. "Most of my friends are more into personal fulfillment than money. I think I'm the only twentysomething yuppie I know. A lot of people my age just aren't as career-hungry as I am."

"Why is that?" asked Hooper. "I mean, why are people like Michael the way they are? The guy is competent enough at his job, but he wants to put in his forty hours a week and that's it. No extra initiative, no drive, no ambition. I don't think he's lazy, exactly."

"No," said Wade. "Michael's not lazy. He did his job and did it well."

"But he has no respect for authority," Tom Hooper growled, bringing one fist down on his desk. "You should have heard the language he used when he told me he was quitting. And he didn't give me any notice."

Wade shrugged. "He always respected my authority. Michael and I got along great."

"I guess it was just me he didn't respect, then."

"I didn't mean it that way," Wade said apologetically.

"I know," said Hooper.

"Maybe it's an age thing," said Perry. "A generational thing. I'm used to thinking of 'Baby Boomer' as the equivalent of youth and young thinking. But lately whenever I talk to my college-age son, Brennan, I start feeling pretty old and creaky. Brennan and his whole generation seem to have a different outlook than I do—different than I had when I was his age."

"Maybe you're right," said Hooper. "Maybe it is a generational thing. These—what do you call 'em? Baby Busters, isn't it?—we've got a lot of 'em working around here. And if there's one thing I've observed about them as a class—present company excepted, Wade—is that so many of them seem to be cynical, unmotivated and self-centered. They don't seem to care about money or promotions. They complain about how hard it is to find a good job. Then they quit a good job rather than getting a haircut or giving up wearing a silly-looking nose ring. Trying to figure out this generation is like trying to nail Jell-O to a wall! I mean, what do these people want?"

A Polaroid-Filtered Perspective

No one sees the world as it actually is. Everyone perceives reality through the lens of his or her own upbringing, experience and beliefs. It is as if we all see the world through different-colored sunglasses. I may see the world through red lenses, you may be looking through green lenses, and the person next to you may have yellow lenses.

As fallen and fallible human beings wearing tinted shades yet arrogantly claiming to have a corner on the truth, we have good reason to learn some humility. Even those of us who steep ourselves in God's perspective by studying the Bible and spending time in prayer and meditation have to admit that our understanding of God's perception is partial at best, and it is adulterated by our own colored perceptions and experiences.

As we seek to share the story of Jesus Christ with others, we would do well to remember that it is the other person's perspective, not ours, that is the most important to consider. This has always been true. In John 4, Jesus encountered a Samaritan woman at a well. Jesus engaged her in conversation. As he dialogued with her, his focus was not primarily on his message but on her needs, her emotions, her issues, her problems. Jesus encountered a despised and disreputable woman and made her feel valued. He didn't preach at her. In fact, if you look closely at the account of their conversation in John 4, you will find that the woman speaks four times as many words as Jesus does; he spends 80 percent of his time listening and understanding this woman—how she thinks, how she lives and how she feels.

Jesus took time to get inside her worldview and look at life through her pain- and shame-tinted glasses. Then, after he had listened to her he was able to tailor his story to her worldview and her needs: she was thirsty and he was living water.

The lesson for us at the end of the twentieth century is clear: From the first century to the twenty-first, much has changed, but biblical principles remain the same. To evangelize effectively we must move into the other person's worldview and look at life through the other person's lenses. That means we need to listen to this new generation. We need to look at the world through Generation X lenses and see how life is colored by their experiences. Then, and only then, will we have the right and the depth of understanding to show them the rich rainbow colors of God's perspective, as seen through the lens of the Bible.

What, then, is the perceptual lens of Generation X? What colors do Thirteeners see when they look at their world? Answer: they look through a dark, bleak, Polaroid-filtered world of grays. The Thirteeners' worldview is a negative one, colored by three fundamental and overwhelmingly negative assumptions:

1. The world is not user-friendly.
2. The world is not simple.
3. The world has no rules.

Let's take a closer look at each of these assumptions.

Assumption 1: The world is not user-friendly. The Boomer generation idolized the movers and shakers who set out to change the world. My generation doesn't believe it's possible to change the world. We set our sights much lower. Our role models are those who survive. The world, as seen through our dark glasses, is a difficult place. We don't want to conquer the world or control it. We just want to get by.

Whereas Boomers are aggressive corporate animals, setting their sights on that big corner office and the Learjet, my generation has settled for less money, less stress, less competition. We stock shelves or run the checkout at Blockbuster Video. We are scavengers and nomads in the low-wage/low-benefit service economy. We look at the career ladders and conclude, rightly or wrongly, that the bottom rungs have been cut off.

Broad generalizations? Sure they are. But these trends are clearly emerging in sociological studies, and I am seeing more and more of my own friends moving in this direction: downsized hopes, downsized ambitions, downsized lifestyles. Whatever ambitions they do have are largely focused outside corporate America, where they feel the opportunities have largely evaporated.

We reject the system. We disregard society's rules and play by whatever rules it takes to survive. We search for simple things to bring order and enjoyment to life, because we have concluded that the career world is a joke. We hang out with our friends. We party. We engage in fast, action-oriented sports that get us in touch with nature—water sports, snow sports, mountain sports, desert sports.

The Xer attitude toward this user unfriendly world is summed up by Rachelle, age twenty-three: "My dad got a Purple Heart in Vietnam. My mom marched in Washington for the passage of ERA. Theirs was the first generation to grow up with the possibility of nuclear anni-hilation. They both remember the A-bomb drills during the Cuban missile crisis, when they had to get under their desks at school because a Russian missile might be coming down. They grew up under this cloud of nuclear fear, just like I did. But at least they had hope that something could be done about it. They thought they could do something about it. But what kind of hope do we have today? The 'evil empire' may be gone, but now they have nuclear bombs in North Korea and the Middle East and who knows where else. It's just a matter of time before one of them goes off. Maybe all of them."

Assumption 2: The world is not simple. My generation longs for simplicity. We are overloaded with information, decisions and prob-lems. Our response is to withdraw from this complex world. If the career world is a meat-grinder, stay out of it. If politics is too complicated to understand or too bureaucratic to be effective, tune it out. If hassles start to get to you, grab the remote control, turn on the dream machine and go channel surfing. Sure the world is complicated, but there's no use in my expending precious brain cells on it.

A friend of mine was observing teenagers in California. He re-marked that the range of their feelings was limited to only two states. Like a light switch that is either on or off, these teenagers were either "stoked" or "bummed." They had achieved a very uncomplicated emotional range.

Many in my generation take a "no problem" attitude to life. At first glance this may seem to be an expression of optimism. Wrong. The "no problem" approach is actually a result of a passive pessimism that others often interpret as apathy. It is an attitude that says, "I can't win, so why worry?"

To my generation, the problems of the world are too complex for us to solve. In response we shun global strategies, ambitious goals and great causes. We disregard political idealism and massive government programs. We tend to pursue fun, money, security and safety rather than the common good. Those of us who are inclined toward do-goodism will perform our do-gooder acts on a smaller, simpler scale: instead of trying to eliminate homelessness in America, we will feed one homeless person in the park. That is an active solution, a tangible solution, a simple solution.

We look at the world and see that despite all the efforts and ideals and programmed solutions of the previous generation, nothing gets done. Lyndon Johnson declared a "war on poverty" in the sixties; in the nineties it is clear that poverty is winning the war. The race riots in South Central L.A. in 1992 were even more angry and devastating than the Watts riots in 1965. If these problems can't be solved after thirty years of trying, then what hope does our generation have of solving them?

Assumption 3: The world has no rules. My generation has come of age in a world without boundaries. For many of us, our parents set no limits, no rules. Instead of giving us structure and a reason to trust authority, Boomer parents experimented with and redefined the parenting role. They became buddies with us, letting us call them by their first names, revealing to us all their quirks and flaws, letting us grow up without a sense of security, rules and boundaries.

In these three assumptions of the Thirteener worldview—the assumptions that the world (1) is not user-friendly, (2) is not simple and (3) lacks rules and boundaries—we catch a glimpse of what life is like as seen through the dark lenses of a Thirteener's RayBan shades. As a consequence of this worldview, the people of my generation value

☐ simplicity
☐ clear action
☐ tangible results
☐ the bottom line, the net-net
☐ survival through self-sufficiency
☐ a sense of boundaries
☐ friendships and relationships

They deeply distrust

☐ authority (actually, they disregard rather than distrust authority—*distrust* is too active a word)
☐ systems and structures
☐ talk (as a substitute for action)
☐ symbolism (as a substitute for substance)
☐ the Boomers, the generation of their parents—a generation that they believe has failed them

Fighting for Survival in a Nintendo World

Grab a joystick! It's time to play Super Mario Brothers! The object of the game is simple: survive and save the princess. Of course few—very few—manage to actually save the princess and win the game. So for most players of Nintendo's Super Mario Brothers, the only satisfaction in the game comes from making it to the next level, and then the next, until they finally get wiped out.

Along the way the player can acquire coins that provide an extra life—a better chance at survival. Hidden treasures and passageways are the secrets to doing well. A good player constantly experiments, constantly tries new strategies each time he plays. The game rewards boldness and risk-taking and punishes hesitation. The only way to avoid the firepower of your enemy is to be quick, agile and aggressive at the joystick.

Frustration is inevitable. Victory, for those few who achieve it, is hollow. Rescue the princess and what have you got? A high score on a video screen and the most fleeting sense of accomplishment.

Super Mario Brothers is a parable for the real world. The world of Generation X is every bit as hostile and risky as the world of the video game. Follow the rules, live by the old traditions, play it safe—and you die. Take a risk and you may die earlier, but you may also gain an advantage. It's worth a shot, dude. The secret to life is to experiment, to keep jockeying for position, to keep trying new approaches and new strategies. Money is not an end in itself. It's just like the coins in the game: you acquire the stuff along the way, and it ups your chances of survival—and helps you have more fun.

The secret to success is to find new ways to do things. Ignore tradition. Be different. Be yourself. Break the rules. Survive!

How does this Super Mario attitude play out in the real world?

Let's say you just graduated from college, and you approach the job market, diploma in hand. You discover that two companies are hiring people in your field, and you are only allowed to apply to one or the other. The two companies are compared side-by-side at the top of page 41.

Remember, you must submit your résumé to only one company, or you forfeit your opportunity with both companies. Which would you choose? There was a time when most people would choose ABC

ABC Corporation	XYZ Industries
☐ Opening: Entry-level	☐ Opening: Entrepreneurial
☐ Salary: $30,000/year with opportunities for promotion every two years	☐ Salary: $50,000/year minimum with unlimited potential for a highly motivated, entrepreneurial go-getter
☐ Percentage of applicants hired: 75 percent	☐ Percentage of applicants hired: 1 percent

Corporation. Given its 75 percent hiring rate, getting hired at ABC is practically a cinch. Sure, the much greater salary potential at XYZ Industries is attractive, but submitting your résumé there—and simultaneously cutting your throat at ABC Corp.—is like putting your whole future on a single spin of the roulette wheel.

This is not unlike the choice that confronted many Boomers as they entered the career market. But times have changed since those days. There are fewer entry-level jobs, and of those that remain, the pay and opportunities for advancement are reduced. Today a side-by-side comparison of these two career possibilities might look like this.

ABC Corporation	XYZ Industries
☐ Opening: Entry-level	☐ Opening: Entrepreneurial
☐ Salary: $20,000/year with opportunities for promotion every five years	☐ Salary: $50,000/year minimum with unlimited potential for a highly motivated, entrepreneurial go-getter
☐ Percentage of applicants hired: 10 percent	☐ Percentage of applicants hired: 1 percent

The odds have shifted. If you can apply only to one company, that risky entrepreneurial position looks a lot more attractive. The Super Mario in us says, *Take the risk! Playing it safe won't get you anywhere! Only a few people are going to get hired for a so-so job at ABC Corp, so why not apply at XYZ and go for it all?*

That is the world of my generation. We look at the world through our dark lenses and conclude that the only way to win is to buck the system, to bypass tradition, to live dangerously in the hope of getting to the next level, and the next, and the next. Who knows? Maybe we'll even get lucky and rescue the princess . . . *Not!*

"I Don't Have to Understand Them!"

"What they want is real simple," said Wade. "They want to do their job, take home their paycheck and have a life. They don't want their job to be their life. They want life to be their life. I hear it all the time from my friends."

Hooper snorted. "Do your friends whine about how brutal the job market is?"

"Well," said Wade, "I wouldn't call it whining, but—"

"They gripe about how tough it is to get a good job, right?"

"Sure. Yeah."

"Well, from where I'm sitting, Wade, these Baby Busters are in the driver's seat of this economy. The air hasn't gone out of the American dream. There's plenty of opportunity for people who are willing to work hard and be a part of the team. I tell you, I interviewed half a dozen of these 'slackers' today, and if just one ambitious, motivated, enthusiastic go-getter would walk through that door right now, I'd give him a job and kiss him on the mouth to boot!"

Wade spread his hands. "If you'd just try to understand them—"

"I don't have to understand them!" Hooper thundered. "I just have to give them an honest day's pay in exchange for an honest day's work, period."

"Look," said Wade. "I'm not defending my generation. Fact is, I don't agree with a lot of what my generation does and thinks. I guess I was born a generation too late, because I sometimes get as annoyed with the 'slackers' in my generation as you do. But I do understand the way they think, and I believe there are ways to motivate them—if you just take the time to understand them."

"Oh?" Tom Hooper was interested.

"Yeah," Wade replied. "This is the MTV generation with a shorter attention span—so why not find ways to give them shorter, more stimulating projects?"

"Now how do you expect me to do that?" Hooper asked with an edge of irritability. "I'm running a business here, not a daycare. If a client comes in here and wants me to run a hundred thousand annual reports, I can't shorten the run to give my people 'shorter, more stimulating projects,' can I?"

"Okay. Bad idea," said Wade. "But these people like flexibility. So why not offer them flex-time or job-sharing?"

"Another bad idea, Wade," said Hooper. "Too many departments have to interlock schedules with each other. Flex-time and job-sharing would be chaos."

"Well," said Wade, "this is also the Nintendo generation, so why not give them feedback every so often—you know, like a video game score? Let them know once in a while that they're doing a good job. Post the names of the top employees each month, together with their performance ratings."

Hooper considered. "Well . . ."

"And they feel shut out of the system," Wade pressed on, "so why not give them ongoing leadership training and a sense that maybe their jobs can lead somewhere after all? They think no one cares about their families, so why not offer them good, well-supervised on-site child care?"

"He may have something there," added Perry. "Make it a Christian child care center—another way of ministering to your employees and their families."

"Hmmm." Hooper looked up at the ceiling. *A hopeful sign,* thought Wade. *Ol' Hoop is actually giving it some serious thought.*

"The people in my generation like fun," Wade continued. "How about making this place a more fun place to work? I mean, everything doesn't have to be so button-down and serious. Let's put up some corkboards around the office and pin up some cartoons. Let's have employee birthday parties. Some unexpected rewards for a job well done. A company picnic at the lake with some softball or volleyball."

"Those are great ideas," added Perry.

"I don't know," said Hooper. "I just don't know."

The Shaping of the Xer Worldview

Why is the worldview of Generation X so dark and gray? What has happened in the experience of my generation to give us such a negative outlook on our own future and the future of the world?

Prior to beginning work on this book I spent many hours talking to individual students and twentysomething career people. I also gathered a number of focus groups on various university campuses to discuss issues and feelings of the Xer experience. Here's a sampling of some of the comments I heard from Xer friends, interviewees and focus group members:

☐ "All I can imagine about the future is the stuff that won't be there for me. Like I look at the FICA line on my pay stub and I do the math in my head and I think, *Jeez, I'm working a whole month out of every year just to pay for somebody else's Social Security—and Social Security won't even be there when I retire!* I mean, what a rip! How am I supposed to foot the bill for myself and the rest of society too?"

☐ "I am supposed to graduate in May, but that's really scary. I'm already looking at the job market and, like, it's a joke. What's out there for me? I just don't know about the future."

☐ "When I'm at school, I worry about school. When I visit my parents at holidays and spring break, I have to worry about their feelings because they're divorced. I walk on eggshells to make sure I don't slight one side or the other. I mean, I want to be fair to everybody, but I have to learn how to be a friend to myself and give myself some time too."

☐ "This is my last chance. If I'm not successful—like if I get kicked out of college and everything—my whole family would all look down on me."

☐ "I'm not out to conquer the world. I'm just out to make do."

☐ "The system has dumped on me. But I don't want to sit and moan about it. I want to get my life together and say to my parents and the world, 'I did it! I didn't need you to do it! I did it on my own!' "

☐ "What am I looking forward to? That feeling that I survived. It's that feeling you get once you get to the top of the mountain, when you're finally safe, you're physically exhausted, your fingers are torn and bleeding—but you've survived."

A large factor in the shaping of the Baby Buster worldview is a revulsion for—and a reaction against—the Baby Boomer worldview. My generation may not have a clear sense of identity, but one thing we do know is that we are *not* Boomers! My generation does not want to be associated with a generational mindset that we consider to be self-indulgent, materialistic and narcissistic. We reject the warped values of consumption and self-absorption that have seemingly robbed us of a chance at a decent future.

The contrasts and antagonisms between Boomers and Busters are deep and profound. In October 1993 a consultation on evangelizing Generation X was held in Charlotte, North Carolina, cosponsored by Leighton Ford Ministries and InterVarsity Christian Fellowship. During that consultation one of the participants, Richard Peace, a professor at Fuller Theological Seminary, drew a stark picture of the differences between the two generations.

"Baby Boomers," said Peace, "are aggressive go-getters who strive to change the world. In the sixties Boomers sought to turn the institutional structure upside down. In the seventies they redefined the structures of relationships. In the eighties they led the way in conspicuous consumption. In the nineties they are busy taking over the spiritual establishment.

"By contrast, the Busters work hard at being low-key and nonaggressive. They tend not to be pushy, preferring to keep things to themselves. 'Whatever . . .' could be their credo. They find it difficult to make decisions, much less commitments. While Boomers like to 'think big,' Busters like to 'think small' and are content with having a comfortable, self-contained world populated by a few good friends.

"Boomers were willing to work long hours to achieve their goals. After the anti-authority sixties they settled down and worked their way up the corporate ladder. They have come to see work as an end in itself.

"By contrast, Busters tend to view their jobs as a means to an end. They take jobs so that they can do important things like earn the money to travel or buy electronic equipment. Boomer employers find Buster employees mystifying at best, aggravating at worst. To them, Busters lack what Boomers see as a normal work ethic. In turn, Busters resent the fact that Boomers got all the good jobs merely by virtue of an earlier birth date, and they refuse to get slotted into McJobs just to make Boomer bosses wealthy.

"According to Busters, Boomers messed up relationships in a major way. In striving to redefine relationships, Boomers shattered the so-called traditional family. They promoted promiscuity, which in turn sparked an epidemic of sexually transmitted diseases—herpes, chlamydia and AIDS. They divorced each other at a headlong, reckless pace. They delayed childbearing and aborted unborn children in record numbers. Busters are still reeling from all this. They see themselves as the victims of the so-called relational revolution. They are the latchkey kids who never had a childhood. As a result, they place a high value on relationships. Boomers network with lots of people; Busters spend a lot of time with a few people. However, Busters lack effective models for relationships, so they are slowly and painfully learning new ways of relating.

"Busters feel that Boomers have snatched all the good jobs and all the good homes but lost their souls in the process. A Buster will tell you that Boomers have *things;* Busters have *integrity.* Boomers traveled the world to get stoned; Busters travel the world to help others.

"Boomers grew up in an atmosphere of great hope. The economy was growing, and even though the world was full of problems, Boomers believed they could solve them. Busters have no such hope. They have grown up in suspense, wondering if the world would be blown up before they reached adulthood. They assume they will never own a home. They wonder if they will ever have a good job. They give every appearance of an entire generation that is clinically depressed."

In the late sixties demographers told us the smaller numbers of our generation would be to our advantage. College tuition and housing would drop, and salaries for entry-level positions would increase. The demographers were wrong.

In *13th Gen: Abort, Retry, Ignore, Fail?* (New York: Random House, 1993), William Strauss and Neil Howe draw some comparisons between the world of Generation X and the world previous generations faced. Some examples: During the Great Depression, household income fell by 25 percent. Between 1973 and 1990 the real median income of families under the age of thirty has dropped 16 percent, according to the U.S. Bureau of the Census. In that same period, home ownership rates have dropped 8 percent for those under the age of twenty-five, according to the Joint Center for Housing Studies of Harvard University. The cost of an Ivy League education has risen from $15,000 in the sixties to over $100,000 today. Fortune 500 companies reached an apex for entry-level jobs in 1979, right before we first hit the work force, then started a steady decline. Looking at these factors, my generation has concluded that *this* is our Great Depression. A 16 percent drop in our standard of living may not mean standing in breadlines, but it is withering to the spirit—and it has driven many of us to move back in with Mom and Dad.

While prior generations were screwing up the economy, they were also gumming up the world. My generation worries that we may have sacrificed our planet's ozone layer on the altar of BMWs, aerosol deodorants and air conditioners. Whereas our Boomer parents used to listen to the morning weather report to see if they needed to carry an umbrella, we listen to find out if it's safe to breathe and if we need to put on our Sunblock 500.

We are, as a generation, bitter toward our parents for divorcing at a rate two or three times higher than our grandparents. They didn't consider how we would feel when divorce tore our entire world apart. They didn't think about how kids tend to internalize and take on the blame and shame for their parents' problems. *Kids are resilient,* they thought. *They'll get over it.* Yeah, right.

We are also, as a generation, bitter about being unwanted, neglected, aborted and resented by our parents. The children of my generation knew how their parents viewed them: as a burden. In the way. Little monsters. My generation hasn't forgotten the movies that appeared during our childhood: *Rosemary's Baby, Carrie, The Exorcist, The Omen, It's Alive, Children of the Corn*—movies about children who were demon-possessed, monstrous, evil, feared and hated. Hollywood simply checked the pulse of society and reflected the Boomer attitude: children were not wanted.

We are angry with the leaders who have let us down. A 1987 *Time* magazine editorial on the ethics of a formative era in the life of Generation X noted: "While the Reagan Administration's missteps may not have been as flagrant as the Teapot Dome scandal or as pernicious as Watergate, they seem more general, more pervasive and somehow more ingrained than those of any previous generation." I remember well the tale of Gary Hart and Donna Rice and their trip to Bimini aboard the aptly named pleasure boat *Monkey Business.* I remember the plagiarism scandal that doomed the presidential hopes of Joseph Biden.

More recently, my generation "rocked the vote" and invested high hopes in a couple of Boomers named Bill and Hillary Clinton, who seemed aligned with us in their attacks on the greed and excesses of the eighties. But our hopes evaporated as revelations of Whitewater and the 10,000 percent return on Hilary's cattle futures investments made their anti-eighties rhetoric seem hollow and hypocritical. The Clintons, we discovered, aren't like us at all. They're just a couple of typical Boomers.

Business leaders have not been great shining examples either. We wonder who got all that money that disappeared in the savings and loan scandals. We remember the lifestyle excesses of Donald Trump and the ethical lapses of Michael Milken, Ivan Boesky and John Z. DeLorean.

Mention the words *evangelism* and *religion* to a typical Xer, and he or she will quickly word-associate a whole laundry list of negative images: Jim Bakker going to prison. Jimmy Swaggart caught with a prostitute—twice. Robert Tilton on *60 Minutes*. Oral Roberts threatening to die if the pledges didn't start rolling in. Ask pre-Christian Xers what it means to be a Christian, and they will probably answer, "a hypocrite," or "someone who's intolerant," or "someone from the religious right." Don't expect to hear "someone who authentically loves people and actively lives out a relationship with Jesus Christ." One cultural barrier that divides pre-Christian Xers from the story of Jesus Christ is the "bad Christian" stereotype—a stereotype that is all too often true.

Again, as in the previous chapter, I should make it clear that when I say "We feel this way or that way," I'm not saying I share all of the attitudes and feelings I am describing. These generalizations do not apply to each individual. However, it is fair to say that there is a general feeling in my generation that our political leaders have failed us, that our religious leaders are a joke and that our Baby Boomer parents have abused or abandoned us. Is it any wonder, then, that my generation has no respect for authority?

Thirteeners are indifferent and distrustful toward societal structures that have let them down, betrayed them or exploited them: the business world, the political structure and organized religion. "What have these institutions ever done for me besides screw things up?" they ask. So they feel no connection, no loyalty, no responsibility toward the outside world, which they view as hostile and rejecting.

The only world my generation feels any allegiance to or affection for is the closer, more intimate world of our friends. We desire friends who will be loyal to us. At the same time we're afraid of commitment. We're afraid of vulnerability. We want to communicate but don't know how. So we surround ourselves with other people just like us.

And we're all lonely together.

Can Boomers Ever "Get It"?

Wade spread his hands. "We could make a lot of adjustments to keep Baby Buster employees happy," he said.

Tom Hooper leaned forward intently. "Such as?"

"Such as not hovering over them. They don't like being watched and having their work scrutinized. And they don't like older people criticizing them and labeling them. They don't like being called 'slackers' just because they're not as driven as their workaholic bosses. They don't like hearing that their generation is inferior to the older generations. They don't like having their tastes and styles ridiculed. They don't like being told they have to conform."

Hooper frowned. "Did I do all that to Michael?"

"Well, I didn't mean to imply—" Wade began.

"Yes, you did," said Hooper. "And you're a hundred percent right." He sighed and turned to the other man. "Perry, you remember what I said about wanting to use my business as a Christian witness? Well, I blew it with Michael. I see that now. I'd like a chance to reach him, and maybe it's not too late."

"What do you have in mind?" asked Wade.

"I'm going to call Michael and invite him back. I'll tell him he can keep his nose ring and ponytail. I'll tell him it's a new policy—a looser dress code. One of several new policies I'm going to implement around here."

Perry raised his eyebrows. "Oh?"

"Yeah," said Hooper, flashing a grin in Wade's direction as he reached up and loosened the knot of his tie. "I've been thinking that we don't have enough fun around this office. Maybe I can put up some cartoons around the office, have some unexpected rewards for good work, start an annual company picnic and—what was that other idea I had?"

Wade chuckled. "Employee birthday parties?"

"Bingo!" said Tom Hooper. "Wade, I'm giving you a new title. Director of Corporate Fun. I'm putting you in charge of implementing all these new ideas. It's a big responsibility. Hope you can handle it."

Wade grinned. "I'll try, sir." He got up from his chair and turned to leave.

"But that's not all!" said Hooper. "I'm going to expect something in return for being such a nice guy. I want to see all these changes producing something for the company. I want to see higher morale translated into higher productivity and performance. These changes don't mean we're slacking off."

"I think you'll see," said Wade, "that a happier crew gets more work done."

"Fine, then," said Hooper. "Go to it."

Perry smiled and thought to himself, *Maybe we're beginning to understand. Perhaps there's hope that a couple of graying Boomers can "get it" after all.*

Straight Up & Plugged In

CompuNet Information Service
21:01 EST Wednesday 20-Dec-95
(Executive Option)
Last access: 22:15 19-Dec-95

Welcome to The Religion Forum

#: 184008 / SPIRITUALITY
19-Dec-95 22:18:36
Sub: Holy Hannah!
Frm: Barry Noonan 56557,3301
To: All

Hi, y'all!
    Say, I've got a problem I've never had before . . .

I'm getting the weirdest e-mail you ever heard of! It comes from a lady who goes by the name of Hannah, and she says she saw my message in the Religion Forum where I described myself as an agnostic. She proceeded to tell me (IN GREAT BIG SCREAMING CAPITAL LETTERS WITH LOTS OF EXCLAMS LIKE THIS!!!!!) that I'm going to hell unless I repent of my sins and get washed in the blood of the lamb!

But that's not the half of it. She sent me not one but *seven* messages totalling over 200 single-spaced pages of print-out, including the complete text of several "how to be born again" tracts, and the first five chapters of the Gospel of John in the King James Version!

I use an automated interface to get my e-mail messages—it normally takes about two minutes for the computer to log on, scoop up my messages, and log off. Last night I had my computer log on, then went off to the kitchen to fix a cup of coffee. Imagine my shock when I came back twenty minutes later and my computer was still connected to the Net! That crazy religious wacko cost me at least ten bucks in connect charges!

Anybody out there have any ideas how to fight this kind of compu-religious terrorism?

Thanks in advance . . .

Barry

There are two replies.

#: 184054 / SPIRITUALITY
19-Dec-95 22:54:02
Sub: Holy Hannah!
Frm: Witch Hazel 56001,0003
To: Barry Noonan 56557,3301

Barry, this lady is hassling everyone in this forum, and over on the New Age Forum, too. She nailed me with the same stack of Xian propaganda and, sure enuf, she burned up about ten bucks of my connect time, too! I suggest you complain to CompuNet via Feedback. They'll cut off her account number if enough people raise a stink.

Blest be!

Haze

#: 184054 / SPIRITUALITY
19-Dec-95 23:30:59
Sub: Holy Hannah!
Frm: Jordy M. 55357,3225
To: Barry Noonan 56557,3301

Hi, Barry!

Welcome to the club. Holy Hannah got me, too.

Like you, I was informed in no uncertain terms that I am consigned to eternal perdition for having the ill manners to disagree with her mythology.

I strenuously object to being forced to pay exorbitant connect charges for the privilege of being told what a damned (*literally*) fool I am. I figure people can believe any kind of foolishness they want, but what right do they have to stuff their theology down my modem?!

All of the most obnoxious, intolerant people I've ever met have been born-againers. I believe if Jesus does ever come back again like the Fundies keep threatening, it won't be to send all us sinners to hell. It'll be to wipe out all the Christians! What an embarrassment they must be to God! I mean, if Jesus had known 2,000 years ago what kind of idiots, morons, and slobbering fanatics his teachings would produce, he would have called the whole thing off right then and there. He's gotta be thinking, "I got nailed to a cross for *this*???"

Good luck with your problem. Lemme know how it turns out.

Cheers!

JM

Straight Up

Thirteeners are the computer generation. We are plugged in and on-line. We communicate by e-mail and fax. We produce videos. We use desktop publishing.

The language we communicate in is blunt and functional. We are not interested in the romance of words. Our generation has not produced poets of protest as the sixties did. Our communicating style is linked to our "bottom line," "net-net," "results-oriented" worldview. We like our communication honest, open and straight up. We are not interested in language for language's sake, but in what language accomplishes in helping us survive.

Thirteener communication tends toward minimalism. Thirteener writers use a blunt, simple style, reflecting our bottom-line approach. Our prose is spare. Our humor is shaded with irony. I remember being told by my high-school English teacher that I was too concise. She said I needed to spend more time in development and description. But development and description take too long.

Enough said.

A Christian Reply
CompuNet Information Service
07:07 EST Thursday 21-Dec-95
(Executive Option)
Last access: 21:01 20-Dec-95

Welcome to The Religion Forum

\#: 184400 / SPIRITUALITY
21-Dec-95 06:05:15
Sub: Holy Hannah!
Frm: Kristin McCabe 56990,1010
To: Barry Noonan 56557,3301

Dear Barry, Hazel, and Jordy:

I saw your notes about "Holy Hannah" and just had to respond.

I've met people like Hannah before. In my experience, they're a minority phenomenon, and certainly not representative of most Christians. I hope you can forgive the excesses of "Holy Hannah" and people like her and that you can keep an open mind toward Christians and toward Jesus Christ himself.

As I look at the life of Jesus and the way he related to people I don't see a single instance where he ever stuffed his message down another person's throat. With people like Nicodemus or the woman at the well in Samaria, he was always courteous and gentle, never pushy or abrasive. I hope someday Hannah will see that.

I'm really thankful that we have a place like this Religion Forum on CompuNet where people of different faiths from all over the world can talk together about their beliefs. IMHO, if Jesus was walking the world today he'd use some of the innovative ways of communicating we have nowadays. I think he might even get a CompuNet account and interact on these forums. What do you think?

I'd invite anyone who's interested to respond and open a dialogue, either by posting a reply to this forum or by private e-mail.

Kris

Plugged In

Most of our entertainment—and a large part of our cultural influence—comes from music and movies. According to *13th Gen*, the average Thirteener watches eighty-nine movies per year (1.7 per week), mainly on video. We watch, on average, three hours of TV per day, and 38 percent of us watch MTV in any given week. We play "king of the remote," zapping commercials and switching programs at the first trace of boredom. MTV has learned how to turn our short attention span to its advantage. MTV videos average one edit every three seconds; edits in MTV commercials are even faster and more frequent.

One of the problems caused by our media saturation is that this constant bombardment by entertainment, music and noise leaves us little time for reflection. We don't like to spend time thinking and reflecting, because most of the things we have to think about are unpleasant—and even scary. Noise drives out unhappy thoughts, but it also smothers productive thought.

Time for reflection is a key component of effective evangelism. Xers need time to reflect on their lives, on their problems and on their pain in order to see their need of Jesus Christ. They need time to reflect on the story of Jesus Christ in order to see that he is the answer to their need. Xers who cannot (or will not) take time for reflection are difficult to bring to a point of trust and commitment.

Paradoxically, our preoccupation with the media comes in part from a longing for family and human connection. The TV shows we grew up with provided a sense of family belonging that our real families often failed to provide. Programs like *The Brady Bunch, The Waltons* and *Little House on the Prairie* helped us get through our lives and gave us something to believe in. Our parents were divorcing and our worlds were coming unglued, but TV showed us families where parents were wise and nurturing and where kids were valued. While Mom and Dad were out working or finding themselves, or in court suing each other for our custody and support payments, TV became our surrogate parent.

Our love of television reflects our longing for community and our desire for simplicity. Reruns of old shows or new shows that present nontraditional familylike groups *(Seinfeld, Friends, Star Trek: Voyager)* provide us with surrogate video families, a simple fantasy world, simple thirty- or sixty-minute solutions to problems and straight-up ways of relating to each other. Even so, many of us who grew up with only three channels on the dial are finding that even entertainment—with one hundred-plus channel capacity on cable and satellite systems— is becoming confusingly complex.

Our choice of music is also simple and straight-up. Xer music reflects the functionalism of today's recycling mentality. Instead of inventing new musical forms, we put retreads on the old ones. In fact, recycled "classic rock"—the music of the late sixties and early seventies—is making a comeback and is almost as familiar to Thirteeners as it was to Boomers. But Thirteeners listen to Boomer rock for totally different reasons than the Boomers themselves did. To Boomers a song like "We Won't Be Fooled Again" by The Who is an anthem of revolution and social idealism about changing society and reshaping the world. But Xers have no Boomer-sized delusions of grandeur and aren't out to "rock the world." So to my generation that song is just a hard-driving, high-energy beat with nostalgic lyrics from some forgotten age before we were born.

The new and original music produced by and for my generation reflects the Thirteener worldview. We favor alternative sounds and alternative messages. Some of today's most popular bands—R.E.M., Stone Temple Pilots, Pearl Jam and The Spin Doctors—began as alternative bands. Now, however, they are big-label bands with large mainstream followings. Alternative bands, in the truest sense, are regional bands that are unknown nationally. In order to be "alternative" a band must appear on an independent label, not a major label. Once a band emerges on the national stage (as when Kurt Cobain and Nirvana got their own MTV "Unplugged" special), it ceases to be "alternative."

Though Seattle is the mecca of the grunge subculture, true alternative culture is regional, not national. New alternative subcultures are arising all around the country, in places like Chapel Hill, North Carolina; Austin, Texas; and Portland, Oregon. *Grunge* is already beginning to lose favor as a label. (We detest labels, remember?)

The twentysomething culture comes from a background of rejection. Xers choose alternative music, an alternative lifestyle and an alternative culture because they feel rejected by the mainstream. They feel abandoned by parents. They are on the fringe of society. So they have connected with a musical form whose lyrics deal with questions of rejection and identity and whose music takes risks, just as they themselves take risks in order to survive.

Alternative music tries new approaches and styles, and alternative radio stations take format risks in order to appeal to the alternative mindset. For example, radio KROQ in southern California interrupts its music format every day for a two-hour call-in show called *Loveline.* The show has become enormously popular, giving listeners in the alternative subculture a place to vent their feelings about life, sex, drugs, family and relationships. It would be surprising if a mainstream rock station dared to take such a programming risk.

The most original music form of my generation is the beat of the urban jungle—rap music. In fact, rap may well be the ultimate expression of the rage and despair of Generation X, which would explain why it has been so enthusiastically embraced and reinterpreted by young whites—both New York hip-hop ("white rap") and black urban rap. Whereas Boomers listened to Martin Luther King's dream of a better future, Busters feel the dream has become a nightmare. They reject the dreams of past futures. Instead of King or his protégé Jessie Jackson, today's African-American Xers applaud voices like these:

I want what's good for me and my people first. And if my survival means your total destruction, then so be it. You built this wicked system. They say two wrongs don't make it right, but it damn sure makes it even. (Sister Souljah, "The Hate That Hate Produced")

I got a twelve-gauge sawed off.
I got my headlights turned off.

I'm 'bout to bust some shots off.
I'm 'bout to dust some cops off. (Ice-T, "Cop Killer")

Rap is angry. Rap is alienated. Rap is blunt as a hammer and as hot as smokin' gunmetal. The language of the streets is like rap itself: rhythmic, functional and straight up. And it's all about survival.

Take an hour; tune in to Black Entertainment Television and see the face of contemporary urban rage. Sure, you'll see a lot of rap that's cool or funky or just plain outrageous. But you'll also see flames and fists clenched and bodies writhing in a half-dance, half-death sequence on Rage Avenue in "Afro Puffs" by Lady of Rage and Snoop Doggie Dog. You'll see nonstop images of hate, rage and frustration set against a mind-grinding chant of "Crush! Kill! Destroy! Stress!" in Organized Konfusion's white-hot hip-hop video "Stress." Rap music and rap video are lurid, low-down, aggressively sexual and violent, and unabashedly antisocial.

Before we jump to condemn rap music, however, we need to understand what these art forms are telling us about this subculture— its pain, its anger, its needs and its values. The black experience is about surviving four hundred years of oppression. Having developed a survival mentality of their own, Xers feel a connection and affinity with African-American culture. White, black, Native American, Asian-American—Xers of every ethnic stripe are fused together in a struggle to survive in an increasingly hostile and user-unfriendly world. The functionalism and simplicity of our language and our music reflect our survival mentality.

The Steam Room

T.J., Josie and Barry sat around a table in the steam room with dewy-cold long-neck bottles of beer in front of them. While Josie and Barry talked, T.J.'s hands drummed the table to the funky beat of Puck and Natty's "Just Wanna Be Your Friend" on the pay-CD player. It was Thursday evening, about 5:15, and the bar was just beginning to fill with the quitting-time crowd.

"You mean you've got a Mac but you don't have a modem?" Barry asked Josie incredulously. "That's like having a brand-new Nissan Maxima without any wheels! It looks pretty, but you can't go anywhere! Josie, if you want to get on the information superhighway, you've gotta have a modem. I'll help you pick one out, and we'll get you on CompuNet and Internet, and you'll be linked to people and information all around the world."

Josie hesitated. "But isn't it expensive to—"

She was interrupted by Lindsey, who had just appeared at the door of the bar. "Hey you guys," Lindsey called out. "Did you hear the news?"

"What news?" asked T.J.

"Michael's coming back to work tomorrow!"

"No way!" said T.J. "Who says?"

"Perry," Lindsey replied, sitting down at the table. "He told me as I was going out the door. He said Hoop offered Michael his job back, and Michael said yes."

Barry threw his hands up. "You mean we threw him a kick-out party for nothing?"

Josie punched him in the arm.

The Cybergeneration

As a generation, we have lost our social and relational center. We have traded relationships for entertainment. We are media-saturated. We are on-line. We occupy cyberspace. The distinction between reality and virtual reality has been lost.

Our media absorption has changed the way we look at the world. By age sixteen, the typical Xer has witnessed thirty-three thousand murders on TV and in the movies. All of those repetitive images of violence have had their cumulative effect, filling us with fear, teaching us that the world is a hostile, dangerous place.

We are plugged into our music. Continually. Obsessively. We carry our boom boxes and Walkmans wherever we go. Our radios are strictly for FM. (What is that AM band for, anyway?) Boomers may want a corner office, a bigger house, a second or third car in the driveway; we want our MTV. As Lisa, a student in one of my university focus groups, told me, "Music is my life. I surround myself with music. Whatever I'm doing goes better if there's music playing."

We Xers have a love-hate relationship with our entertainment media. We love it because, above all else, we want to be entertained. But we don't trust it. We don't rely on what we hear on the news. We are wary of the products big business tries to pitch at us. We want to be cool, but we are suspicious of any advertising that says, "Buy this and you'll be cool."

Because we are easily bored, we view everything in life as potential entertainment. And we sometimes mistake entertainment for real life, and real life for entertainment. The pervasiveness of entertainment media sometimes confuses our sensibilities. We get confused because we believe that (1) everything is image and image is everything and (2) the medium is the message.

Everything Is Image, Image Is Everything

Boomers thinks in terms of issues and agendas. My generation thinks in terms of personality and is impressed by image.

I don't know if candidate Bill Clinton understood this fact in 1992, but it's clear that his handlers did. And many of Clinton's top handlers (such as George Stephanopoulos and Mandy Grunwald) were brainy, savvy Xers. The Clinton campaign grasped the fact that Generation X was a much-underestimated reservoir of potential votes and that their candidate had something to offer those potential voters that the Bush campaign didn't have: a youthful image. That is why Bill Clinton wore cool shades and played a wailing sax on *Arsenio*. And that's why Clinton did interviews not only on *60 Minutes* and *Meet the Press* but on MTV as well. The Clintoneers understood that everything is image and image is everything, especially if you are trying to reach Generation X.

My generation is so inundated with information that we don't know what truth is anymore. We suffer from information overload. We see the political ads on TV and we are confused. We will vote for the one who projects the most trustworthy or caring image, or the one with whom we most identify. We vote out of feelings, not convictions. We don't know who's lying and who's telling the truth. So we vote for the one with the most attractive image.

Issues are complex. Image is simple. Thirteeners like it simple.

The implications for evangelism of our "everything is image" generation are enormous. As my friend Spencer Burton, a student and lay evangelist at James Madison University, recently told me,

"Even if I were the best biblical scholar in the world and could prove to my peers that the Bible was true, I don't think it would make a difference in their response. For people today, everything has become virtual reality." In other words, everything is an image. Reality is an image. Even logical proofs are an image. The issue for Xers is not "Is it objectively true?" but "Does it excite me?"

Read the great writings of Christian apologetics of our times—C. S. Lewis's *Mere Christianity* and the works of Francis Schaeffer, Os Guinness and Josh McDowell. They are filled with convincing arguments, logical proofs and powerful evidence. There are hundreds of thousands of Baby Boomer Christians who can point to these great thinkers as major factors in their conversion. But these books and these arguments don't reach Generation X. Why? In part because reality is virtual, everything is an image, and logical proofs don't pack the power of persuasion they once did.

"You say you can prove Jesus lived and died and rose again," says a typical Xer. "Fine. I've seen proof that UFOs exist, that Elvis is alive and that there is a mile-long human face carved in stone on Mars. I can't argue with you, but I also can't relate to your evidence. I'd rather just believe what I want to believe. You have your truth and I have mine."

Our "everything equals image" mindset has a lot to do with our media fascination. We see our entertainment media as a way of escape from our hopelessness about the future. TV, movies and music anesthetize our pain and assure us that everything will be okay. Since nothing in the media is real, we can surround ourselves with images that make us comfortable. Despairing of carving an identity and a life for ourselves out of the cold, hard stuff of reality, we find our identity and our hope for the future in the alternative flavor of our music, in the fantasy characters in our movies and in the synthetic images of TV.

If we turn on CNN and take a hard look at the face of famine, war, AIDS, racial polarization, overpopulation and environmental disaster, we become depressed. If we open the newspaper and read about our economic future, we begin to panic. But if we flip the TV tuner over to MTV or pop in a video or turn on the CD player, reality disappears. The world of images and unreality returns. We are able to believe and hope, if only for a while, that life is not as bad as it seems.

"Baby Boomers were the first generation to grow up with television," observes Richard Peace, "but they were raised to view entertainment as a reward, not a right. Boomers feel guilty about excessive TV watching. Baby Busters, by contrast, live in a media world like fish live in water. Entertainment is their environment. Massive media input is seen as a right, just like food, shelter, and freedom. Generation X owns twice as many CD players as the Boomer generation. Two-thirds of Xers have VCRs, and they account for over half of all revenue from movie ticket sales. Xers outspend all other age groups on concerts and recorded music.

"Boomers tend to watch movies from beginning to end. Busters tend to catch snatches of films. Boomers watch a film once. Busters watch favorite 'cult' films over and over again and can quote dialogue verbatim. Boomers find commercials annoying. Busters are more tolerant of commercials, because commercials inform them of trends. Boomers grew up with three networks dominating the TV dial. Busters grew up with forty or more channels on cable and perfected the art of channel surfing. Whoever controls the remote control has the power."

What are the implications for evangelizing a culture that is fascinated with image and entertainment? "First," says Peace, "Xers are sophisticated about their media. If we want to use media as a tool for evangelism, we dare not do something hokey, that lacks authenticity or that is done poorly."

Bob Fryling, director of campus ministries for InterVarsity, agrees. "If you don't use media, you lose a major communication link. Xers expect it and assume quality. If you don't have it or don't have quality, you've lost an opportunity."

The second implication for evangelizing this media-fascinated generation is that media can't do the whole job. "Entertainment media can't bring people to the Lord," Fryling observes. "They just help identify the issues and questions they are facing, so that they will become more receptive." A powerful Christian film or concert can move the heart and provoke a sense of openness, but it rarely cements a commitment in and of itself. The most effective role for media in evangelizing Xers is not to preach or evangelize, but to pose the question, to state the situation, to create an atmosphere where the individual can say, "Yes, that expresses the core problem of my life. I see now that I can't handle life on my own. I need some kind of intervention."

Dieter Zander, founding pastor of the Xer-oriented NewSong Church in Walnut, California, and currently on the staff of Willow Creek Church in Illinois, expresses the role of Christian media this way: "Christian entertainment media can get at a person's heart. It sneaks up on people, and they enter into it. The world of story and music is a safe place where people allow their emotions to be touched.

"For instance, one Father's Day we showed a scene from the motion picture *Hook,* a powerful scene in which Robin Williams plays a father who has forgotten what fatherhood and childhood are all about. This scene goes straight for the heart. It poses a very personal question. You can't watch this scene without wondering, *Am I this kind of father?* It reaches a father's heart in a way you never could by simply talking about it. Media is great at posing such questions, but you can't give a media answer. You have to give a flesh and blood answer to the questions that entertainment media can raise."

Searching for Meaning on the Net
CompuNet Information Service
13:47 EST Saturday 23-Dec-95
(Executive Option)
Last access: 07:07 21-Dec-95

Welcome to The Religion Forum

\#: 184699 / SPIRITUALITY
21-Dec-95 23:04:44
Sub: Holy Hannah!
Frm: Barry Noonan 56557,3301
To: Kristin McCabe 56990,1010

Hi, Kris,

Hannah left a bitter taste in my mouth, no question, but I'll try to heed your advice and not let her sour me on all Christians. I should add that I'm not at all soured on Jesus Christ.

A couple years ago, when I was going through a really rough time, I did some spiritual searching. Read the Urantia book, the I Ching, parts of the Qur'an, some Alan Watts, some Robert Pirsig, some Scott Peck, and of course, I read the Bible—specifically the Gospel of Mark and the Gospel of John (so there, Hannah, I *have* read it, nyahhhh!!). I was really impressed by the Jesus I found in the Gospels—a totally different impression of Jesus than I remember from my few trips to Sunday school in my early daze.

But is he the Son of God, as you Christians would say? Or *a* son of God, as a lot of other faiths say? Or just a very good, very wise human being who has been reinterpreted and misinterpreted a lot by his followers over the centuries? Who's to say? I sure can't with any certainty.

As to your comment, «IMHO, if Jesus was walking the world today, he'd use some of the innovative ways of communicating we have nowadays. I think he might even get a CompuNet account and interact on these forums»—Kris, I sure wish he would! I've got *a lot* of questions I'd like to ask him! [g]

Regards,

Barry

There are two replies.

#: 184729 / SPIRITUALITY
23-Dec-95 00:53:28
Sub: Holy Hannah!
Frm: Eric E. Eichelson 53887,5422
To: Barry Noonan 56557,3301

Barry—

A few more resources to suggest on your spiritual search. I've also done a lot of reading about Jesus. I've made a hobby of collecting books that debunk the myth of Jesus as God. Some recent additions to my collection: *The God-Man Heresy* by Anthony Friedman, *The Jesus Deception* by Hockman and Thomas, and *God's Lies* by Knight and Funk.

BTW, the day after Xmas, we're holding an on-line conference on the subject "Demythologizing Jesus" over in the New Age Forum. Feel free to join us. It oughta be fun, especially if the Bible-thumpers show up.

Have a good one,

EEE

#: 184798 / SPIRITUALITY
23-Dec-95 09:30:05
Sub: Holy Hannah!
Frm: Kristin McCabe 56990,1010
To: Barry Noonan 56557,3301

Dear Barry:

I can see you've made quite a thorough search for the truth, not just about Jesus, but about life in general. Reading a stack of books can be confusing. I tried it in my pre-Christian days and felt it got me nowhere. Maybe because so much of what I read was conflicting, or maybe just because so much of what I read just leaked out of my head a few hours later.

I've always been much more impressed by a reality I can touch and feel than by a reality I can only read about.

I don't know what kind of "really rough time" you were going through, but my "really rough time" was a combination of a disastrous relationship (I was living with an abuser) and substance abuse (mostly alcohol, plus some cocaine). After one particularly nasty beating by this (ahem!) wonderful man I was living with, I went to the hospital with a shattered cheekbone and a dislocated jaw. After I was released I went to a women's shelter where I met a counselor, a domestic violence survivor who was also a Christian, and I received a quality of caring and genuine concern I never knew before. She got me into a Twelve Step group, where I met several more authentic, caring Christians who loved me through the worst time in my life and helped me to finally beat my addictions.

Sorry to bore you with my past, but the important part of the story is that I have been rescued from it all. If God wasn't real, if Jesus Christ wasn't alive, I would not be where I am today. I was able to do

it *only* through dependence on him.
Have a great Christmas, Barry!
Kris

There are two replies.
#: 184808 / SPIRITUALITY
23-Dec-95 10:14:21
Sub: Holy Hannah!
Frm: Lori Paige 50011,3567
To: Kristin McCabe 56990,1010

Dear Kristin:
Thanks for being so honest and vulnerable in sharing your life with everyone here on the Net. I'm not a Christian, but I have a friend, Sandi, whose story is a lot like yours. I've always been amazed at how her reliance on a "higher power" accomplished what all the aversion therapy, drug therapy, hypnosis, and other "cures" never could: freedom from addiction.
Sandi and I talk a lot about these kinds of issues—God, eternity, guilt, painful memories, healing. I still have a lot of questions. Maybe you and I could correspond about some of these questions by e-mail and I could compare your answers with the answers I'm getting from Sandi. Would you be open to that?
Lori

#: 184854 / SPIRITUALITY
23-Dec-95 11:30:21
Sub: Holy Hannah!
Frm: Shizuye Murashima 63303,0003
To: Kristin McCabe 56990,1010

Dear Kristin McCabe
I thank you for you story. I'm really rough time too write now. Some day I maybe tell you about it not write now. Sorry my english no good. I'm still learning to it. But I want to say thank you for you story. I'm 22 year old japanese. Talk to Jesus about me if you think about me, okay?

Thank you, please.
SHIZUYE MURASHIMA
Nagoya, Japan

The Medium Is the Message

On Thursday, July 28, 1994, *The Real World* came crashing into Ron Wilkerson's life.

The Real World is a "staged documentary" produced by the cable channel MTV. The show's producers put a group of Generation Xers in a San Francisco apartment, pay their rent and living expenses (five thousand dollars a month), then follow them around with video cameras and put the edited results on TV every week. Why such an unreal scenario is called *The Real World* is a mystery in itself. How this show intersected with Ron Wilkerson's life is an even stranger story.

Wilkerson is a stunt biker and the owner of a bike-customizing business in San Francisco. He has no connection whatsoever with MTV or the producers of the show. But he does (slightly) know an English stunt biker named Geoffrey Cain. And Cain knows David "Puck" Rainey, a bicycle messenger who is one of the "real world" stars of the show. After visiting Wilkerson at his apartment, Cain went to visit Rainey at his apartment, where *The Real World* is taped. In front of the video cameras, Cain kidded with Rainey and flirted with one of the female regulars. Then he gave her a note that read, "Call me anytime," along with a phone number. Problem: it was not his own number! It was Wilkerson's unlisted home number. The MTV camera zoomed in on the number and broadcast it to the world.

Within minutes after the show was aired, Wilkerson's phone began ringing. And ringing and ringing. Wilkerson couldn't even call out, because his phone was equipped with call waiting and his outgoing calls were interrupted by incoming calls every few minutes. Calls came from all over the country, asking for Cain—though Cain had long since blown town. Some calls were suggestive. Some were downright obscene. Some were tinged with unreality—many callers wanted to speak to *The Real World* cast members.

"I want to kill all TVs now," Wilkerson told *The San Francisco Examiner* in a front-page story (August 1, 1994). One of the ironies of this whole disaster is that Wilkerson doesn't even own a TV.

This story illustrates a crucial dynamic in the thinking of many Generation Xers: some find it hard to distinguish entertainment from reality. The medium and the message have fused. A camera is not a disinterested observer; it affects and alters what it observes. Put a video camera in an apartment full of young people, and you don't get the real world. You just get an unrehearsed rip-off of *Melrose Place*. The "staged documentary" is every bit as phony and fictional as anything that ever came out of Aaron Spelling's Burbank studios.

You cannot separate a message from the medium used to communicate that message. The medium is not neutral. It alters, affects and even becomes the message.

For example, TV has conditioned us to expect programming to be interrupted at various intervals for a series of flashy, fast-paced, often funny miniprograms called commercials. We see these commercials on sitcoms, soap operas, movies and the news. We are so used to the presence of commercials in our programs that we fail to recognize some of the truly bizarre juxtapositions commercials create alongside the stories and scenes on the nightly news. A TV reporter can be showing us a starving African baby with a jutting rib cage and flies walking across her dying eyes. Seconds later Ronald McDonald is romping through McDonaldland, showering smiling, well-fed American kids with boxes of Happy Meals. What's wrong with this picture?

What if we were actually in Somalia or Rwanda, holding dying, malnourished little children in our arms, and a rubber-nosed clown came bouncing along, shouting, "Hah-hah! Come on, boys and girls! Follow me to Happyland!" I mean, is that tasteless or what? But on TV such juxtapositions are normal—and they can be confusing to people in their formative years as they are learning to sort out reality from media fantasy.

On reflection, we have to recognize that TV cannot give us an undiluted, unfiltered, unaltered message. The messages that TV conveys are squeezed by time slots, filtered by human bias, skewed by image and sound editing, colored or discolored by surrounding advertising and fragmented by the viewer's restless thumb on the remote control.

This is a bigger issue for younger viewers today than it ever was for the previous generation. Boomers found it much easier to distinguish television formats: news was news, sitcoms were sitcoms, and fantasy was fantasy. Today the various formats are merging and blurring those distinctions. We have docudramas, infotainment and infomercials. TV news, once as staid and gray as the front page of *The New York Times,* is now full of flashy computer graphics and MTV-style fast-cut images.

Can you blame Thirteeners for being confused when they see the president of the United States answering questions about his underwear on MTV right after the twisted grunge commentary of *Beavis and Butthead?* No wonder we have trouble distinguishing *The Real World* from the real world!

This common problem was illustrated for me during a conversation I had with a college graduate in California. We were talking about books when she said, "I like reading fiction more than nonfiction." Then she stopped herself. "Wait a minute—which one is true?"

The media fascination of Generation X provides Christians with a great opportunity—and a great danger. We can use various forms of entertainment media to tell the story of Jesus in new and effective ways, but we have to recognize the perils posed by the fact that the medium itself becomes the message. What happens to the story of Jesus when we use it to light up "the dream machine," the same electronic box on which people view Leno and Madonna and HBO and pornographic videos? Will the medium alter our message? Will it trivialize our message? Will it turn our message into just another form of entertainment—even low comedy?

I remember how some of my college friends loved to watch TV evangelists. They enjoyed mimicking their "Praaaaaaise Jesus-uh!" preaching style. Some even called the number on the screen with fake problems so they could talk to the phone counselors. It was all a big joke to them. My suspicion is that traditional forms of mass evangelism through television and other mass media are on the wane.

What, then, is the evangelistic medium of the nineties and beyond? Us!

Individual Christians need to become the medium for the message. This means that our lives need to be authentic. Integrity is the key to effective witnessing among today's youth generation, because (1) Xers are highly suspicious of fakes and of people who want to exploit them,

(2) a story that is told without authenticity and integrity is a lie and doesn't deserve to be told, and (3) Xers are hungry for the kind of authenticity and integrity that they can't find in the systems of this world. Only when we have shown by the quality of our own lives that we have something to offer will our message have power and credibility.

Is there any role for Christians in the mass media? Absolutely! In fact the critical need right now is for Christians to move out of the "evangelical ghetto" of Christian-only entertainment and to move into the secular media, where they can truly have an impact on the world. Our tendency as Christians is to "preach to the choir," to form tight-knit, inbred little colonies of Christian entertainers and Christian fans. But we need Christian actors, writers, producers, musicians, songwriters, singers, dancers and journalists to emerge from the Christian subculture and to fan out into the culture at large, living lives of authenticity and integrity, doing work that honors God by its excellence, making the story of Jesus Christ known to the world through the story of their own lives.

Pilgrims on the Information Superhighway

"It says Gateway 2000 on the front of your computer," said Josie as she sat down at the desk in Barry's apartment. "What kind of computer is this?"

"It's IBM-compatible," said Barry, standing behind her.

"Oh. Well, mine is a Macintosh. Does that make a difference?"

"Not when you're communicating on a computer network. People on the Net use all kinds of computers and operating systems—Mac, MS-DOS, Windows, OS/2, Novell, NeXt, Amiga and even those humongous mainframes. I've encountered people on CompuNet who are still using ten-year-old Commodore 64s and Apple IIs. There are a lot of different computers and operating systems, but they all speak ASCII, and that's why they can all talk together on the Net."

"So what do I do first? How do I—what do you call it—log on? How do I log on to CompuNet?"

"Well, I use WinComm, which is a mouse-driven interface like you have on your Mac, so you should be able to do it pretty much like this once you get your modem." Barry reached around her, moved and clicked the mouse. "There, you can see it working. The computer logs on automatically, grabs my e-mail, visits the forums I'm interested in, checks the headlines in the CompuNews section and logs off. The whole procedure takes four, five minutes, and the computer stores all the information it gathers in a file on my hard drive. Once I'm off-line I can either read the information right here on the screen or I can output it as hard copy from my printer. Here, look." He took a stack of pages from the top of his laser printer and handed them to Josie. "That's from my last session."

"Wow!" said Josie, flipping through the pages. "They have all these forums? Science Fiction! Rock Music! Human Sexuality! Religion! New Age! And you can connect with people from all over the country?"

"All over the world. There are people I 'talk' to on a regular basis from the West Coast, Canada, England, Germany—"

"Awesome! It's like a big on-line community. All these people have one place where they can all get together and talk over the things that really matter to them." She glanced through the session transcript, then pointed to something on the page. "IMHO. What does that mean?"

"That's Netspeak. It means 'in my humble opinion.' People on the Net use a lot of shortcuts to save typing. BTW is 'by the way.' And ROFL is 'rolling on the floor, laughing.' "

"How fun!"

"Sure it's fun! And see that *g* with the carets around it? That's short for 'grin.' You use that when you want to make sure someone knows you're kidding."

"Hey, here's a note from you! Okay if I read it?"

Barry shrugged. "Sure."

As Josie read, Barry picked up a computer products catalog from his desk and began flipping through it. "Hey, here's a killer fax-modem for under two hundred bucks!" he said. "Fast, too. Twenty-eight-dot-eight kilobaud."

"Barry," Josie said softly, looking up from the transcript, "you say here that you went through a really rough time a while back. I guess you wouldn't wat to talk about it." There was the faintest hint of a question mark at the end of her sentence.

Barry closed the catalog. "Josie," he said, "I'll tell you about it sometime . . . just not right now, okay?"

Josie smiled. "Sure, Barry," she replied. "You don't have to talk about it if you don't want to."

Barry smiled—a tight, forced-seeming smile. He put the open catalog down in front of her. "What kind of modem would you want—internal or external?"

Society Versus Generation X

It was an old two-story white clapboard house, one of a cluster of six empty houses sitting behind the dunes on Sunset Beach about halfway between Myrtle Beach and Cape Fear. It was perfect. "Well, this is the living room," said Lindsey, unlocking the door and holding it open for the others to enter. "There are six bedrooms in this old house. Didn't I tell you this place was great?"

There were eight in all—Lindsey and her boyfriend Grant, T.J. and his girlfriend Marisa, John and Kim Takeda (a married couple, friends of Lindsey's), Josie and Barry.

Josie wrinkled her nose. "Smells musty in here."

"That's because the place has been closed up for two months," said Grant. "People don't go to the beach in the middle of winter."

"Unless they're crazy like us," laughed Lindsey.

"Hey, I'm starved!" announced T.J. "It's lunchtime! Let's get some food on the table, man!"

"How can you think of food when it's so cold in here?" Josie asked, shivering and rubbing her arms.

"Why don't you build a fire in the fireplace, Josie?" said Lindsey. "There's wood and newspaper and kindling in the corner. The rest of us can bring in the food and stuff from the cars. Guys, this is gonna be such a cool New Year's Eve!"

As everyone went back out to the cars, Josie looked around the living room. "Hey!" she shouted. "Where's the TV?"

The Marginal Generation

We are the generation at the margins of our society. The media has played up this image, and for many of my generation it has become a self-fulfilling prophecy. At the same time much of this is rooted in reality. The media has simply made us aware of the facts.

We have a disregard for society because we think society has disregarded us. Believing our culture has dealt us a losing hand, we are at odds with that culture. We disregard authority, don't trust our parents, seek friends who will be authentic and loyal, and neglect the world at large in order to take care of our own.

Thirteeners have little tolerance for anything that smacks of "the system." We are convinced we are getting screwed by society. For the first time in American history, the younger generation will not surpass its elders in terms of wealth and living standards. Benefits for the elderly have increased at our expense. It is us against the system, and we give our allegiance to any individual or enterprise that challenges the system.

This "society versus Generation X" mindset creates an enormous problem for evangelism, particularly the evangelistic efforts of those of the Baby Boom generation (or older) who would like to reach out to Xers. My generation is less likely to respond to older adults because they remind us of the system. We are unimpressed by degrees and position, such as Pastor So-and-so or the Reverend Doctor So-and-so. We are wary of the techniques and approaches of Boomer strategists who make us feel like targets of some marketing strategy. We distrust religious leaders as much as or more than politicians.

Who, then, do we trust? People we can identify with. People who have made it by going outside the system. We don't idolize JFK, who was part of the political system, or Martin Luther King Jr., who was part of the religious system. They might as well be faces on Mount Rushmore. Our heroes are people like Deion Sanders, Andre Agassi, Howard Stern, Shaquille O'Neal, Madonna, Christian Slater, the pop star formerly known as Prince, Mariah Carey, Dennis Rodman, and even twentysomething Hollywood madam Heidi Fleiss—people who have succeeded on their own terms, by their own efforts, often by bucking the system and violating the rules.

We distrust the big "change-the-world" idealism of our Boomer parents. Though we are still, like most young generations of the past, essentially liberal, our Xer liberalism doesn't look anything at all like the Boomer liberalism of the sixties. In fact, many people mistake our liberalism for conservatism. We are pragmatic, not idealistic. We think locally rather than globally.

On some specific issues such as defense spending and welfare, we actually appear to be more conservative than our Boomer forebears— but not because we lack liberal compassion. Rather, our view of the Pentagon has been shaped by the successes of the Gulf War rather than the fiasco of Vietnam. And we have grown suspicious of government's expensively failed attempts to solve America's social problems. We Xers are still liberal, but our liberal compassion tells us it's time to rethink the bloated, wasteful government programs that Boomer liberal compassion began—programs that are bankrupting the country and stealing our future. Boomer idealism, we conclude, hasn't saved the world; it has only made things worse.

All of this leaves Baby Boomers shaking their heads in bewilderment. The average Boomer just doesn't get it. As Richard Peace observes, the antagonism between the generations is rooted in a dramatic contrast between the Boomers' formative experiences and the Xer experience.

Look what happened to the Baby Boomers, the post-World War II generation born between 1945 and 1960. They grew up in the innocent years of the Eisenhower administration, lost their innocence when JFK was shot, turned into hippies during the Woodstock sixties, became yuppies in the seventies and eighties.

Now, in the nineties, the Baby Boomers are gray at the temples, and they realize they have become the very thing they once rebelled against: bewildered parents of an angry generation. The same Baby Boomers who used to astonish and provoke their elders with long hair, outrageous clothes, loud music, peace symbols, and "flower-powered" VW vans are now astonished and provoked at the sight of a new generation of gender-indeterminate youths with earrings, nose rings (and rings in places too personal to mention), tattoos (both his and hers), baggy pants, reversed baseball caps, MTV gestures, rap talk and an attitude. Boomers are especially exasperated by the attitude. ("Just chill, man." "Back off." "Be cool, dig?")

New Year's Eve with Friends

After lunch they had all walked along a cold, windy beach under an iron-gray sky. That evening they gathered by the fireplace. Lindsey and Grant had decked a coffee table with plates of different breads, cheeses, fruits, vegetables and wines. Marisa had brought candles—at least forty of them in candelabra and candlesticks—and they were all lit, giving off a festive scent and a soft glow. Barry had brought a massive CD stereo boom box, and he had stacked the changer with enough discs to carry them into the new year.

"This is what it's all about," said Grant as he put another log on the fire. "Good food, good wine and most of all good friends."

"Let's drink to it," said Kim, holding up her glass. "To good friends."

So they did.

On the stereo, the cool jazz-rap voice of Brian McKnight was laying down, "If you don't want her, don't waste her time, I'll take her." Barry and Josie got up and slow-danced while the others talked.

Marisa leaned over and whispered to Lindsey and Grant, "I thought those two were just friends."

"They are," said Lindsey. "People can dance when they're just friends."

Sitting on the floor behind Lindsey, Grant reached an arm around her and pulled her close. "People can fall in love when they're just friends too." He kissed her playfully on the neck.

"This is so cool," said Marisa with a sigh, "seeing the New Year in with good friends." She leaned back against T.J.'s chest. "What time is it, baby?"

T.J. checked his watch. "Eight-thirty. Three and half hours till next year."

"I really want to savor this moment," said Lindsey. "A night as perfect as this may never come again."

"What do you mean?" asked John.

"I mean . . ." Lindsey paused thoughtfully. "I mean, there aren't many people in this world you can really depend on, you know? Like, you go through your whole life, and your friends come and they go. I think about my friends from grade school and high school and college, and I have no idea where they are tonight. They're gone from my life. But you all are my friends now, and we're all together, and it's really, you know, special. I don't know if I'm making any sense, but—"

"Go on," John Takeda said softly.

"I mean, three or four years from now, who knows? People move. They drift apart. You all may not be in my life anymore. So I want to savor this night, this special night with my special friends, because a night like this may never come again."

"Gee, Lindsey," said Marisa, "that seems like such a sad thought."

Lindsey was about to answer, but Grant spoke up first. "No," he said. "It's not sad, not the way Lindsey means it. What she's saying is that this is our moment right now. Right now is all we ever have. But this is a wonderful now—the best possible now. She wants to enjoy it fully while it's now."

"What do you think makes a good friend, Lindsey?" asked Marisa.

T.J. laughed. "Risa, you're always analyzing things. Friends just are. If you try to dissect a friendship and see what makes it work, it stops working."

"I don't know," said Lindsey. "There are some things that all good friendships have to have. Real friends are people who are willing to listen—people you can tell secrets to and know they won't tell them to anyone else. People you can have good times with, but you can also get serious with them—like we're doing right now. Mostly I think a good friend is someone who's there for you in the bad times . . . when you're really hurting."

"You've had friends like that?" asked Kim.

"Yeah. In high school," replied Lindsey, resting her head on her knees and hugging herself thoughtfully. "They got me through a really awful time in my life. I hated school, and my home was a living hell. My parents were going through this intense battle. They eventually got divorced when I was in college, but first they put me and my sisters through these years of agony while they kicked and clawed at each other. Dad later told me that he and Mom stayed together until my sisters and I left home for our sake! I thought, *Like, don't do me any favors, okay?*

"My friends were my refuge. After school we'd go to my house or a friend's house and sneak some vodka from the liquor cabinet. I knew where my parents kept a stash of pot in their bedroom, and sometimes we'd roll some joints and smoke 'em in the basement. I lived for weekends and parties, where I could escape from home and school and just be with my friends. I loved those guys. They were always there for me when my life was falling apart. I really miss them."

"The thing I always look for in a friend," said John, "is acceptance. It's hard to find people who will really accept you as you are. Like, when I was in college, there was this guy who lived down the hall in the dorm. And, like, he had a TV and he would invite me to his room to watch movies and football and stuff on the weekends. And I thought we were getting to be pretty good friends. He started talking to me about religion. He talked about being a Christian, and I talked about being a Buddhist.

"After a couple days, I realized he was pressing me pretty hard, arguing about how wrong Buddhism is, how Jesus Christ is the only way to heaven, stuff like that. I tried to change the subject, but the guy was relentless. All of a sudden I realized he wasn't coming around my room anymore, and when I'd say hi to him, he was really cool to me— you know, aloof. I finally asked him if I had made him mad or what, and he said something about not hanging around with 'unbelievers.' I mean, I was really pissed! I told him what he could do with his Christianity.

"I was mad—but I was also hurt. I had thought he was a real friend, but I found out I was just some kind of missionary project to him. He saw a Japanese-American heathen living down the hall, and he thought I was someone he could convert. When I didn't become his convert he dropped me as a friend. Ever since then I've always tended to test new friendships a little to see if people are really accepting of me or not."

"That's so stupid," said Lindsey. "I mean, why does religion have to be so divisive? Why should it matter to people if you are a Christian or a Buddhist or a Druid? Religion should bring people together, not pull them apart. Like, I had these two friends in high school. One was Buddhist, the other was Catholic, and I was 'none of the above.' And we all got along great! We never even mentioned religion. My Buddhist friend would never dream of trying to convert me and my Catholic friend. Why do Christians always have to be so pushy? Why can't these Christians just try being your friend?"

A Longing for Belonging

Like Lindsey, many Thirteeners have grown up with little emotional nurturing or support from their families. Many have even sought a refuge from their families. For them, relationships have brought more pain than comfort during their formative years.

Does this mean that the concept of family is any less important to Thirteeners than to other generations? On the contrary. Many of my generation—particularly those who come from dysfunctional backgrounds—have a special hunger for family. They look for a sense of community wherever they can find it. They have a longing for belonging. They may not know what a "healthy" relationship is like, but they deeply want to experience it.

One of the most destructive social factors to affect my generation is the disintegration of the family. Whatever you care to blame for the troubled state of the American family—moral relativism, the decline of values, the sexual revolution, the selfishness of the "me decade" of the eighties—there is no question that our troubled families have produced a troubled generation. And the more trouble the American family is in, the more important relationships are to us in Generation X. For many of us, our friends have become the family we never had.

We hear this longing for belonging in the words of Lindsey, my fictional character who echoes the words I have heard again and again on campuses and elsewhere in the Generation X culture:

"There aren't many people in this world you can really depend on
. . . My friends were my refuge . . . Why can't Christians just try being
your friend?" For Lindsey and the others in that big beach house on
the Carolina coast, the longing for belonging took on a pattern that
most of us would easily recognize: good friends having good times
together. They had found a special moment of bonding and community together.

But for people who find themselves in extreme situations—extreme
danger, extreme deprivation, extreme emotional crisis—their longing
for belonging and community can take some very dangerous and
excessive forms. An intense desire for community coupled with intense anger, hatred or paranoid fear toward society tends to produce
communities that are massively dysfunctional caricatures of authentic
families: religious cults (such as David Koresh's followers in Waco),
violent secret societies (such as the Ku Klux Klan) and street gangs.

Many people look at street gangs as nothing more than roving
mobs of gun-toting, dope-peddling thugs. But the truth is that gang
members are, in their own distorted way, pursuing relationships and
satisfying their need for belonging and community. Gangs aren't just
about drive-by shootings and carjackings. These individuals are creating a "family unit" in complete opposition to the system. In this family
unit the gang looks out for its own, protects its members and, when
a member is injured or insulted, avenges its members.

Initiation into this alternate family system usually involves an antisocial act—literally, an act against society—such as a random murder
or other violent crime. The attitude is "If you attack the system then
you are one of us." Gang members know that life in the gangs can
be short and violent, but they often prefer a year or two of being
respected and feared in the 'hood to a long but dreary life of flipping
burgers or washing cars. In some ways the counterfamily of the gangs
is the ultimate Xer response, since it involves hostility toward the
system, finding a place of belonging and day-by-day survival.

In fact, while inner-city life may seem far removed from the mostly
white world of suburbia and higher education, we are beginning to
see the growth of a new phenomenon: white middle-class gangs. Suburban violence, suburban graffiti tagging and suburban vandalism
now stand at an all-time high.

This is not to suggest that gang activity is the normal behavior for most Thirteeners. Gangs are at the extreme end of the twentysomething scale. But even the socially respectable Thirteener tends to feel alienated from—and angry toward—society and the system. Gang members take visible, aggressive action on that anger. You can see the gang member's anger in his eyes. You can hear it in his shout. You can feel it in the muzzle-flash of his gun.

The socially respectable Thirteener tends to carry out his or her anger in what psychologists call passive-aggressive behavior. They don't attack society directly and aggressively as the gang member does. They get back at society in ways that appear passive but that are truly expressions of anger. They express their anger by ignoring authority and breaking the rules. They express their anger by ridiculing and scorning the system and its icons through iconoclastic surrogates such as Wayne and Garth of *Wayne's World,* Beavis and Butthead, and the Brothers Grunt. And many express their hostility by extending their adolescence and delaying adulthood.

To many Xers the oppressive social expectations of the system are symbolized by our parents. Together, our parents and our society have made all the rules, set all the limits and imposed all the punishments. "Don't do that!" "You can't have that!" "You're wrong!" My generation heard these statements throughout childhood from parents—and now we hear the same statements from the system. Our parents expect us to graduate from college in four years, get a decent job and make it on our own. Some of us can't find jobs and can't make it on our own; others refuse to do so.

I was on the slopes at the Alpine Meadows Ski Resort, Lake Tahoe, when I heard one Thirteener say to another, "Get a job!"

Laughing, the other called back, "Why?!"

The first Thirteener was parodying the "get a job" work ethic of the system, while the second was stating the attitude of Generation X: "Why should I participate in the system when I can have more fun ignoring it?"

We see this attitude lived out by students who stay in school for six, seven or eight years instead of four. Sure, part of it is that they don't want to leave the safe refuge of their friends to face the tough realities of life alone. But part of it for many Thirteeners is that staying in school is a statement of rebellion against the expectations of their parents. "I don't have to get a job" is the message they are sending to both parents and the system. "I am enjoying my extended adolescence."

There is a major difference in the way young Baby Boomers viewed relationships in the sixties and the way my generation views relationships today. Boomers sought out friends who would join them in the cause, march in the same protest and talk endlessly and passionately about the same issues. Baby Busters don't think that way. We approach relationships from the standpoint of feelings and individual needs, not issues and causes. We seek out friends who will be there with us as we struggle to survive our oppression by the system. Our friendships are functional; they act as stabilizers in a world where everything is up for grabs.

Resolutions

Barry turned off the CD player, and his voice was sober and emotional as he said, "Hey, guys, we're down to the last two hours of the year. I don't know about you, but I get kinda choked up thinking about my friends here in this room tonight. There's a song about friendship that has always meant a lot to me, and I'd like us all to sing it together." He paused, looking from face to face. Then, in a low voice, he began singing,

Here's to good friends
Tonight is kinda special . . .

Grins broke out around the circle of friends as everyone joined in.

The beer we pour
Must say something more somehow
So tonight, tonight
Let it be Lowenbrau.

The song dissolved into gales of laughter.

"Hey," said Lindsey, "does anybody have any New Year's resolutions?"

Grant rolled his eyes and groaned. "New Year's resolutions, Linz? That's so lame!"

"No it's not!" John protested. "I've got a killer resolution for the New Year." He held up his right hand. "I hereby resolve to spend less time on my butt at the office and more time on my skis and my mountain bike."

"Hear, hear!" cheered Lindsey, clapping.

"I also resolve," John continued, "to spend more time making wild, passionate love to my beautiful wife."

"Hear, hear!" cheered Kim, wrapping her arms around John.

"I resolve," said Barry, assuming a body-builder's pose, "to take even better care of this gorgeous body than I already do."

Jeers and catcalls.

"I resolve," said Marisa, "to stop trying to please other people and to start pleasing myself for a change. I resolve to be less tolerant of other people's B.S. And I resolve that the next time my boss makes a pass at me, I'll tell him what he can do with himself!"

Cheers, whoops and clapping.

Then, unexpectedly, a voice spoke up in quiet and somber tones. "I resolve," said Josie, "to put my brother's suicide behind me. I resolve to be happy again." She began to cry.

There was stunned silence for several seconds.

Then Barry reached out, folded Josie in his arms and held her tightly.

Social Issues and Agendas

Xers have a very simple approach to social issues: people should be treated fairly. There should be equality between the sexes, between the sexual orientations and between the races. We believe in "live and let live." To us, sexual harassment, homophobia and racism are just plain wrong, and we are impatient with a society that has failed, decade after decade, to cure these destructive social attitudes.

My generation sees abortion not as an issue of right or left, but as a purely personal decision. We aren't inclined to march for life or for choice. While political correctness (PC) is important to some in my generation (especially on the campuses), PC is really more of a Boomer thing, and you find passionate PCism more prevalent among college profs than among college students. PC is a movement, and we're not into movements. We want to be ourselves, not part of a thundering herd.

We are less likely than Boomers to polarize to either traditional left or right positions. We pick and choose positions on individual issues, and many issues we simply ignore. If it doesn't affect us personally, why get involved?

I recently talked to a group of Thirteeners at the University of Wisconsin. "We're going to start an environmental organization here," they said. "This is the best way to bring together all different kinds of people." That's a striking statement. In one sense these students are doing the same thing their Boomer forebears used to do: band together to do something to help save the environment. But notice the motivation these Thirteeners gave for starting a green organization: bringing people together. Their motivation is not the issue of the environment, but a desire for relationships.

Studies show that Xers are less likely—by as much as 13 percent—to volunteer for a humanitarian agency or organization than previous generations. This shift can be observed even among Christian Xers, who are less likely to support world missions than to take a group of students or young career people downtown to help some homeless people. We don't want to save the world; we want to help that old guy in the park. We can't relate to Bosnia or Rwanda; we care about that neglected kid down the street. We don't want to write a check and drop it in the mail to soothe our conscience; we want to do something tangible and see the results.

Race is not a hang-up for most of us in Generation X. In fact, ours is the most ethnically diverse and accepting generation in American history. Our ethnic and gender consciousness is reshaping our society and setting important trends for the future. In the next century the Caucasian population in America will remain approximately the same. However, the number of African-Americans will double, the number of Hispanics will triple, and the number of Asian-Americans will increase fivefold.

What will interracial relationships be like over the next hundred years? We see the answer, in part, in the attitudes of Generation X, a generation that is largely less racist, more ready to embrace differences and more hospitable to immigrants than prior generations.

Here we find another potential window of opportunity for the story of Jesus Christ. Because our story is one of reconciliation and peace, it is a story with enormous appeal to a generation that detests division and violence. Generation X is ready and eager to hear about a new way of life, a new family system in which there is "no division into Jew and non-Jew, slave and free, male and female. Among us you are all equal. That is, we are all in a common relationship with Jesus Christ" (Galatians 3:28).

Surviving Under the System

Midnight was approaching, and the mood among the circle of friends at the beach house had mellowed to a gentle and introspective melancholy. The bond between them was a thing you could almost reach out and touch.

"It's been a tough year for T.J. and me," Marisa said wistfully. "I've had a lot of hassles on the job. I've got a boss who's a creep. He's a sexual harasser and a bigot. He knows I have a black boyfriend, and he's always ragging me about it." She sighed. "And I've got problems with my parents too."

"What kind of problems?" asked Lindsey. "If you don't mind my asking—"

"Hey, no, I don't mind," Marisa replied. "My folks are hung up on the race thing."

"You mean," said Lindsey, "your folks can't handle it because you're white and T.J. is black?"

"You got it. I mean, they are such hypocrites! They raised me to be open-minded and accepting of other people—but the moment I started actually dating a black guy, they absolutely lost it! Can you believe that? My mom actually broke down crying! When I asked her what she was so upset about, she said, 'What if you and this T.J. boy get married? We always thought our grandchildren would look like us! How would we explain to our friends that our grandchildren are half-black?' I mean, give me a break! Did you ever hear anything so stupid in your life?"

"What did you say to that?" asked Lindsey.

"I said, 'What makes you think I'm planning to have children?' That's when my dad had a meltdown! He went into this long thing about my generation not wanting to take responsibility for bringing the next generation into the world."

T.J. laughed. "It's really kind of funny," he said, pulling Marisa to him and stroking her hair. "Marisa's momma is about to pass a pineapple 'cause some nigga's gonna call her Grandma, and her daddy's about to have a stroke 'cause he may not get to be a grandpa at all!"

"I don't think it's funny," said Josie. "I think it's sad. Why does a person's race mean so much to people? Why can't we just be—people?"

T.J. shrugged. "My momma's just as bad," he said. "She won't even let me mention Marisa in her house."

"Yeah," said John. "Kim and I know exactly how you feel."

All eyes turned in John's direction.

T.J. grinned. "Are you kiddin' me, man?"

The look on John's face was completely serious. "I'm not kidding you. Kim and I have had to deal with the same kind of prejudice you all have. You know, the interracial thing."

"What interracial thing?" said T.J. "You're both Asian-American!"

John and Kim looked at each other. "You mean," said Kim, "you don't see any difference between us?"

"What difference?" said Marisa.

"I'm Japanese," said John. "Kim's Korean."

The room exploded in laughter—all but John and Kim. "John," said Kim, "they think we're kidding."

"You mean," Lindsey asked incredulously, "you're serious?"

"Totally! My parents can't stand John!" said Kim. "They threatened to disown me if I married him. Well, they backed down on that when they saw I was serious, but they still won't let John in the door."

"That's incredible," said Lindsey.

"Oh yeah," said John. "This is a big deal to our parents. I mean, for a Japanese and a Korean to fall in love, it's like the Montagues and the Capulets all over again."

"The what?" said Grant.

"That's from *Romeo and Juliet*," said Lindsey. "You know—Shakespeare."

"Oh yeah."

"Racism is everywhere, man," said T.J. "It's in the air we breathe and the water we drink. You can't escape it, man. I know. 'Cause I've tried. I mean, I may not be some bad-ass gangsta from the 'hood, but I know there's no future out there for the black man, and I've got a belly full of anger about that. The white power structure has tried to whack us up and hack us up and chain us down. I grew up in the welfare system and the public housing system, and if there's one thing I've learned it's that the system is a meat grinder. But I survived it, man, and I still decide what I think and how I live."

"I can't imagine what it's like," said Barry, "knowing that your ancestors were stacked in ships like firewood and shipped to a strange country where they were kept in chains and worked like animals. I can't imagine what it's like to know that the descendants of those slave masters still want to keep you in social and economic bondage."

"The only way to survive four hundred years of oppression, my man," said T.J., "is by stayin' just a little bit crazy."

"What do you mean, 'crazy'?"

T.J. bugged out his eyes and gestured with his hands like a wild man. "I mean *craaaaaazy!* You want to make out in this world, man, you gotta go up against the system, man. You gotta bust it, like Shaquille O'Neal grabbin' the hoop and bustin' up the backboard, you dig? And I don't just mean the black brothers. I mean we all gotta get crazy. We're all of us livin' under oppression, right? Barry, Josie, Linz, my man Grant, John, Kim—we're all in this together, man. Check it out. It's us or the system, and the system holds all the cards and makes all the rules. If we wanna beat the system we gotta break the rules, man. We gotta be crazy." His head and his hands started moving to a rap beat only he could hear. Syncopating with the beat, he said,

When you're living in poverty,
Crazy you gotta be,
'Cause ain't nobody here
looking out for me
but me . . .

Outside the house a wind arose, rattling the shutters and moaning under the eaves like the last gasp of the dying year. It was a quarter to midnight.

The Coming Craziness

Generation X is the rule-breaking generation, the generation that leads the way to chaos and craziness. Rules represent the system. Break the rules and you break the system.

The rage and frustration many Xers feel threatens to rupture the seams of society. While it is true, on the whole, that members of my generation tend to be more accepting and open toward other races, there are also segments of my generation that are becoming more polarized, angry and violent. We see this in the rise of white neo-Nazi "skinheads" and in the racially motivated gang warfare in our cities. Observing these societal trends, Win Manning, the Gallup Scholar in Education at the George Gallup Institute, suggests that the drive-by shootings and gang warfare of our inner cities may soon begin spreading into suburbs and smaller towns.

But some of the rage and craziness that threaten to rip the lid off our society is actually generational and reflects Xer frustration with the Boomer generation. Twentysomething writer Eric Lieu was interviewed by Bruce Morton in a CNN special report ("Boomers and Busters," August 8, 1994). "The real problem," Lieu observed, "isn't that Boomers are criticizing twentysomething people. I mean, that's gonna happen. The real danger is that we're kind of lurching toward really explicit generational warfare. Oppression leads to violence, and Xers feel oppressed. As our society becomes increasingly fragmented and Balkanized along generational, ethnic and gender lines, we may actually begin to see Bosnia-like warfare breaking out in American cities in the not-too-distant future."

Mine is an angry and alienated generation that will soon move into positions of political and cultural leadership. It is a media generation that emphasizes images over logic. This could dramatically change the way our society processes information, perceives reality and makes crucial decisions. How will these changes shape the church of the future? Will churches become less of a force for dynamic social and individual change and more of a source of entertainment? Will virtual reality churches and on-line churches replace real experience and authentic human touch?

We are in the midst of a major cultural shift, quite possibly a cultural war. Generation X is riding the wave of that shift and is worried about being caught in a large-scale cultural breakdown or meltdown. We're tired of the wars—the political wars, the ideological wars, the abortion wars, the gay-straight wars, the racial wars. We just want to find a place of peace in a bullet-riddled, pockmarked cultural landscape.

As the various conflicts in our society continue to heat up and boil over, there is no telling where they will lead. But one thing is sure: these radical cultural changes will demand a flexible response from the Christian church.

Midnight

At midnight in the big house on the beach no one blew horns or threw confetti. No one sang "Auld Lang Syne" or shouted "Happy New Year!" That's the way previous generations celebrated the end of an old year and the birth of the new, because previous generations were always expectant about the future.

Barry and Josie, Lindsey and Grant, John and Kim, Marisa and T.J. did not think about the future as the clock struck twelve. They couldn't envision the future. They couldn't imagine a promising tomorrow. They inhabited only a brief and ever-changing moment called now.

As the new year dawned, Barry cranked up the music—Soundgarten's ugly, raucous, hard-rockin' "Black Hole Sun." They all got up and danced the night away.

5

"Just Do It!"

Things have really changed in

twenty-five years," said Grant as he polished the chrome on his cycle—a massive Harley Shovelhead with a big 1200cc vee-twin engine. "My dad hitchhiked to Woodstock in '69, and he got in for free. To get to Woodstock '94, Lindsey and I took a plane and rented a car, and we put the whole thing on her VISA card. My old man tells me that at the first Woodstock you could score a joint for a quarter. At Woodstock '94 a lousy Coca-Cola cost you five bucks, and it was mostly ice. The first Woodstock was about free love. But Woodstock '94? Man, it was all about capitalism.

"It's sort of symbolic of the way things have changed, you know? In the sixties being young was all about 'sex, drugs, and rock 'n' roll.' But what do we have today? AIDS, crack and Michael Bolton! I mean, have we gone downhill or what?

"Life sucks, but what can you do? I mean, you gotta deal with it, right? So you grab your fun where you can. You take it to the limit. I've got friends who hang-glide or race speedboats. I have one friend who's climbed the face of El Capitan in Yosemite. Me, I like taking my Harley out on a two-lane and running her wide open, or racing cross-country on my Suzuki motocross bike—that one there." He thumbed over his shoulder to a lightweight, weathered-looking bike in the garage.

"Lindsey rides with me sometimes," Grant continued, running the chamois over the passenger seat, "but she hates this bike. She hates my Suzuki even more, 'cause it's for racing. Hey, I can understand that, but it's something I gotta do, you know? She keeps raggin' on how dangerous it is, but hell, no one lives forever.

"Do I think about death? Sure I do. All the time. But thinking about death doesn't make me live more carefully. It makes me want to live more intensely.

"People like me aren't looking to avoid death. We want to cheat death and spit in its eye. We want more excitement, more sex, more fun. If you want to have fun in life, man, you can't hit the brakes and play it safe. You have to throttle up and take the risks.

"If you really want to live you can't waste time thinking about it. You have to just do it."

The "Just Do It" Generation

Nike, manufacturer of sports shoes and accessories, understands the Xer mindset. Two of Nike's most effective advertising slogans are "Just do it!" and "Life is short. Play hard." Nike's ads tend to combine images of athletic competition, sexual energy and stark, grainy black-and-white photography. Nike understands that my generational peers are conscious of death, fascinated with risk, obsessed with playing hard, fanatical about pumping up and looking good, and at the peak of their sexual energy. They know how to set a hook in the Xer psyche.

We are the "just do it!" generation. We are bombarded by sexual messages during most of our waking hours, and our bodies rage with the hormones of youth; so when it comes to sex, we *just do it*. We are haunted by thoughts of death and the fear of failure as we zig and zag our way through this Nintendo game called "life," so when it comes to risk, we *just do it*. We are narcissistically attentive to our own bodies and our physical appearance, so when it comes to maintaining an image of physical perfection, we *just do it*.

The Sex Life of Generation X

We are confused about sex because the values of our society keep shifting under our feet. Arguments keep flying and rules keep changing. What is sex? "An emotional and spiritual commitment of one's entire self to another person," say some. "A form of recreation," say others. Should I do it? "Only within the safe enclosure of a monogamous marriage," say some. "Go ahead," say others, "but don't forget to use a condom." Are condoms safe? "Yes," say some. "Not always," say others. Whom do I believe? For most in my generation, the choices are troubling and confusing.

In their book *13th Gen* (New York: Random House, 1993), William Strauss and Neil Howe observe that the World War II generation associated sex with procreation, the Baby Boom generation associated sex with free love, and today's generation associates sex with self-destruction. Sex used to be an issue of right or wrong. The sexual revolution of the sixties and seventies stripped away the question of morality for most people. The AIDS epidemic and the mounting gender warfare of the eighties and nineties add two new questions to the sex equation: "Is sex worth the risk?" and "Is sex worth the hassle?"

Today's generation has both learned about and experienced sex at an earlier age than its predecessors. Peer pressures, media pressures, marketing pressures, cultural pressures and biological pressures all help drive people to be sexually active at an increasingly earlier age—and the paradox for most Thirteeners is that all of these pressures come to bear at a time when sex can make a person hideously, terminally sick. This creates confusion for the Thirteener—a sense of being both pulled and pushed by society, being caught in the crossfire of conflicting expectations and demands regarding his or her sexuality.

Though sex has become a painful issue for many Xers, the sex life of Generation X gives us in the Christian church several windows of opportunity for communicating God's story to young pre-Christians. Here are some examples.

Sex and emotional commitment. A 1994 *Parade* magazine survey (conducted by the Mark Clements Research Organization and reported in the August 7, 1994 issue) indicates that more people than ever before report that emotional involvement is a necessary ingredient of sex. Casual sex is losing ground to committed sex—and not just because of the threat of AIDS. Rather, there is a growing awareness that truly satisfying sex can be found only as a component of a committed relationship.

This is an enormously important fact, because it means that pre-Christian people are stumbling onto Christian truth. They are edging closer and closer to an understanding of why the gift of sex and sexuality was given to us by a loving God. This gives us an opening to tell the story of a God who understands (as Genesis 2:18 tells us) that the human beings he created should not be alone. We all have a desire to love and to be loved, and the gift of love God gave us is three-dimensional:

1. *Agapē*-love is spiritual, unconditional love that is rooted in the will, not in the emotions.

2. *Philia*-love is affectionate, emotional love. It is the strong and self-sacrificing love that creates strong families.

3. *Eros*-love is romantic and physical love. This ecstatic and passionate love bonds a man and a woman together in an intense emotional and physical fusion.

Each of these dimensions of love is a beautiful, God-given dimension. When all of these dimensions of love are working together at once in a marriage relationship, each of them is heightened to the absolute maximum. That's why an *eros* (sexual) relationship that is surrounded by the safe enclosure of *agapē* and *philia* can be so supremely satisfying—and it is one of the reasons that (according to the 1994 *Parade* survey) 67 percent of married people report being sexually satisfied, versus only 45 percent of sexually active single people.

Sexual activity and God's grace. Tim Conder, youth pastor at the Chapel Hill Bible Church, reports that my generation's openness in discussing sex and sexuality creates a window of opportunity for sharing the story of God's grace and forgiveness.

Ten years ago I would never have had a student come into my

office and confess to sexual activity. There was an unspoken consensus that to be a sexually active teen was not only wrong but shameful. Today kids are less hesitant to admit their sexual behavior, particularly in a safe setting such as a counseling situation. I've even had a thirteen-year-old girl come in for counseling about a family problem and casually mention her sexual activity—almost as a footnote to her story!

At first you think, *My gosh! Don't these kids have any sense of morality or of respecting their own bodies?* But deep down, even those who appear unconcerned about the moral component of their sexual behavior really do experience guilt and unease. And that sense of guilt is the doorway to their souls, because we have a story that is all about how God can change their lives, erase their guilt and replace their old desires with new desires. The story of the woman caught in adultery (John 8) is a story with enormous application to the lives of Generation Xers. Because so many of them have experienced pain, betrayal, shame, confusion, guilt, exploitation and even violence through their sexual behavior, the story of God's grace collides with their own story at a very basic emotional intersection. Sexually active Xers are frequently very hungry for the grace of God.

Sex and justice. We are seeing a rise in tensions and outright warfare between the sexes. Many women are becoming increasingly hostile and militant over what they see as male oppression and violence. A long list of crimes are generally committed by men against women, including spousal abuse, stranger rape, date rape, statutory rape, incest, sexual harassment and sexual exploitation by therapists and other professionals. The feelings of fear and anger expressed by many women today are justifiable—and they are rising.

Women are responding to these threats and fears in a variety of ways. On the campus many heterosexual women are choosing not to date but instead to pursue their studies and their career. This accomplishes two objectives: (1) it enables women who fear men to avoid contact with men, and (2) it allows them to indulge in a common Xer behavior pattern—prolonging adolescence.

Another way women are responding is by attacking men and maleness at every turn. On one American campus a women's group decided to raise awareness of the problem of date rape. So the group purchased a full page in the campus newspaper and ran an ad with the headline "Each of These Men Is a Potential Rapist." Below that headline was the name of every male student on campus. Though the anti-date rape intentions of the group were laudable, the antimale tenor of the ad raised a predictably angry storm of protest—and a defamation suit.

Some women have taken the position that all women are victims, that all sex is rape and that all men are abusers. They seek to obtain power by pleading powerlessness. This approach offends both men (who object to being automatically labeled and stereotyped as victimizers) and women (many of whom object to be automatically cast in the role of a helpless victim).

Antioch College in Ohio has gone so far as to create a school policy requiring students who are dating to obtain permission before advancing to a deeper level of intimacy: "May I hold your hand?" Verbal permission. "May I kiss you on the cheek?" Verbal permission. "May I soul-kiss you?" Verbal permission. Those who advance to a new level of intimacy without permission can be kicked out of school. The assumption behind this policy is that every man is a potential predator.

The problems of sexualized violence and sexual injustice provide yet another opportunity for the story of Jesus Christ. As we look at stories of Jesus dealing with women, such as the woman at the well in Samaria (John 4) and the woman caught in adultery (John 8), we see that Jesus reached out to women who were despised, exploited and oppressed by an unjust, male-dominated society—and he elevated those women and gave them back their dignity and their self-esteem. The women of Generation X, many of whom have been hurt and exploited by men, are hungry for a community in which there is mutual respect and equality between the genders and in which there is "neither Jew nor Greek, slave nor free, male nor female, for [they] are all one in Christ Jesus" (Galatians 3:28 NIV).

Gender identity and grace. One of the biggest issues in the consciousness of the "just do it!" generation is the issue of gender identity. My peers are less gender-specific than previous generations. Xer culture is becoming increasingly androgynized, with men wearing ponytails and earrings and women wearing traditionally male clothing and moving into traditionally male roles.

Perhaps this is in part because women are coming to have a larger role in our political and cultural institutions. As their influence spreads, it may well be that men begin to become more "feminized" at the same time that women are inserting themselves into traditionally male-dominated places in our society. Clearly, some in our culture have placed great hope for social justice and advancement in an erasure of the differences between the sexes. Some have believed that, obvious physical distinctions aside, there is really no innate difference between men and women, boys and girls. The differences, these people believed, are only the artificial categories we impose on them when we give them Barbies or G.I. Joes to play with, and when we otherwise stereotype their roles during childhood.

Research clearly indicates, however, that men and women are born different. Even brain structure is different in men and women; the average woman's corpus callosum (the nerve bundle that connects the left and right hemispheres of the brain) is thicker in than in men, which may explain why men tend to be left-brain-dominant and analytically oriented while women tend to have a more right-brain (or whole-brain), feelings-oriented quality of thinking.

The androgyny experiment of the eighties and nineties, which sought to erase gender distinctions, has largely proved to be a failed hope. Despite the fact that the trappings of androgyny are still very much apparent—ponytails, earrings, body rings and the like—the androgyny experiment can't overcome the cold hard fact that men and women are intrinsically different. So now we see men and women increasingly moving apart and segregating into opposing camps, demonstrating not only a wariness toward each other but an outright hostility. A men's movement is arising to challenge the perceived onslaught of the women's movement, and many feminists are reacting by becoming even more radical and extremist than ever before.

Left out of the battle between men and women, but feeling equally hurt, angry and alienated, is the homosexual population. Despite the existence of a vocal and visible gay rights movement, the homosexual community is not a single, united, monolithic community. There are male homosexuals and there are lesbians. There are vocal gay-rights advocates, and there are gays who quietly pass as straight, practicing their sexual orientation while avoiding controversy or scrutiny. Many thousands of people struggle with homosexual tendencies but are not involved in an active homosexual lifestyle.

The problem homosexuality poses for Christians is, How do we respond? Is homosexuality always wrong? Is it merely an alternate lifestyle, as our society is coming to accept? Clearly, the courts, our political institutions and the media have elevated homosexuality to a status on par with racial minorities, entitled to respect and protection under the law. Those who claim that homosexuality is a sin are criticized as "intolerant" and "homophobic." What should the Christian response be? And does the issue of homosexuality offer another window of evangelistic opportunity in reaching Generation X?

The Bible gives us both general warnings against sexual immorality (see, for example, 1 Corinthians 6:13-20 and 1 Thessalonians 4:3-6) and specific warnings against homosexual behavior (see Leviticus 18:22; Romans 1:21-32; 1 Corinthians 6:9-10; 1 Timothy 1:8-10; Jude 6-7). Though the Bible is totally clear in condemning homosexual behavior, these passages should be understood within the context of God's love for sinners and his power to change lives. In John 8:1-11 Jesus freely forgave a woman who was guilty of sexual sin, yet he also held her accountable. "Go on your way," he said. "From now on, don't sin." The key to responding to the issue of homosexuality is to express God's full personality in our response: both God's grace and God's truth, forgiveness and accountability.

One of the tough questions regarding homosexuality is "Why?" What makes a person homosexual? Are the causes of homosexuality genetic or environmental? Research indicates that both genetic and environmental factors produce a tendency toward homosexual behavior. Certainly God does not condemn a person for having homosexual feelings—and neither should we. Homosexual behavior is sin, but homosexual tendencies are not. Perhaps our evangelistic influence in the gay community would be greater and more positive if Christians focused less on political legislation and focused more on caring for gay individuals.

But what about those who are deeply immersed in homosexual behavior? Christlike unconditional love calls us to offer help, hope and a way out to those who feel trapped in the homosexual lifestyle. If we can learn to separate the sin from the sinner and to see homosexuals as people who have experienced great pain and shame in their lives, we may be able to have a redeeming and healing influence on their lives.

What about AIDS? Many Christians view AIDS as "God's curse" on the sin of homosexuality. But is AIDS a curse from God? If you believe so, then perhaps you also believe that herpes is a curse on sexually promiscuous heterosexuals. And that heart disease is a curse God visits on people who compulsively overeat. And that melanoma is a curse God inflicts on people who spend too much time in the sun.

AIDS is not a curse. It is a consequence of a certain kind of behavior, just as other forms of behavior have their consequences. In fact, it may well be that God's moral sanctions regarding sexual purity are actually guidelines for good health and good hygiene. God designed monogamous marriage as a protective enclosure for his gift of sex. When we use and abuse that gift outside of marriage, with either same-sex or opposite-sex partners, we bring emotional, spiritual and physical harm to ourselves, our marriage partner and our extramarital sex partner.

Here, then, is our window of opportunity with the homosexual community: to reframe the issue of morality in more complete and fully biblical terms. God's moral law is not designed to limit our fun, to damage our self-esteem or to oppress us in any way. God's moral law is a demonstration not only of God's judgment but of his love and grace for us. God wants to heal us, not to hurt us.

Now we have a story of love and a heart full of love to take to homosexual Xers. Instead of condemning the gay community, we can reach out to gays with the affirming, accepting love of Jesus Christ.

Whoop-de-do

Fourteen bikers and about a hundred spectators gathered at the MX track on a breezy Sunday afternoon. "I don't do this professionally or anything," Grant shouted over the blatting of his idling engine. "It's just great fun!" He was sitting astride his Suzuki, holding his bright yellow helmet in the crook of his arm.

"This is a killer track," he shouted, then pointed toward the starting gate. "It starts right there, and over there's the first turn. The trick is to get out in front right away, because if you let some other guy hit that water bog before you do, he'll fling up a bunch of mud on you, and it'll be ten times as hard to get ahead later. The mud coats your goggles so you can't see, and it clogs the fins of the engine, which can cause overheating. So I'm gonna try to get out in front, first thing.

"Now, right there is the second curve—a real tight one. That brings you up a rise for the first jump, then a short straightaway, then another jump that really sends you flying. I mean, you really gotta have your weight distributed just right when you're in the air. If you land too far back, you go into a shimmy. Too far forward and you nose down and go right over the handlebars, man. How do I know? Ha! I've done it! That jump always gives me trouble.

"Now, see those ripples right after that next turn? That's called a 'whoop-de-do.' You have to come outta that turn and hit those ripples at a perfect straight-on angle or they can turn your front wheel and send you right off the track. And right over there—"

Lindsey interrupted. "Grant," she said, "they want you at the starting gate!"

"Later!" shouted Grant, strapping on his helmet. He flashed a big grin and gave two thumbs up. Lindsey smiled wanly and waved as he took off for the starting gate. She folded her arms and hugged herself nervously. "I hate motorcycles," she said. "You know, motocross bikes don't even have brakes. No brakes! They say it's safer that way, but why it should be safer to not be able to stop if you want to, I'll never understand."

Fourteen cycles lined up at the starting gate—a long piece of welded pipe. The bikers pushed their front wheels up against that pipe. This kept anyone from jumping the starting flag. At the drop of the flag the pipe would fall and all fourteen bikers would throttle forward into a massive, revving, roaring, fishtailing, dust-churning, oil-burning traffic jam.

Fourteen two-stroke engines powered up, eager to launch forward. The smell of gasoline fumes and hot oil drifted on the dust-laden air. Lindsey bit her lip. The flagman raised the starting flag.

The tension held for several eternal seconds.

The flag dropped. The gate fell. Clutches popped and wheels spun.

The racetrack roared with thunder . . .

Risky Business

"I mean, what are we living for if not to have fun?" said Brett, a twenty-four-year-old Californian. "To me, having fun means being in motion with the wind in your hair. Wind-surfing. Sky-surfing. Board-surfing. If it moves, I do it. Of course, that kind of fun is kind of dangerous, isn't it? But hey, you only live once."

"When I relax," said Kerry, a student in Virginia, "I don't want to use my mind at all. So I do physical stuff that is totally mindless."

Brett and Kerry express the attitude behind a key Xer behavioral pattern: the tendency to escape from thinking by plunging into physical action and taking physical risks. By engaging in risky behavior—whether motorized, athletic or sexual—we hope to escape our pain, anxiety, anger and fear. Since life is a Super Mario Brothers game, since the odds are already stacked against us, risk is a way of life for us.

But there's another reason Thirteeners engage in risky activity. Risk has shock value. And my generation (which is still living out an extended adolescence) loves to shock and outrage the older generation. We get pumped up when people say, "I could never do what you just did," or "Weren't you terrified?" or "Why on earth do you do things like that?" There is a perverse sense of independence and pride (some may call it cockiness) that comes with getting out on the edge and experimenting with forms of "fun" that the older generation looks upon with horror and dismay.

We like to try new experiences, bizarre sensations, unheard-of thrills. We know there's no percentage in jumping off a bridge with a bungee cord around our ankles—no records to be set, no prize money or endorsement money, no coverage on ESPN. Bungee jumping is just the kind of meaningless, garbagy thrill that appeals to our weird and risk-loving sense of adventure. It's like surviving suicide—the ultimate leap into the unknown. After all, something could go wrong and you really might die! Awesome!

It almost seems as though Thirteeners are seeking to launch themselves out of this reality and into another, beyond the pain of their everyday existence and their memories of a dysfunctional past. They bungee jump off a bridge. Or skateboard off a ramp. Or throttle up a motorcycle to a hundred miles an hour. Or climb sheer mountain walls, then rappel back down again on a rope attached to a piton hammered into a cleft in the rock.

Even when these activities are pursued with friends, they are ultimately solo achievements. Part of the motivation for such risky activity comes from a desire to prove one's ability to survive by one's own daring and strength.

"I like spending time by myself," one university student told me. "I don't mean sitting in the lap of luxury, soaking up the comfort, but actually getting out there in the wild and just doing it. When I was in high school I used to go to the beach without any money, without a place to stay, and I'd just camp there and rough it. I mean, just from doing it alone you learn a lot about yourself and how important it is to physically and mentally prove yourself."

Luxury and comfort represent the safety net of our parents. We want to validate ourselves as individuals, as warriors and survivors in a hostile world.

Risking Everything for "Love"

Another reason Thirteeners take dangerous risks with their lives is that they are hungry for love and belonging. According to an August 1994 story carried by the Associated Press, two different surveys show that while an overwhelming majority of homosexual and bisexual youths are knowledgeable about the AIDS virus and safer sex practices involving condoms, a huge segment still choose to practice unprotected sex. One survey conducted in Minnesota revealed that 63 percent of respondents practiced risky sex. The other study, conducted in San Francisco and published in *The Journal of the American Medical Association,* found that one-third of subjects ages seventeen to twenty-two reported having unprotected anal intercourse in the previous six months, and 12 percent reported intravenous drug use. Almost 10 percent of respondents were HIV-positive, and most of those were not aware that they were infected until they were tested and surveyed by the San Francisco Department of Public Health.

Psychological studies indicate that one of the primary sources of male homosexual tendencies is a distant, absent, unloving or rejecting father, especially when combined with a smothering, dominating mother. Young boys crave affection from their fathers and hunger for a male role model to emulate. When their fathers fail to provide that affection and that role model, boys will often unconsciously substitute sex for the missing affection and substitute a male lover for a father figure.

People who are empty inside and hungry for the love that was denied them in childhood will often risk anything—even the suffering, degradation and death of AIDS—in order to grab just a little fleeting affection. Some will even risk their lives for the counterfeit affection of an anonymous encounter in a bathhouse or a public restroom.

Why, when they know that unprotected sex is nothing more than a game of Russian roulette, do people risk everything for a momentary experience of pleasure? "I saw a standup comic on TV one time," says Terry, a gay twenty-six-year-old who is HIV-positive. "He said, 'Having sex with a condom on is like eating steak with a balloon over your tongue.' And that's really true. I mean, the whole idea of a condom is to place a barrier between you and another person—and who needs that? 'Safer sex' is just a code word that means 'Don't feel anything when you have sex. Don't feel anything physically, and don't feel anything emotionally.' Well, that's not even sex, and that's not for me."

We have a message for those who are risking their lives for the false (and ultimately shame-producing) "love" of promiscuous sex or homosexual sex. Our message is "You can experience true love, affirming love, unconditional love—the love of a caring, understanding heavenly Father—through Jesus Christ." Experts in the recovery field will tell you that compulsive and addictive behaviors—compulsive sexual behavior, compulsive drug abuse, compulsive alcohol abuse, compulsive overeating—are really substitutes for love and for God. That is why Twelve Step programs for all of these addictions are so effective. The steps teach addicted individuals to replace their compulsive behavior with reliance on a loving and powerful God.

Our message to love-hungry, sex-addicted Xers, both hetero- and homosexuals, is the beautiful story of a loving Father who sent his Son as an expression of his affirmation, grace and forgiveness.

Deadstick Landing

Grant jockeyed for position in a rumbling herd of cycles. Fourteen machines, their riders hunched low, jostled and nudged each other, handlebar to handlebar. For several seconds as the riders scrambled down the straightaway and approached the first turn, there was no one leading, no one trailing. There was just the pack. But as they went into the turn, nerve, skill, grit and grim determination pulled several riders out ahead of the pack. One of them was Grant. There was room in the turn to squeeze cycles through four abreast. If the lead cyclists had been the four horsemen of the apocalypse, Grant would have been the third horseman from the outside.

They roared out of the turn, splashed into the first bog, then lunged into the tight second curve. Coming out of that turn they roared straight up a big mound for the first jump. With balletic grace, a flight of motorcycles took to the air, wire wheels spinning and glinting in the sun. They landed gracefully on the short straightaway and began spacing out along the track. Grant and another competitor were jockeying for second place behind a black-helmeted rider who had pulled one cycle-length into the lead.

They gunned it up the second jump, a bigger and trickier jump than the first. From behind the retaining ropes and hay bales, Lindsey watched anxiously as Grant took to the air, conspicuous in his flashing yellow helmet. He kept his weight back on the seat as his wheels cleared the ground, then moved his weight forward through the arc, standing up on the footpegs to move the front wheel down a bit, flying the bike through the air like a space shuttle coming in for a deadstick landing.

The bike touched down on the rear wheel right on cue, but the front wheel was a few inches too low. It was a jarring landing, and it put Grant a little off his pace. He slipped half a bike-length into third place.

Grant gunned it over the jolting undulations of the whoop-de-do and held his own going into the third turn. Accelerating for the second bog, he edged to the right to avoid the splashback from the first and second cycles—but with limited success. A wall of mud exploded in front of him, drenching his goggles and leaving him half-blind. He didn't even have a moment to spare to wipe at them with his gloves.

He was halfway through the first lap, and he had a long way to go.

Daring Death

Robert Heinlein expressed it well in *Podkayne of Mars*. "Each one of us," he wrote, "faces up to the universe alone, and the universe . . . always wins and takes all." Heinlein was talking about death. So was twentysomething actor Charlie Sheen, who told a TV interviewer, "Death is a pretty heavy trip. They save it for last, you know." And the Eagles were talking about death in "Hotel California" when they sang, "You can check out anytime you like, but you can never leave."

My generation thinks about death a lot. And thoughts of death lead us to despair and depression. "I often think that life lacks meaning," one student told me. "When you're heading toward death you wonder what anything really means—what anything is really worth. Everything just seems dead and stale." As one Xer standup comic observed, "I've just seen the light at the end of the tunnel. It's a train."

The extreme fringe of Thirteener culture is fascinated with death imagery. We curiously explore Satan worship. We read books like *Final Exit*. We play real-life versions of Dungeons & Dragons to the death. We love dark comedies. We have proved a hard-core cult following for the garishly sadistic filmmaker Quentin Tarantino, writer and/or director of such blood-spattered films as *Reservoir Dogs* and *Pulp Fiction*, and Oliver Stone's *Natural Born Killers*. We laugh and slurp it up when Tarantino hits us with a hideous torture scene, a bam-splat shootout or a drug overdose scene, all colored by his trademark irony and a smirking twist of farce.

Our preoccupation with death is displayed on our skin: we avoid the sun, we cherish our pallor, we look like ghosts or corpses. Xer women often favor makeup in shades of white, black, blue and purple—the colors of death and lividity and corpsehood. Our preoccupation with death is displayed in our lifestyle: we take crazy risks and dare death to come and get us.

In the popular movie *What About Bob?* Richard Dreyfuss asks his Thirteener son, "Why are you always wearing black? What is it with you and this death fixation?" His son replies, "Maybe I'm in mourning for my lost childhood."

Later in the movie Thirteener moviegoers howl as Dreyfuss (who plays a homicidally frustrated psychiatrist) tries to kill an annoying patient (Bill Murray) by tying him up and surrounding him with explosives. As the fuse is lit, Murray joyfully exclaims, "Oh, I get it! Death therapy!"

Free Falling

Lindsey had butterflies in her stomach. Grant had caught up with the number-two biker in the middle of the fourth lap, and now the two of them were battling it out, their front fenders just inches behind the rear fender of the number-one biker. The three leaders flew in triad formation over the first mound, roared up the short straightaway and powered up the mound to that tricky second jump.

Lindsey's breath caught. This jump always gave Grant trouble. Always.

A trio of shiny helmets—black, red and yellow—bobbed upward in unison. Six wire wheels clawed the air, reaching for altitude. Three mighty two-stroke engines roared angrily.

In horror, Lindsey watched the yellow helmet wobble and falter out of formation. Grant was wrestling with his machine, struggling to correct his weight distribution as the bike descended to earth. His lead wheel was too low and turned slightly. The bike was tilting, listing, twisting in midair. Grant's machine clattered against his side-by-side competitor's machine just as they were touching the ground. The other biker slewed, skidded and fishtailed, but finally regained his balance and roared off after the black-helmeted leader.

Grant was not so lucky. His machine came down on a shimmying front wheel. His weight was too far forward. The rear wheel hit, bounced and flew into the air again. Grant was thrown forward, his legs flying up even as his hands maintained a death-grip on the handlebars. The bike veered off the track and flipped toward the restraining ropes as a small knot of spectators scattered. Grant left the bike, soaring over the handlebars. Both he and the roaring Suzuki cartwheeled end over end.

Lindsey gasped as Grant disappeared behind a hay bale. The bike landed in a heap in the tall grass, sputtered and stalled. People were yelling and running, but Lindsey was rooted to the spot. She stared, unmoving, her face pale and stricken, for several seconds.

Then slowly, unsteadily, she began walking around the track toward the place where Grant had come to rest.

Death over Life

Kurt Cobain wanted to call his next album *I Hate Myself and I Want to Die,* but the record company rejected the title. He tried to kill himself more than once with drugs, but he survived the attempts. Why was this young man so hell-bent on self-destruction?

Any way you cut it, Cobain had a lot to live for. He had a beautiful one-year-old daughter. As the lead singer-guitarist-songwriter for the grunge-rock band Nirvana he had achieved the pinnacle of success: Nirvana's album *Nevermind* had sold ten million copies, and the follow-up album *In Utero* was following close behind. He had more money than any human being could reasonably spend in a lifetime. Yet he scorned it all.

"Teenage angst has paid off well / Now I'm bored and old," he sang in "Serve the Servants," a cut from *In Utero.* A lot of people who knew Cobain were saddened but hardly surprised in April 1994 when they heard that he had blown his brains out with a shotgun.

Why was Cobain so unhappy that he had to end a brief, successful, promising life? Maybe his past had something to do with it. His parents divorced when he was ten. He was passed from relative to relative throughout his adolescence, and for a while he even lived under a bridge. Perhaps he saw no way out of his addiction to heroin. Perhaps he couldn't take the pressure of living as the media-appointed spokesman for the angst- and anger-ridden Xer generation.

The really tragic thing about Kurt Cobain's suicide is that there is nothing particularly unusual about it, except for Cobain's notoriety. Xer suicides are as common as fleas on dogs. As Xer columnist Dennis Romero, cofounder of X Journalists Association, writes in *The Charlotte Observer* (April 15, 1994, p. 15A),

Cobain's suicide can help America finally take note: Youth unhappiness is more than a fad, the product of a temporarily dull economy, or the whining of another generation of post-war brats.

It's pathological. . . .

Self-destruction is to Generation X what playing chicken was to fifties rockers, what taking hard-core drugs was to flower children.

It's the ultimate rebellion in a world of youth culture where the forms of rebellion have been exhausted. At the same time, it can be the only way out of a life made crueler by the pressures and pessimism of modern-day America.

Here, then, is the most tangible demonstration of our preoccupation with death: we choose death over life at an astonishing rate. As youth and family counselors Stephen Arterburn and Jim Burns observe in their book *When Love Is Not Enough*, the suicide rate for today's young Xers is triple the suicide rate for Boomer youth in the sixties. About three-quarters of all teenagers have contemplated suicide, and over one-quarter have attempted suicide. Suicide is the third leading cause of death among young adults.

General George S. Patton once said, "Did you ever stop to think that death could be more exciting than life?" Many of today's Xers apparently agree with the general. As one university student told me, "Death would be pretty cool. Not mass suicide or anything, but for certain people it's a good option." Pretty cool? A good option? What kind of experiences and philosophies does it take to produce a heartfelt belief that extinction could be "pretty cool" and a "good option"?

Life is complicated. Death is simple. Xers, in their drive to simplify their lives, often choose to extinguish their lives.

As Christians, we have a story of life and meaning and hope. We have a story of love and affirmation and self-worth. For Xers who see no hope in life, who see only death ahead, whose only light at the end of the tunnel is an onrushing train, we have the story of the God who came to bring us the true light and the true life. As John 1:4-5 tells us,

What came into existence was Life,
    and the Life was Light to live by.
The Life-Light blazed out of the darkness;
    the darkness couldn't put it out.

On the Ground

"Careful! Careful! Get back! Give the man some air!"

"Don't move him! His back may be broken!"

"Is he dead? He looks dead!"

Lindsey pushed her way through the crowd of gawkers. Grant's body was a shapeless heap. His legs were twisted at odd angles. His face was hidden beneath a muddy helmet and goggles. He wasn't moving.

"Grant!" Lindsey called chokingly.

A man was bending over him. "Can you hear me, buddy? Are you in there? Hey! Talk to me, man!"

A groan bubbled between Grant's mud-spattered lips.

Lindsey gasped.

"Hang in there, buddy," said the man. "You're gonna be okay!" The man reached out, dug his fingers into Grant's knee and squeezed hard. "Can you feel that?"

"Hey!" Grant moaned. "Cut it out!"

The man chuckled. "You'll be okay, cowboy."

Grant tested his limbs and winced. "Sure I'm okay," he said through clenched teeth. "I think my leg's broken though. How's my bike?"

Lindsey dropped to her knees at Grant's side and called him something unprintable. Then she began to cry.

Hard Bodies

Christian Slater, one of my generation's leading film stars, has been an alcoholic since his early teen years. His motto expresses the outlook of an entire generation: "Live hard. Die fast. And leave a good-looking corpse." We are the hard body generation. We are leaner, stronger, more pumped-up and toned-out than any previous generation. We look good. Looking good is our life, our obsession, our religion. An Xer in one of my focus groups put it this way: "I lead a very healthy life. I run. That's spirituality for me."

My generation spends more time in the gym than any previous generation. Whereas the Boomers of the sixties and seventies had their mind-altering hallucinogens, our drug-of-choice is body-altering. More college athletes than ever are using steroids. Even more startling, many average Thirteeners who have no professional or Olympian athletic aspirations are turning to steroids to build body mass. Why? To look good.

The "just do it!" slogan of our generation comes straight from our desire for hard, beautiful bodies. Boomers are always trying to find ways to motivate themselves to exercise or diet. Xers don't ponder motivational gimmicks or techniques. In typical straight-up Xer fashion, we say, "Just do it!"

A hard body is a beautiful body—and image is everything. Live hard. Die fast. Leave a good-looking corpse. Hey, the shape of my body may be the one thing in this out-of-control life that I can control.

Back in the Saddle

"What was going through my head as I was going over those handlebars?" Grant chuckled. "I thought, *Whoa, momma! This is it!* I was just hoping it wouldn't hurt much. But it did. I mean, I never knew that such pain existed! The moment I stopped bouncing, man, I began to rethink my philosophy of life. I thought, *Oh, this is stupid, man. This is really dumb. If I live, man, I'm never getting on a bike again. Never, ever, ever.*

"Then I turned my head and saw my bike, and it was all twisted up. And I thought, *Aw, man! Look at that! It's gonna take months to get it back in racing shape!* And that's when I knew I could never give up biking.

"Lindsey thinks I'm crazy. She's all, 'Are you telling me you're gonna go right on racing after what just happened to you?' And I'm like, 'Sure, why not?' As soon as I get out of this hospital and get my leg out of this cast I plan to get right back in the saddle. I don't intend to let this thing mess up my head. Life is short, man. If you don't jump in and just do it, man, you're not living."

• • • • • • • • • •

6

The Postmodern Generation

Brennan clicked off the TV with

the remote control. He was stretched out on the family-room couch. "So, Dad, what do you think? Is that a great show or what?"

"It's not *Star Trek*," said Perry, frowning at the blank TV screen from his overstuffed chair.

"It's *Star Trek: Voyager,* Dad. You have to take it on its own merits," Brennan sat up and leaned forward—an aggressive, engaged posture that Perry recognized from previous philosophical debates with his twenty-year-old son. "You can't keep comparing today's *Trek* to the old series," Brennan continued. "I mean, the original Gene Roddenberry *Star Trek* show is more than a quarter of a century old!"

"Ouch! Don't say it like that! You make me feel old! That's my favorite show you're talking about! Jim Kirk, Spock, Bones, going where no man has gone before . . . But this show! I tell you, son, the future sure isn't what it used to be."

"You didn't like *The Next Generation*. You didn't like *Deep Space Nine*. And now you don't like *Star Trek: Voyager*. You're hopeless, Dad. Face it: you're stuck in the Nixon era."

"I am not! I just know good TV when I see it! It's easy to be wowed by all those whiz-bang special effects and the stereophonic sound on the new series, but what grabbed me about those original *Star Trek* episodes was the stories . . . the characters . . ."

"Don't give me that, Dad. The stories and characters on the new shows are way better! You know why you're stuck on the old Trek? Because it was *your* Trek, and the stories were about your times! Those old episodes are just a bunch of sixties morality plays, all about the Cold War and Vietnam and the flower children. And a lot of the stories are pretty lame. Like the one where that hippie guru is leading all those young people to a planet called Eden. And the one where—"

"Okay, okay, so not every episode was a classic! But what about 'Charlie X'? Or 'City on the Edge of Forever'? You've gotta admit, that's great TV!"

"I'm not talking about individual episodes, Dad. I'm talking about the whole premise. The new Trek shows operate on a totally different set of assumptions and cultural attitudes. Take Spock, for example."

"What about Spock?" asked Perry defensively.

"He's a human who wants to be a machine."

"He's Vulcan!"

"Half-Vulcan, half-human. He continually struggles to repress his human emotion, always trying to become as mechanical and emotionless as his Vulcan father, right? And several episodes turn on the fact that his emotions don't stay repressed."

"What's your point?"

"Just follow me, Dad. Cut to *Star Trek: The Next Generation*. Instead of Spock, a human who wants to be a machine, we have Data, a machine who wants to be human. And there are other major differences in the premise from the old series to the new. The old Trek is about the conquering hero, the rugged individual, Captain James T. Kirk going from planet to planet, always sneaking around the Prime Directive so he can right wrongs and make the universe safe for democracy.

"*The Next Generation* is totally different! It's not about the individual, it's about the community. The new shows are about what it means to live together as a society, about redefining our cultural values. There is a greater respect for nonhuman realities and for alien ways of thinking. There's more of a multicultural feel. In *The Next Generation* the Prime Directive isn't just a plot device to be cheated by the captain. It's a moral guide to keep the *Enterprise* crew from screwing up other cultures."

"So what you're telling me," said Perry, "is that the big difference between the original Trek and the new Treks is that the new shows are politically correct?"

"It goes deeper than that, Dad. Kirk's mission was 'to explore new worlds, to seek out new civilizations'—and to bring those civilizations into the Federation. It was really a conquest thing. The new shows are really about learning from alien cultures rather than assimilating them. That's a major shift in worldview."

"Okay, let me see if I'm tracking with you, Brennan. To boil it all down, you're telling me that the reason I like the old Trek and don't like the new Treks is that I'm a hidebound old fossil, my thinking is stuck back in the tie-dyed sixties, my worldview is hopelessly out of date, and there's a whole new generation with a new way of perceiving reality."

"Right."

"All of which adds up to the fact that I just don't get it, and I probably never will."

"Congratulations, Dad. I think your porch light just came on."

Shifting Ground

"It's pre-postmodern, guaranteed!"

"Nick-at-Nite, better living through good TV!"

So goes the Nickelodeon cable channel's self-promo ad for its evening lineup of "classic" reruns of *I Love Lucy, The Dick Van Dyke Show* and *Bewitched.* These old shows are "pre-postmodern" indeed. They reflect a time when our society was radically different—a time when families were much more functional and whole than they are today, when choices were simpler, the future brighter and issues as black and white as the shows the themselves.

The pre-postmodern era is gone (except in reruns). The postmodern era is here to stay. If we want to continue evangelizing in the postmodern world, we need to understand postmodern realities. We need to adopt postmodern strategies. Reruns of outdated, black-and-white, pre-postmodern strategies just won't work anymore (except on TV).

A profound shift in thinking has taken place in the space of a generation. Generation X is the first to see the world through postmodern eyes. Very few of those who were born prior to Generation X understand how radically the thought patterns of Xers differ from their own ways of thinking. The ground has shifted under the feet of the Baby Boomers, and they don't even know it. My generation doesn't just look and dress and act differently from previous generations. My generation truly thinks differently, perceives differently, believes differently and processes truth differently from any previous generation.

Skeptical? Stay tuned.

The Postmodern Revolution

The word *postmodernism* may sound ominous. The term may make you feel you're taking college history all over again. But understanding the impact of postmodernism on our society is really not that hard. A short course (Intro to Postmodernism 101) follows.

Modernism (or what Nick-at-Nite would call "pre-postmodernism") came into being during the death of the Middle Ages and the birth of the Renaissance. The defining achievement of the modern period was the Age of Enlightenment, a European intellectual movement of the seventeenth and eighteenth centuries that celebrated human reason and human values. The Enlightenment experiment produced revolutionary developments in science, philosophy, politics and the arts. One of the leading proponents of the Enlightenment was Thomas Jefferson, who helped lay out one of the great success stories of the Enlightenment project: the United States of America.

The massive shift in thinking that produced the shift from modernism to postmodernism can be traced to the beginning of the twentieth century, when Einstein's theory of relativity overthrew the Enlightenment-spawned physics of Isaac Newton. As my father, Leighton

Ford, explains in his analysis of postmodernism in *The Power of Story* (Colorado Springs: NavPress, 1994), Einstein's theory completely upset all previous assumptions of the nature of reality. The implications of relativity included the following:

☐ There is no such thing as an objective point of view in matters of physics; all viewpoints are relative in space and time.

☐ Under some conditions, subjective experience supersedes objective measurements.

☐ Space and time are relative, not absolute, concepts and depend on such factors as relative motion and the point of view of the observer.

Of course Einstein wasn't the only influence on the evolution of the postmodern worldview. Friedrich Nietzsche's late-nineteenth-century attacks on Christianity and his negation of morality in favor of the "will to power" also hastened the breakdown of the modern worldview. Nietzsche preached a gospel of rejection of the story of God, asserting that the human race "must learn to live without its gods" and the consoling mythical stories of religion.

Charles Darwin contributed to the rise of postmodernism by substituting evolution by natural selection for the narrative of Genesis. His theory was soon applied not only to science but to society and economics as "dog-eat-dog" social Darwinism.

James Joyce contributed to the end of modernism and the rise of postmodernism with his "antinovel" *Ulysses,* a book with no dramatic coherence and no possibility of occurring in the real world. The world of *Ulysses* is a world apart from storytelling.

Obviously I'm not suggesting that most people in the grunge culture have studied the implications of Einstein's theory, Darwin's theory, Nietzsche or Joyce. Rather, the implications of these various influences have slowly filtered from the scientific community and the intelligentsia to the arts, the entertainment media and the news media. Over a period of sixty or more years these implications have gradually solidified into the present foundational framework for the way our culture thinks and perceives reality. They have saturated our society's view of ethics, morality, philosophy and religion so that the average person of my generation now believes the following:

☐ There is no such thing as an absolute, objective point of view in matters of morality and religion. A common expression of this assumption is the statement "You have your truth and I have mine."

☐ Subjective experience supersedes logic and objective facts. We are free to choose what we will believe according to what makes us feel comfortable. Don't confuse us with the facts.

☐ The nature of truth and the nature of God are relative, not absolute, concepts: "You have your god and I have mine."

This postmodern perceptual framework is a totally different way of looking at the world from the modern framework that reigned from the Enlightenment all the way to the Baby Boom generation. Unlike previous generations, Generation X doesn't see itself as occupying a meaningful place in creation under the guiding hand of a benevolent God. My generation seeks only to survive in a godless, mindless universe where there are no rules, no right, no wrong, no meaning and no absolute truth.

In the 1994 Charlotte symposium on Generation X, Stanley J. Grenz of Regent College in Vancouver, British Columbia, defined four assumptions of postmodernism that are deeply entrenched in Xer thinking and the Xer worldview.

Feelings and relationships supersede logic and reason. The postmodern mind rejects the philosophical assumptions of the Enlightenment and modernism. The transrational, the paradoxical and the supernatural are not unquestioned by Xers; they are automatically assumed to be real.

To Xers it is feelings and relationships that matter, not dispassionate knowledge and logical arguments. This fact would only bolster some people's conclusion that my peers are a bunch of "slackers," that they are not only lazy on the job but intellectually lazy as well. But Dieter Zander, founding pastor of NewSong Church in Walnut, California, disagrees. "This generation," he says, "is not lazy in any sense of the word. Intellectually and in every other way they are very active. They reject logical arguments not because they won't or can't think, but because there are so many conflicting arguments. Staying out of the 'logic wars' enables them to mentally survive in a confused and chaotic world."

Pessimism. The postmodern mindset of Xers is in sharp contrast to the optimistic cultural forecasts of modernism. The Enlightenment spawned the notion of inevitable human progress, the belief that knowledge is inherently good and leads to social betterment and that science and education will free us from social bondage and lead us to utopia. Such thinking, while still common among Baby Boomers and their parents, is completely alien to my generation. As Walker Percy observed in *The Thanatos Syndrome,* "This is not the Age of Enlightenment but the Age of Not Knowing What to Do" (New York: Farrar Straus Giroux, 1987, p. 75).

"For the first time in three centuries," observes Grenz, "today's youth do not share the conviction of their parents that we will solve the problems of the planet or that their lives will be better than that of their parents. They know that life on the earth is fragile and that the continued existence of humankind is dependent on a decrease in consumption and a new attitude toward the earth, an attitude that replaces the model of conquest with one of cooperation."

Jimmy Long, Blue Ridge regional director for InterVarsity Christian Fellowship, was (to my knowledge) the first person to link an understanding of postmodernism to an understanding of Xer thinking. "I believe that the Baby Boom generation was the last true modern generation," he observes. "The Boomers thought they would save the world. The Baby Busters have abandoned that notion. They only want to survive in a world that can't be saved. Just look at the different ways Boomers and Busters perceive the ecology issue. Boomers are trying to restore and re-create the creation. Busters are just trying to survive the demise of creation." The sense of pessimism and powerlessness of Generation X is a major generational and cultural shift—and it is a direct result of the postmodern influence.

Holism/wholism/community. Modernism compartmentalized knowledge and exalted the individual. Postmodernism seeks to reunify knowledge and exalt the community. The watchwords of postmodernism are *holism* and *holistic,* which *The American Heritage Dictionary* (electronically accessed on CompuServe) defines as follows:

Holism. *n.* The theory that living matter or reality is made up of organic or unified wholes that are greater than the simple sum of their parts.

Holistic. *adj.* 1. Of or relating to holism. 2. Emphasizing the importance of the whole and the interdependence of its parts. 3. Concerned with wholes rather than analysis or separation into parts:

holistic medicine; holistic ecology.

The word *wholism* is sometimes substituted for *holism* because the concept involves looking at the whole rather than the parts. Holism represents a postmodern desire to reunify what modernism has dissected and torn apart. Holistic postmodernism rejects the radical individualism of modernism and seeks to replace that individualism with community. The individual is an isolated component; the community is the whole.

"We see an example of the shift from the modern to postmodern mindset," observes Grenz, "in the transition from *Star Trek* to *Star Trek: The Next Generation.* The original show was about modern individualism, about Captain Kirk's heroic autonomy in the universe; the 'next generation' series is about a postmodern community, about the close-knit heteronomy of the *Enterprise* fellowship. In our transition from a modern evangelistic enterprise to a postmodern evangelistic enterprise, our challenge is to discover how we can embody the gospel story in a way that appeals to the community-oriented postmodern mind."

Truth is relative. The postmodern mind views the issue of truth from a completely different perspective from that of the modern mind. To the modernist, truth is rational and can be judged and apprehended by the human intellect. The postmodernist has ousted the intellect from that position of authority, believing that truth can be nonrational and even emotional and intuitive. To the postmodernist, truth is relative at best and possibly nonexistent. If truth is no longer an absolute concept, then there is no longer one truth. There are many truths. There is your truth, my truth, his truth, her truth. No one truth is more valid than any other—and the postmodern mind sees no contradiction in such a viewpoint.

I once shared my faith with a University of Virginia student named Paul. He had a lot of questions about the reliability of the Bible, and I thought we were having a very good dialogue. I had just finished grad school at that time, so I was armed with dozens of sound arguments that he could not refute. He should have been completely convinced. I had clearly "won" on debating points. But the conversation ended with Paul saying, "So what?" and walking away.

That conversation was a real eye-opener for me. The truth issue is not *the* issue for Xers, because truth, to them, is relative.

The "truth is relative" assumption offers a powerful challenge to the Christian faith. If truth is relative, then morality is relative. The Ten Commandments become "the Ten Suggestions." If truth is relative it doesn't matter what people believe or what faith they embrace. Since logical reasoning is not important to the postmodern mind, apologetics is meaningless. There is no more reason to believe in biblical Christianity than in Zen or Scientology or the Flat Earth Society or Satanism or druidical tree worship; all beliefs are equal. In fact, Christianity comes off as distasteful to the postmodern mind, especially when compared to other faiths, because Christianity is evangelistic. Because they seek to evangelize and convert other people, Christians are seen as "dogmatic" and "intolerant"—and these are the unforgivable sins to the postmodern mind.

Instructions from a Son

"Here," said Perry, handing a triplicate form to Lindsey. "Get Mr. Bordon's signature on the 'received' line and he's ready to go."

"Okay." Lindsey grabbed the form and dashed out to the loading bay, where T.J. and Barry were muscling the last cartons of brochures into the bed of the client's Chevy S-10.

"Hey, Dad!" said a voice behind Perry. He turned and saw his son, Brennan, approaching.

"Hi, son!" said Perry. "What are you doing here?"

"Old Hoop—I mean, Mr. Hooper called me and asked if I had time to do some fill-in work again. He's a little short-handed in the bindery department, so I'm gonna run the collating machine this evening. I take over the shift in ten minutes."

"I'll bet it's that Apex Industries report," said Perry. "Tom's in a real crunch on that job. What about your studies?"

"Things are kinda slack right now. I can handle it."

"Good. I'm sure you can use the extra money."

"You got that right." Brennan hesitated. "Say, Dad?"

"Yes?"

"You know that guy Michael over in the pre-press department?"

"Sure."

"I invited him over to our place tomorrow night."

"Great!"

"Yeah, well—" Brennan seemed uncomfortable about something.

"What is it?"

"Well, would you do me a favor? Don't try to convert Michael when he comes over, okay?"

"Huh?"

"I mean, I want people to find Christ as much as you do, Dad. But the way you go about it . . . I mean, people like Michael don't . . . The thing is, Dad, could we just have, like, a normal evening? I mean, let's just get to know Michael. I invited him over to shoot a few baskets and have dinner with us. Let's just leave it at that, okay?"

"Okay, son, I get the picture."

Brennan smiled. "Thanks, Dad. Hope I didn't hurt your feelings."

"Heck, no!" said Perry with a grin.

His feelings weren't hurt. They were *stinging*.

A Deconstructed Generation

If the centerpiece of the modern era is the Enlightenment experiment, then the centerpiece of the postmodern era would have to be deconstructionism. The concept of deconstruction was first proposed by French philosopher Jacques Derrida in the 1970s as a theory about language and literature. Derrida's central tenet is that words have no objective content. His goal was to empty words of their meaning, and we see this clearly in the word itself. *Deconstruction* is a combination of two words, *destruction* and *construction*. Derrida sought to deconstruct language, to turn words inside out and drain them of objective value. Today deconstructionism has been applied to a wide range of disciplines including not only literature but also the law, journalism, politics, theology and sociology. The new feminism of the eighties and nineties has been heavily influenced by deconstructionism. The essential principles of Deconstructionist theory are as follows.

The whole world is "text." To the deconstructionist, language exists not only in literature but in our history and our culture; it shapes our thinking and creates our reality. There is no objective reality, only the reality that our language creates in our minds. The words we use take on subtly different shades of meaning depending on who is speaking, who is hearing and the context in which the words are spoken. Words are also invisibly linked to a larger cultural and conceptual history that further drenches them with hidden content, connotations and codes. Thus any text is made up of words whose meaning is indeterminate and whose content is not objectively verifiable. Words do not have objective meanings. To interpret the meaning of a given text is to impose meaning on it. To say "This is what it means" is to misread it.

There is no objective truth. Derrida criticizes modern Western thinking for its attachment to "logocentrism," the belief that "words mean things," the idea that truth can be assigned to *logos,* the word. There is no truth. There is no objective point of view. There is no "voice of reason," no logic, no meaning. Derrida specifically attacks the doctrine that the Word of God—God's *logos*—is truth. The words of Jesus in his high priestly prayer, John 17:17, are pathetically absurd to the deconstructionist mind:

Make them holy—consecrated—with the truth. Your word is consecrating truth.

Jesus' prayer is meaningless, according to Derrida's theory. God's word consecrates nothing. It proves nothing. It accomplishes nothing. It is only a text. There is no objective truth.

The polarity of Western logocentrism is divisive and destructive. Western thought divided the world into a framework of polar oppositions, such as good-evil, truth-falsehood, male-female, positive-negative, being-nonbeing, thing-word, presence-absence, reality-image. In the standard logocentric systems, the first word of each pair is always stronger, greater, more highly valued: GOOD-evil, TRUTH-falsehood, MALE-female and so forth. Thus, Derrida said, we use language to create destructive, oppressive hierarchies. By saying some things are good and some are evil, we make moral judgments and set ourselves up as morally superior. By placing male over female, men use language to keep women in sexual, economic and social bondage.

The average person—including the average Xer—has never heard of deconstructionism. However, this arcane theory captures the rough-and-ready thought forms that pervade the postmodern air—thought forms that have largely been absorbed and accepted by my generation. You see the tendrils of the deconstructionist mindset in the way journalism—both print and electronic—is conducted today.

The search for truth, for the objective facts, used to be the essential goal of journalism. Opinion used to be reserved for the editorial pages, but no more. Now opinion is woven right into stories on the front page—and done so openly.

In the late seventies and early eighties a debate raged in the journalistic community over "advocacy journalism." The "old guard" journalists wanted the news media to report the facts and seek the truth; the "new wave" journalists wanted the news media to advocate for social change and a point of view. The advocacy journalists, inspired by deconstructionist thinking and the belief that there is no objective truth, won the debate. Today virtually all major outlet journalism—both broadcast and published—is advocacy journalism.

Deconstructionism poses a major challenge to those who would communicate the Christian story to this generation. We come to this generation with a story that we say is objectively true, a story about a Person who claims to be the Word and the truth. But this generation responds, "A word has no meaning, and there is no objective truth." We come to this generation claiming that salvation is by grace through faith. But this generation responds, "I'm not interested in salvation, only in survival. And as for faith, well, that is only a matter of perspective and interpretation." We come to this generation with an urgent mission to evangelize. But this generation responds, "You're being intolerant. Why do you want to impose your belief system on me? Leave me alone."

The postmodern mindset and the deconstructionist mindset challenge the very foundation of the act of evangelizing—of telling the story of God. How can we meet this challenge? How can we carry the story of ultimate truth to a generation that cannot even conceive of the existence of ultimate truth?

One-on-One-on-One

Brennan and Michael were shooting baskets in the driveway when Perry got home, so he parked his car on the street. He walked up the drive and stood watching for a couple of minutes while the two young men went at it, one-on-one. Brennan was near the basket, while Michael was in the middle of the driveway.

"Here's a shot I worked real hard on," said Michael, "when I played pivot man for the Cougars. Give me some hands-up defense, okay? Now I'll come charging at you for the jump shot, so watch for it, right? Right! Here goes!"

Michael came in hard and fast. Brennan raised both hands to keep Michael from getting a good line of fire at the basket. Michael paused, dribbling, looking left and right around Brennan, seemingly unable to get a good shot. Suddenly Michael feinted to the right, and Brennan moved toward the feint. Michael jumped for the shot—the ball sailed in a perfect arc, kissed the backboard and slid through the basket like grease through a goose. Michael came down from the jump shot, blundering right into Brennan, who staggered backwards.

"Hey, sorry, man," said Brennan. "I fouled you."

Michael laughed.

Perry was surprised to see Michael laugh. He had worked in the same building with Michael for six months and had never seen him laugh before.

"Dude, you didn't foul me!" said Michael, clapping one hand on Brennan's shoulder. "I fouled you!"

"No way!"

"Listen, man, I used to get away with this little trick all the time!" said Michael, more animated than Perry had ever seen him before. "This jump shot is a great way to draw fouls! Check this out, dude. I fake you out, right? You move out of position and I go for the jump shot, right?"

"Yeah? So?"

"So I get a three-point opportunity, man! The ref sees you out of position, shoving into me while I'm in the air making my shot. Who gets the foul call? You do, my man! It's a beautiful setup. They're wise to it in the NBA, and the refs call an offensive foul when they see it. But when you're playing high-school or college roundball you can usually get away with it. I mean, I even fooled you into thinking you had fouled me!"

"Cool!" laughed Brennan. "Let me try it on you. Get in position where I was and I'll—oh hi, Dad! Watch this!"

Perry watched as Brennan tried the jump shot that Michael had just demonstrated. Then Perry joined in for a little "twenty-one" until Perry's wife, Heidi, called them in for dinner.

While Michael was in the bathroom washing up, Perry took Brennan aside. "Son," he said, "I showed you that three-point fake-and-jump-shot trick a long time ago, didn't I?"

"Sure, Dad. But I'd sorta forgotten how it went. Besides, I'm letting Michael show me some stuff."

"Why? You know all there is to know about basketball, Brennan."

"Don't you get it, Dad? I don't want to know about basketball. I want to be his friend."

Window of Opportunity

We have seen that postmodernism poses a challenge to Christian evangelism. But might it not also, if properly understood, offer us a window of opportunity?

Stanley Grenz suggests that postmodernism may well be an opportunity in disguise. It would be ironic and tragic, he suggests, if evangelical Christians were to position themselves as the last defenders of modernism! After all, it was the Enlightenment project of the modern era that produced the radical scientific belief system that has waged such a successful war against Christianity in the twentieth century. It is the modern rationalist, materialist, scientific mindset that claims nothing exists if it cannot be quantified and examined within a scientific framework.

The postmodern mindset represents an abandonment of the rationalist belief system. The postmodern framework allows for the existence of realities that science cannot measure—the supernatural, the transrational, the spiritual, the eternal, the ineffable, the numinous. These are all realities that are central to the biblical story, and Christian writers such as Henri Nouwen, Eugene Peterson and Richard Foster help us get in touch with the mystery of God. The collapse of the modern worldview has given the Christian worldview a beachhead in the postmodern mind.

In fact, modern science has produced the seeds of its own downfall. Einstein's theory, with its emphasis on relativity and the subjective viewpoint of the observer, undermined the concept of absolute truth. Quantum physics, with its uncertainty principle, further undermined the materialistic view of reality, replacing it with a worldview in which matter is information. John Wheeler, the physicist who gave "black holes" their name, said the "nuts and bolts, if you will, out of which the world is made" is *logic*—the word—an intelligent thought. And physicist James Jeans said, "The universe begins to look more like a great thought than a great machine."

As Win Manning of the George Gallup Institute observes,

The revolution in physics has totally undermined the modern conception of science. It's commonplace to hear scientists saying that the physicists' grounding for a quark is no different than Homer's belief in the gods on Olympus. If postmodernism is a breach in the fortress of scientism, it can't be a bad development, since it opens up the ability to deal with spiritual and metaphysical issues on a level that was not possible twenty years ago.

The story of Jesus has a natural appeal to postmodern sensibilities. Jesus spoke in a way that plugs directly into the postmodern psyche. To Nicodemus he said, "You know well enough how the wind blows this way and that. You hear it rustling through the trees, but you have no idea where it comes from or where it's headed next. That's the way it is with everyone 'born from above' by the wind of God, the Spirit of God" (John 3:8). Whereas most modern-minded evangelists would have attempted to logically persuade Nicodemus with rational arguments or the Four Spiritual Laws, Jesus gave Nicodemus a mystery— a taste of something elusive and intangible. In so doing he aroused within Nicodemus a hunger for spiritual awakening.

"As Christians," says Grenz, "we've always said there are some things which are ineffable. God himself is beyond the capacity of reason to fathom. 'My ways,' says God, 'are not your ways.' This acknowledgment that there are some things more than just the rational can be a powerful framework for reaching the postmodern generation."

The Christian worldview intersects with the postmodern worldview at several key junctures:

☐ *An acceptance of the existence of the supernatural.* The modern era disregarded and ignored the spiritual dimension of our humanity in favor of the scientific method. By contrast, the postmodern era reaffirms a belief that Christians have always held to be true: the world of spirit is real, and we are spiritual beings.

☐ *The questioning of the autonomous self.* Modern man was a rugged individual. Postmodern people are interactive parts of a larger whole.

☐ *The emphasis on a communal reality.* The Christian faith, according to the Bible, is to be lived out within a context of healing relationships. The Christian community is called the church, and when the church functions as it was intended to according to the Bible, it is the deepest and best form of community possible. The Christian church is the communal reality that postmodern pre-Christian people hunger for.

☐ *The emphasis on responsible stewardship of the environment.* The modern mindset sought to master and tame nature. The postmodern mindset challenges this worldview and seeks to live in harmony with nature. The biblical Christian sees a need to carefully balance these two worldviews. Biblically, the human race has been given a mandate by God to exercise dominion over nature—not in an abusive or exploitative sense, but as responsible caretakers of God's creation.

While postmodernism does intersect with Christianity in some of its assumptions, Christians should be careful not to buy into all of its concepts. For example, we cannot agree with the notion that there is no objective truth, no transcendent center of existence. If there is nothing at the center, we are left with a godless nihilism. Nihilism leads to despair. The light and life of Jesus Christ gives us hope.

The church has a great opportunity to open a life-changing, society-changing dialogue with my generation. While postmodernism poses a challenge to the Christian story, it is also a point of connection between Christians and Generation X. It is like the water that was Jesus' point of connection with the woman he met at the well in Samaria.

In John 4, a Samaritan woman comes to draw water at the well where Jesus is resting. He says to her, "Would you give me a drink of water?" She is taken aback, since he is Jewish, and Jews have nothing to do with Samaritans. But Jesus goes on to say to her, "If you knew the generosity of God and who I am, you would be asking me for a drink, and I would give you fresh, living water." The "living water" Jesus spoke of was the life-giving, refreshing gift of himself.

How can we use the postmodern mindset in the same way that Jesus used water from a well? By bridging from postmodern yearnings and postmodern thirst to Jesus Christ, who fulfills those yearnings and satisfies that thirst. Our message to this postmodern generation is

"You have a hole in your postmodern soul; Jesus is the One who fills it. You accept the existence of a supernatural reality. Come experience the deepest and most transcendent reality of all. You question the autonomy of the self and seek to become part of a larger community. Come with us to the beach for a weekend of fun, real relationships and real caring. You care about the environment and wonder if creation can survive what humanity is doing to it. Our church is having a recycling drive, and we're cleaning up trash along the river as a celebration of God, who created the environment."

That is the challenge my generation presents to the Christian church at the end of the twentieth century: "Understand how we think and how we feel. Reach out to us on our own terms. Like Jesus, put yourself in our reality and see the world through our eyes and feel the world through our feelings. Then you will have something authentic to say to us. Then we will listen."

A Connection

They all sat down around the table—Perry, Heidi, Brennan and Michael. Perry glanced at Michael and winced inwardly. He had gotten used to the ponytails young men wore nowadays. He had even gotten used to earrings—though it had been a struggle for him the first time he saw Brennan wearing one. But a nose ring—ugh! It wasn't just how it looked, but he couldn't help wondering what it must feel like! The thought made him shudder. *How do you blow your nose with one of those things hanging down in your nostril?*

"So, Michael," he said, instantly feeling awkward, "in our house we say grace before a meal—" That was terrible. It sounded condescending. Both Heidi and Brennan shot pleading looks in his direction.

"Dad," said Brennan, "I'll ask the blessing."

"Well, sure. Go right ahead."

"God," said Brennan, "thanks for this good food. And thanks for letting Michael be with us. Amen." Short and sweet.

Heidi had fixed her specialty—a melt-in-your-mouth prime rib roast au jus, with baked potato, sour cream and horseradish. Michael was quiet, even withdrawn, as the food was passed around. Perry remembered how animated he had been shooting baskets. *Isn't there some way to draw him out?* Perry wondered. *Isn't there a subject I could think of that*

*would get the guy to come out of himself a bit? Maybe talk about things at
the print shop? No. He's only been back on the job a couple weeks, and that
subject is probably still a bit touchy.*

As he spooned a dollop of sour cream into the hollow of his baked
potato, Perry prayed for guidance. In the next moment an answer
came: *Keep your mouth shut. Just listen.*

So Perry listened.

As he listened, he began to notice a dynamic in the interaction
between Brennan and Michael. They talked about basketball. They
talked about music. They made plans to get a couple of dates and hear
Steven Hobb, a local acoustic singer-songwriter, at the Wild Blue Yonder the following week. They talked about problems Michael was
having with the landlord at his new apartment.

"He's been hassling me because I turned the bedroom closet into
a darkroom," said Michael. "The guy's a real dweeb. I think he's been
using a passkey and snooping around while I'm at work. I mean, how
would he know I've got a darkroom if he's not spying on me?"

"That sucks," said Brennan. "There oughta be something you could
do to keep that guy out. Change the locks or something."

Perry looked sharply at Brennan. His son knew he didn't like terms
like "that sucks," especially at the dinner table, in his mother's presence. But Heidi didn't seem to care—and Brennan didn't seem to
notice the "ahem!" in Perry's glance.

"So, Michael," said Perry, "you develop your own pictures?"

"Sure," Michael said, shrugging. "Develop 'em. Print 'em. Just black-
and-white, though. Actually, I prefer black-and-white for the aesthet-
ics. I like the silvery tone of a really crisp, high-contrast print."

"What kind of camera do you use?" asked Brennan.

"I've got about half a dozen, mostly SLRs," Michael replied, "but I
do have this old Hasselblad large-format camera that I'm fixing up.
That's the way I get my cameras—mostly used and busted. I pick 'em
up for next to nothing at estate sales and stuff, then I work 'em over.
My best camera is a Minolta 9XI QD—it's, like, a thousand-dollar
camera body that I got for twenty bucks!"

"No way!" said Brennan.

"Almost new too! This rich dude dropped it in a rock crevice when
he was hiking in Utah. He said the camera shop wanted four hundred

to fix it and he wasn't gonna 'let those robbers get their mitts on it.' He decided to get a new camera instead. So he sold it to me cheap, and I opened it up. There was nothing wrong with it but a cracked prism. I cannibalized another busted Minolta for the prism, and I had me a thousand-dollar camera for next to nothing!"

"I didn't know you were so handy with cameras, Michael," said Perry. "I've got a Yashica ZoomTec that's been giving me fits. I've been meaning to take into the shop for weeks, but I just haven't had time—"

"What's the matter with it?" asked Michael, his eyes alight.

"The autowinder sticks or something," said Perry. "The film seems to jam, and the images overlap and double expose."

"I've seen that before," said Michael. "Sounds like a slipping cam in the winder. Want me to take a look at it?"

"Gee, would you, Michael? I mean, I'd pay you for it—"

"No way!" Michael laughed. "Unless you're gonna charge me for this dinner!"

Amazing, thought Perry. *I've just seen Michael laugh twice in one day!*

"Whatever . . ."

Postmodernism is not just a new way of thinking. It is a worldview that elevates feeling to a level on par with, or superior to, rational thought. The postmodern worldview has intuition and emotion at its center, not intellect. The first question asked by a postmodernist is not "What do you think?" but "How do you feel?"

"I discovered that a major cultural shift had taken place after Clinton was elected," said Kyle, a self-styled twentysomething New Democrat (that is, a Democrat who is neither a liberal nor a conservative but who picks and chooses his positions on an issue-by-issue basis). "I knew that there were a lot more people of my generation in the White House when I wrote a letter on the health care issue. When I used to write to the Bush White House, I'd get a letter back on classy rag bond that said, 'Thank you for telling us what you think.' When I wrote to the Clinton White House, I got a postcard on recycled paper that said, 'Thank you for sharing your feelings with us.' That's important to me—an administration that not only cares what people think but how they feel."

We are an emotive generation. We are not impressionable, but we are impressionistic. We are perfectly comfortable with paradox—with keeping two contradictory thoughts in mind at the same moment. Polls show that 98 percent of us want to be married but that 75 percent of us would abandon marriage if it came into conflict with our life aspirations. That's a contradiction.

Our thinking is nonlinear. You can't convince us, persuade us or convert us with logical arguments and linear reasoning. Many of us feel confused because deep down we recognize that there are inconsistencies and contradictions in our beliefs. Yet we resist digging into our belief structure and attempting to reconcile those contradictions out of a fear that there really are no answers.

Traditional, modernist oriented, evidential apologetics relies on creating a sense of "cognitive dissonance" within the other person— a sense that his or her own belief structure does not logically square with reality. You create this cognitive dissonance by building a case, much as a lawyer builds a case in court by piling up evidence on evidence. At some point in the process this person is expected to resolve the cognitive dissonance by saying, "You're right. I need to become a Christian." Traditionally that is the point where an individual can be led to Christ.

But the modernist, evidential approach just doesn't cut it anymore—not with Generation X. With my generation you're unlikely to arouse any cognitive dissonance in the other person. You won't hear "You're right." You'll hear "Whatever . . ."

Our philosophy is summed up in the slogan for Bud Dry: "Why ask why?" Philosophies? The meaning of it all? Who knows? Who cares? It doesn't matter why. We only ask, "How can I get through my life?" "How can I duck the hassles?" "How can I stay alive?" My plugged-in, up-linked, on-line generation sifts through tons of information every day. We discard the unusable, the ideological, the intrusive, the exploitative, the manipulative. We process only that which is useful to our survival.

All people and all cultures have the ability to think. Some think more clearly and logically than others. Each individual and each culture has its own way of processing information. Boomers prize logic, argument, assertiveness and grand strategies. Thirteeners prize feelings, harmony, speed and invisibility. We stay low to the ground, beneath the radar, so that no one can trap us into intellectual arguments we just can't win.

If you think that this is just lazy thinking or ignorance or a "slacker attitude," than you just don't get it. Try thinking of it as alien thinking. Think of yourself as a missionary to another culture, or even another planet. You wouldn't expect to go among the Watusis or the Martians and make them alter their thought patterns before you would share Jesus Christ with them. Why, then, would you want Xers to adopt a new worldview before you evangelize them?

Accept the fact that Generation X is "culturally deprived" (if that is how you wish to view it). Accept the fact that my peers have no fundamental starting points for thinking linearly and logically about God, about reality, about their own meaning and place in the universe. As Win Manning says, "Xers are intellectually impaired without even being aware of it." It is as if my generation was expected to do arithmetic with Roman instead of Arabic numerals. Quick—what is MMMDXLVIII divided by XXIX? You can't do it without converting Roman to Arabic. You have to move from one mode of thinking to another.

How will you reach this postmodern generation—a generation that cannot conceive of objective truth, cannot follow your linear arguments, cannot tolerate anything (including evangelism) that smacks to them of religious intolerance?

Answer: first, if you want to reach Generation X, move toward the Xer's worldview. Underscore those aspects of the Christian story that intersect with the yearnings of Generation X: an acceptance of supernatural, spiritual realities; an emphasis on belonging to a healing, accepting community called the church; and an emphasis on a responsible attitude toward the environment.

Second: avoid overintellectualizing the gospel. Xers are bright. They are informed. They have a keen intellect. But if we package our story as a philosophical argument or an intellectual thesis we will lose them as an audience. Xers have more interesting and enjoyable things to do with their minds than listen to a lecture on religion or philosophy. If you start sounding like PBS, they will switch over to MTV. To an Xer the Christian story is just another information channel demanding access to his or her already overloaded mind.

Third, and most important of all: you must demonstrate authentic love to Xers. It's not easy to reach my generation by arguing with them, but it is very easy to reach them by loving them, by sticking with them and standing by them, by befriending them and letting them into your own life. My generation hungers for friends who will be loyal and genuine. We long to belong to a community of acceptance and affirmation. We hunger for models of authenticity, integrity and transparency. We are searching for other people who are like us and who will build a relationship with us so that we don't have to feel we are alone.

The Porch Light Is On

It was dark outside when Michael climbed into his ten-year-old Toyota Celica, waved and drove off. Standing on the front porch, Perry and Brennan waved back. A few seconds later Michael was out of sight, leaving a thick plume of exhaust smoke rising toward the streetlight in front of the house.

"Thanks, Brennan," said Perry.

"For what, Dad?"

"For showing me how it's done."

"Huh?"

"I figured it out. I understand now why you let Michael show you some basketball moves you already knew."

Brennan shrugged. "I was just trying to be a friend, Dad."

"I know. That's what I mean. You can't be a real friend to somebody if you're in a superior position to him, if you're 'one-up' on him. If someone else is 'one-up' on you, then you feel 'one-down.' Your self-esteem is dented, and you don't see the other person as a friend. He may be your benefactor, your boss, maybe even your mentor, but he's not your friend. In a real friendship both sides have to be at street level."

"Yeah, Dad," said Brennan. "So I guess that's why you asked Michael to take a look at your camera. If he does you a favor, then you're not one-up on him, right? You're at street level with each other."

Perry nodded. "He sure seemed to loosen up around me after that."

"Yeah."

"And I got my camera fixed for free."

Brennan chuckled, turned and went inside. Perry followed him, closed the front door behind him and locked it for the night. He started into the kitchen to help Heidi with the dishes.

"Hey, Dad," said Brennan.

Perry stopped. "Yeah, son?"

"I think the porch light is on."

Perry grinned. "You mean you think I'm finally starting to 'get it' about Michael?"

"No, Dad," said Brennan, grinning and pointing to the light switch next to the front door. "I mean the porch light really is on."

7

Adrift in the Universe

Lindsey was bored. She was tired

of watching Grant sleep.

Sitting in the chair at the side of his hospital bed, she heard singing coming from across the hall. She got up and wandered over to find out what was going on. In the room across the hall she saw a group of young men and women gathered around a bed. They were singing something about "the mercy of the Lord." The music was sweet, low and harmonious. Lindsey paused, listening, with one foot inside the room. One of the women in the group turned, saw Lindsey and came walking toward her.

Lindsey realized she had been caught eavesdropping.

"Losing My Religion"

"Religion isn't something that has been on my mind over the four years that I've been here at the university," one Wisconsin student told me. It's a fairly typical statement. Religion doesn't have much of a place in the Xer schedule or the Xer psyche.

Listen to the music of my generation and you'll find references to religion, but they are usually negative references—allusions to a faith that has been lost, as when R.E.M. sings on the album *Out of Time,* "That's me in the spotlight / Losing my religion." Sometimes our music preaches a nonreligious or antireligious "new religion" to replace the failed faith of the past. When you hear that throbbing sexual bass beat and hear Alannah Myles singing in her boozy, bluesy style about sex and hard liquor, you know she's sure not singing "give me that old-time religion." Instead she sings,

A new religion that'll bring ya to your knees

Black Velvet, if you please.

Our view of God is relative. Our view of religion is skeptical. Our view of commitment is wary. Our view of reality is survivalist. Our thinking is relational and feelings-oriented, not intellectual. We live in the now; we can't imagine eternity.

One of the reasons we take a utilitarian, survivalist view of our lives and our belief systems is that we have been brought up to believe we are nothing but temporarily animated matter. We are animals who think, create, procreate and die. We have a diminished sense of our own self—our own soul. When that is all there is to one's view of life, eternal values are meaningless. All that matters is enjoying life while you can, all the while knowing that death is coming at you like a big supercharged steamroller.

In a message posted on the Science Fiction and Fantasy Forum bulletin board on CompuServe (May 31, 1991), Xer science fiction writer Michael Kube-McDowell observed, "I have serious doubts that there's anything more to my personality and 'selfness' than a synergy between genetics, neurochemistry, and the environments and experiences to which I've been exposed. And my expectation concerning death is that it will be both corporeal- and ego-death." In other words, both his body and his soul will cease to function. He continues by saying that this awareness of the finality of death "is part of the reason I write, to be honest. Like everyone who finds existence interesting and occasionally enjoyable, I want to live forever. And I'm pretty sure than 'I' won't. The best I can do is to see that my genes live on through my children, and that my thoughts live on through my writing."

A university student made a similar comment to me in one of my focus groups. "The only thing you know for sure," he said, "is that you are alive and that it's your lifetime and you're existing for right now. So you have to do everything you can and basically try to enjoy as much as you can and try not to worry about what is going to happen afterwards."

The Xer perspective on God, faith, religion and life is shaped by the Xer experience. Our distrust of religious authority stems directly from having been let down by leadership figures in the past. Our willingness to commit ourselves to a specific religious view of God is hindered by our desire to be tolerant and inclusive.

For many of us, spiritual conflicts are rooted in the conflicts of the family systems in which we grew. Our inability to trust and make commitments is directly related to having been emotionally bruised by our parents' marital conflicts and divorce. In many cases, our ability to conceive of a loving heavenly parent is impaired by having grown up with an abusive earthly parent.

Some of us have developed a psychological ambivalence from seeing mom and dad at war with each other and experiencing the pain of both sides tugging at us and demanding our allegiance. Since kids naturally want to love both of their parents, even when the parents hate each other, children of divorce usually learn coping techniques that are not logical but that enable survival in the hostile environment of a broken home. One coping technique involves becoming a "problem child" who "acts out" in order to focus both parents' attention on the child so that the parents will forget their own disagreement.

Another coping technique involves learning to agree with both sides. The child learns it is possible to hold two conflicting opinions in one mind at the same time, and that by doing so he or she can help a rocky family maintain a precarious homeostatic balance. To this child, maintaining relationships is infinitely more important than sorting out logical arguments about who is right and who is wrong. The child will later carry this coping technique and these "relationships-supersede-issues" values into adult relationships. In matters of religion he or she will follow the same procedure as in childhood: agree with everybody and try to get everybody to get along with each other.

"I'm not religious or antireligious," said one Xer I talked to. "Maybe there is a God. I sure wouldn't rule out the possibility. But I don't rule it in, either. I mean, how does anybody really know? How can anybody say that Christians are right and Moslems are wrong? To criticize or condemn other religions, to say that some people are going to go to hell because they call their god 'Allah' instead of 'Jesus'—I mean, that just seems totally ridiculous to me." What is this Thirteener saying? In effect, this means, "I'm more interested in peaceable relationships than in spiritual realities."

This is a major shift from the perceptual framework of Boomers who sought "true truth" and objective reality. Thirteeners will affirm contradictory realities and accept multiple and competing religious views if it will enable them to maintain the kind of stable relationships they longed for—and often never experienced—in childhood.

How do Xer religious perceptions affect evangelism? The implications are enormous! This means that old-style evangelism in which we defend the gospel as absolute truth will no longer be very effective. It worked with intellect-oriented Boomers but it is an alien way of thinking to my generation.

This is not to say that the intellectual dimension of our faith is unimportant. I believe reasonably argued apologetics is an enormously valuable tool—not for evangelism, but for discipleship. One of the best-received speakers at the Urbana 93 missions and evangelism conference was Ravi Zacharias who gave a powerful intellectual defense of the Christian faith. I believe his message was so well received because Christians have a sense of security about the reasonableness of their faith. I am convinced that while apologetics is no longer as effective as a witnessing tool, it is very important as an anchor for securing the faith of new and growing Christians. "True truth" is no longer as persuasive as it once was, but it does keep Xers from skipping from one community to another.

In our effort to reach Generation X we would do well to spend less energy defending the 'fortress of truth" and more energy providing a safe and nurturing haven of relational stability. We need to show that the church is not only logically credible but relationally relevant—and user-friendly. We need to present the church as a place where community and secure relationships can still be found.

Boomer youth used to stream to L'Abri in the sixties and seventies, seeking the meaning of life. Buster youth at the end of the second millennium are not looking for the meaning of life. We are looking for secure relationships. Our parents split our world apart when they divorced. Our politicians and religious leaders betrayed us and disillusioned us with their scandals and lies. Our bosses exploit us and oppress us. We don't want anyone to tell us what to do or how to believe. We don't want to achieve satori or nirvana or epiphany. We just want to survive and have a place to belong.

"I do believe there is a God," one twentysomething student told me. "I don't believe in a Catholic God or a Muslim God or a Buddhist God. Those ideas are ridiculous. I think we're all really the same and there's really only one God, no matter what you call him—or her."

According to George Barna of the Barna Research Group, 91 percent of Thirteeners claim to believe in God and many of those claim to be Christians. Few, however, fit a definition consistent with any traditional religious faith. While we accept the idea that God exists (at least superficially), we don't spend much time thinking deeply about God. We don't so much reject religious faith as neglect it. We have more important and more tangible things to think about. If we can't see, hear, touch, or taste it, it doesn't have an impact our lives.

Natalia

Standing at the doorway of the hospital room, Lindsey realized she had been caught eavesdropping. Embarrassed, she muttered to the approaching woman, "I'm sorry." She turned to leave.

"No, don't go!" said the woman. She was dark-eyed, dusky-skinned and young—about Lindsey's age.

Lindsey stopped and turned to face the woman. "I didn't mean to intrude."

"You're not intruding. I hope our music wasn't bothering you."

"Oh, no! It's beautiful. I just heard the singing and had to find out what was going on."

The singers had finished singing, and one of the people by the bed, a young man with an earring and long blond hair pulled back in a ponytail, began praying.

"They're friends of ours from church fellowship," the woman continued softly. "They came to comfort my husband." She put out her hand. "My name's Natalia Perales. That's my husband, Emilio." She pointed to the man in the bed.

Lindsey took the woman's hand and introduced herself, then nodded toward Emilio. "Is he very sick?" she asked.

"Emilio has liver cancer," said Natalia. "It's spreading very fast. The doctor says a few weeks, that's all."

"Oh!" said Lindsey. "I'm so sorry."

"It will be hard, but Emilio will be safe in the arms of Jesus," said Natalia, smiling despite her quavering voice and glistening eyes. "The one I am more concerned about is our little boy, Oscar. He's at his grandma's house right now. He's just six years old and he's going to miss his daddy." Natalia looked past Lindsey, to where Grant was sleeping. "Is that your husband?" she asked.

"My boyfriend," said Lindsey. "His name is Grant."

"Why is he in the hospital?"

"Because he's totally stupid," she said disgustedly. "He was motor-cycle racing and took a header over the handlebars. He broke his leg and may have done something to his back—he's still having a lot of pain and the doctors aren't sure why."

"That's too bad."

"No. Cancer's too bad. What your husband is going through is too bad. Grant just got what he was asking for. Boys and their toys." She shook her head.

Xers and Organized Religion

"Organized religion kills the living beauty of God," said Christian writer-philosopher Malcolm Muggeridge. Many of my generation would agree.

"I don't believe in God," one university student told me. "But even if I did, I wouldn't go to church because it's my life, they're my beliefs and I don't need anybody telling me what to do. I can read the Bible for myself or I can think whatever I want to think. I don't need a church telling me what's wrong and what's right."

"I think there is something beyond this reality," said another twentysomething student, "something you could call God, I suppose. I wouldn't say I'm an atheist, but I can't imagine being a Christian and going to church every Sunday. I don't believe in the church with all its rules and doctrines and stuff like that. Churches are too restrictive. They take away your freedom to believe what you want to believe."

In my recent work on campuses with InterVarsity Christian Fellowship, I rarely encountered students who were in search of the ultimate truth. Those who had any interest at all in religious faith tended to be more "me-oriented" than that. They wanted a faith that was tailor-made for their practical and emotional needs. They were looking for a "Rent-A-Religion" where they could choose the colors, the options, the horsepower and the upholstery of their faith to suit their tastes and comfort level. Witness to such people about the story of Jesus Christ and you'll likely hear the question, "So what does your religion have to offer me?"

My generation is not seeking out the church as an institutional gathering place where we can find comfort and an absolute moral authority. We don't care about theology. We don't care about denominational affiliation. We don't care about rites and liturgies and traditions. And we are turned off by hard-nosed doctrinal stands on nonessential issues—mode of baptism, charismatic gifts, women in ministry, and petty rules and attitudes about dress and lifestyle.

With our survival mind-set, we are seeking only that kind of faith which will make a practical difference in our everyday lives and in our communities. We are very results-oriented, and a faith that doesn't tangibly improve our lives and our immediate surroundings is quickly discarded. If that makes us "liturgically impaired," so be it. That's who we are.

"Trust in God helps me more than anything else," one twentysomething woman told me. "I believe that he works out his plan through my life. He has a hand in what happens in my life, and the lives of other people. To me, God is a tangible reality—though sometimes a mysterious reality. I can't always understand why God does things the way he does. But as long as I can get the same positive results, let him work in mysterious ways. It doesn't bother me in the least."

In a telephone interview Bill Strauss, author of *13th Gen,* told me, "Thirteeners require that religion be useful." I've seen this truth borne out again and again in my research and focus groups. My generation wants to know that God will bring about reconciliation, that he will heal our hurts and that he will accept us unconditionally. Unfortunately, most of us Thirteeners have not found this in church.

We come into church with our self-esteem already bruised. Then we find that church makes us feel even more guilty and unworthy. The preaching is judgmental or irrelevant to our lives. The music is lame. The liturgy is boring and meaningless. Everyone dresses in a Sunday-best evangelical "uniform," making us feel shabby, inferior and out of place. We see the church taking hard-nosed doctrinal stands that divide people and put certain groups down. We see hypocrisy. We agree with Gandhi, who said, "I like your Christ. But I don't like your Christians—they are so unlike your Christ."

What would happen if Thirteeners could see a faith that works in the lives of people? If pastors would talk across to us, not down to us, about issues and problems we face every day? If we could see people living what they say they believe? If we could hear music and experience other aspects of worship that are geared to our tastes, needs and attention span? If we could experience church as an inclusive and affirming experience, rather than an exclusive and dreary experience?

Perhaps—just perhaps—we might be more open to a spiritual commitment.

What is the greatest obstacle to the story of Jesus Christ? I believe it is Christians. Xers hear our message, watch our lives, then they say, "This Jesus thing is lame, man. It's not real." Christian recording artist Barry McGuire recalls spending an entire year of his life believing that Jesus' story was true, wishing he could become a Christian, yet unwilling and unable to make the commitment. Why? There were several reasons, but one of the biggest was the hypocrisy of Christians. "I would read the Bible, the story of Jesus," says McGuire, "and I'd think, 'Man, I want to be like him.' Then I'd look at Christians and I'd say, 'But man, I don't want to be like them!' "

Thirteeners have no heroes—no role models. They are looking for practical examples that will show them how to live their lives. They are hungry for faith and religious reality, but they have no interest in organized religion. As one University of Wisconsin student told me, "You can't learn good morals by going to church. I've developed my own sense of morality." Yet, underlying that profession of moral independence you can hear a longing for moral role models. If they are disillusioned and turned off by organized religion, where will my generation find these examples for which they hunger?

"I'm Not a Church-Type Person"

"Your boyfriend doesn't get many visitors," Natalia observed. "Does he have many friends?"

"Sure," Lindsey replied. "Grant and I have lots of friends—but I guess they're all kind of busy right now."

"What about your friends from church? Do they come to visit?"

"Church? Oh, Grant and I don't go to church."

"Well, maybe you'd like to visit our church sometime," Natalia said, her face alight and her hands gesturing expressively as she talked. "It's really different from what you'd think of as 'church,' you know? I mean, the music, the teaching . . . it's fun and exciting. It's for people like you and me."

"I . . . I don't think so," said Lindsey. "Thank you anyway, but I'm really not a church-type person."

"That's okay, Lindsey," Natalia said, smiling sweetly. She opened her purse and pulled out a used envelope and a pen and began writing. "But remember, you're always welcome. If you ever want to try it, or if you'd just like someone to talk to, give me a call. Anytime. Here's my number."

"Sure," said Lindsey. "Thanks." She tucked the envelope into her own purse and snapped it shut.

"Lindsey!" It was Grant calling from across the hall. "I'm thirsty!"

"Hold on," Lindsey called back over her shoulder. "Well," she said, turning back to Natalia, "my big dumb baby just woke up. It was nice meeting you."

"It was nice meeting you, Lindsey," said Natalia. "And I meant what I said. Call me anytime."

"Thanks."

Natalia turned away and went back to her husband's bedside.

As Lindsey turned and crossed the hall to Grant's room she wondered why she felt such a sense of uplift and pleasure after talking to Natalia—a woman whose husband was dying of a wasting disease. *You'd think it would be depressing to be around people like that,* she thought. *Instead, I feel—well, how do I feel? I don't think I have a word for a feeling like this.*

It was a good feeling . . . a light feeling. Like someone had put some extra spring in her soul.

A "Reality Religion"

We need to offer my generation a faith that works in the conflicts, pressures and pain of their everyday lives. Thirteeners need the tools to help them deal with their families and friends. They need mentors who can model for them what healthy adulthood is like. They need to see authenticity and transparency in relationships so they will know how to relate to others.

We are tired of "commercial Christianity" with its televangelists and Christian celebrities, its merchandising and T-shirts, its slick packaging and insincerity. All that is part of The System which my generation rejects. Xers are an underground movement, listening to alternative music, maintaining an alternative lifestyle, living at the margins of society. Christians must learn to identify with the Xer experience. Properly and biblically understood, we, too, are an underground movement—a persecuted church serving a tortured and murdered Christ, telling our story to oppressed and marginalized people. Instead of simply advertising our faith, we need to focus more on living it and embodying it. Instead of grand strategies, we should rely on relationships.

Like Xers themselves, we Christians should stay low to the ground and under the radar, employing covert rather than overt tactics. Before launching any evangelistic effort or program, we might do well to ask, "Could I get away with this in communist China?" If not, then maybe that effort or program is too commercial, too overt, too much like The System to be effective with a marginalized generation.

Thirteeners need to see that Christians can identify with them in their low estate—their marginalized condition. They need to hear that Jesus himself was despised and marginalized, a man of sorrows, acquainted with grief. His "illegitimate" birth was questioned. He went up against The System, and The System had him crucified. Instead of claiming to be a "moral majority" as we have in the past, we Christians would do well to return to our roots as an oppressed and persecuted minority. Then Xers will see a church that identifies itself with them.

That is the outline of a "reality religion"—a faith that works and that my generation can identify with and commit itself to. Not coincidentally, that is also Christianity in its truest, purest, most distilled and most biblical form.

A Number on an Envelope

Saturday afternoon. Nothing to do.

Lindsey had tried calling Kim, just to talk about nothing. No answer. Oh, yeah. Kim and John were going skiing this weekend.

She tried Marisa's number. No answer.

Everyone's got something to do this weekend but me! Stupid, stupid Grant and his stupid, stupid motorcycles. Just because his leg is in a sling why does my social life have to be laid up? She swore aloud.

Lindsey decided to call Josie, then remembered that Josie had just moved to a new apartment. Lindsey had Josie's new number in her purse. She took her purse from the kitchen counter, opened it, pulled out a scrap of paper, went to the phone and started dialing.

After four digits, she realized she had the wrong piece of paper. This wasn't Josie's number. The name written in a fine hand above the number said Natalia Perales. *Oh, yeah,* she thought, *the woman at the hospital.* Her finger paused over the phone buttons—then she dialed the last three digits and listened to the ringing at the other end of the line.

Why am I doing this? she wondered. *I don't know this woman! I don't even know what to say to her!*

She almost hung up on the third ring, when . . .

"Hello?"

Xers and Evangelism

If someone comes along claiming to have the secret of ultimate truth or the key to life, we are skeptical. *What's his motive?* we wonder. *What does he want from us? Talk is cheap, dude. We don't want your theories or your high-blown rhetoric. Prove to us that it's real and that it relates to our lives and our survival.*

To Generation X, evangelists represent religious bigotry and intolerance. "Their attitude," says IVCF's Bob Fryling, "is, 'You cannot impose your value system on someone else!' After all, we live in an age of relativism. Evangelists are the heretics in an age when everything is relative."

A typical dialogue between an evangelist and an Xer might go something like this:

Evangelist: "Jesus said, 'I am the way, the truth, and the life.' "

Xer: "That's your truth."

Evangelist: "That's not *my* truth. It's *the* truth."

Xer: "Hey, dude, there are many truths."

Evangelist: "No, there is only one truth. Everything else that claims to be the truth is deceptive."

Xer: "Why do you have to be so intolerant? Why do you have to try to change people? Why do you judge other people's beliefs? Why does everybody have to believe like you? I believe in 'live and let live.' "

Evangelist: "I'm not intolerant. I'm just trying to show my love for you. I don't want you to have to go into eternity without Christ."

Xer: "Why don't you just say it straight up, man? You're saying I'm going to hell, right?"

Evangelist: "Well, er, yes, apart from Christ, but—"

Xer: "You see? There you go with the judgment and the intolerance, man. I don't force my beliefs on you, I don't condemn you, but there you are telling me I'm a sinner, I'm bound for hell! Who died and made you the judge of my soul, man?"

Evangelist: "Never mind. Have a nice day."

Many evangelists come claiming to have the truth. Thirteeners dislike that. That truth is divisive, separating those who have faith and life and God from those who do not. Thirteeners dislike that too. Evangelists won't just accept the "fact" that there are many beliefs, many truths, many ways to God. Thirteeners really don't like that. They call that "intolerance."

Moreover, spiritual issues tend to seem rather remote and unreal to people who are scratching for a living, worrying about relationships, and trying to survive in a user-unfriendly world. Why get embroiled in a divisive debate over things that are so invisible—so unreal?

To a Thirteener evangelism is nothing more than trying to persuade people into switching ideologies. Evangelism starts fights. Many

Thirteeners had their fill of such struggles when they were growing up in their dysfunctional families. They are tired of fighting. They don't care about ideologies. They are into relationships. If ideologies, such as evangelism, are going to destroy relationships then those ideologies are wrong.

To many Thirteeners there is only one virtue: Tolerance. "The thing I can't tolerate," they say, "is intolerance."

Evangelism by its very nature is intolerant. It is the light that cannot tolerate darkness. It is the good that cannot tolerate evil. It is the truth that cannot tolerate deception.

But Xers aren't ready to hear that. They will not examine the story of Jesus if it appears to be coming from a heart of intolerance. The old evangelistic approach—"I have the truth and you need to hear it"—won't fly anymore. To reach Generation X, a different approach is needed.

Starstream

"Hi. Natalia?"

"Yes."

"This is Lindsey. We met at the hospital, you know? My boyfriend is in the room across the hall—"

"Lindsey! How are you? I was just thinking about you!"

"You were?"

"How is Grant doing?"

"He's okay. I was just—I mean—I was wondering . . . Do you—"

"Lindsey, are you busy this evening?"

"Me? No, not really. Why?"

"Would you like to go to a concert with me?"

"Well—sure, why not?"

"I'll pick you up at quarter to eight. Where do you live, Lindsey?"

The Starstream Concert was held in the auditorium of a junior high school. The stage was strung with thousands of tiny white Christmas-tree lights, and when the house lights were brought down low, the effect was dramatic. A blue spotlight came on, illuminating a lone acoustic guitarist who began singing about the pain of living in a unloving world.

Lindsey and Natalia sat side-by-side near the front. Lindsey recognized the singer-guitarist—his name was Steven Hobb, and she had seen him perform at the Wild Blue Yonder and other local alternative and "grunge" clubs. The spotlight widened to include a keyboardist and a percussionist—not a drummer-percussionist, but a soft-percussionist, surrounded by instruments like bongos, wood blocks, vibes, charango, and melodica. The music was gentle, intimate and plaintive, and it reached into the tortured regions of her soul, expressing pain and sadness that she did not know how to put into words. The sad and sometimes angry songs of Steven's opening set reminded her of the songs of Kurt Cobain, yet without Cobain's toxic bitterness.

After Steven and his backup musicians finished their first set, a guy named Judd came up and did a wild mix of stand-up comedy and storytelling. He had the audience laughing uproariously one moment, stunned to silence the next. His stories wove a complex pattern of emotions and created visions in her mind of transcendent realities: of love beyond her imagining, peace beyond her experience.

After the storyteller, Steven Hobb, the acoustic musician, came back and performed a second set, beginning with a slip-slidy, deeply melancholy piece on the dobro. Then he picked up a twelve-string guitar, and with the first chord, a change came over the auditorium. People shifted in their chairs. The air tingled. A spirit—no, *the* Spirit—began to move through that place. The beat was joyous, contagious, outrageous and fun.

A smile spread across Lindsey's face. Her hands began clapping to the beat, almost as if they had a will and a rhythm all their own. As Steven, the guitarist, began to sing, Lindsey didn't understand all the words—not because she couldn't hear them clearly, but because they spoke of a reality that was foreign to her. Yet the song was so full of hope and power that her spirit was swept up in it—wrapped in its glow, exhilarated by its joy. The rest of Steven's second set was like that: joyful, upbeat, exultant, exuberant.

The last song received a standing ovation, and Lindsey was one of the first to jump to her feet. The hour had flown by too quickly, and Lindsey was sorry to see it end.

As they walked out to the car, Lindsey turned to Natalia and said, "Thanks for inviting me! That was so cool! But you know what? Some of those songs were about God and stuff, and it kinda reminded me of church!"

Natalia laughed. "Lindsey, that *was* church. Our church has Starstream Concert every Saturday night. It's a regular weekly program."

"That was church? No way!"

"Well, we have a Sunday-morning service that is a bit more traditional, but it still has a lot of the same music and stuff you saw tonight."

"Awesome!" Lindsey said, more to herself than to Natalia. "I just spent an hour in church . . . and I didn't even know it!"

Xers and Commitment

Richard Peace says this about commitment:

> Thirteeners can't make commitments because they've never had much experience with commitments working out. Whenever they've made commitments in the past—to family, school, employers, relationships—they've gotten burned and bruised. You see this inability to make commitments in even the most mundane areas of life.
>
> Thirteeners will talk endlessly about a decision that's facing them, such as, "What do we do now?" After hours of negotiation, they may decide to order takeout. Well, what kind of takeout? That means another hour of negotiation to decide whether it's going to be pizza or Chinese food.
>
> This is a generation that has a big problem making commitments. And that's a real challenge for evangelism, because evangelism is about conversions, and conversion is a commitment.

One comment I've heard in many forms from many Thirteeners is, "It's just too hard to be a Christian." Commitment to a specific belief system with hierarchies and doctrines and rules looks like a lot of hassle. We've been hassled enough. We don't want to make the same mistake twice. We want spirituality. We want the power for living that only comes from a supernatural source. We want something to believe in—but we don't want the structure and stricture of an organized religion. That, we believe, would be morally and spiritually suffocating. We want our spiritual freedom.

"I believe there is some kind of higher purpose," one Xer student told me, "or something that's controlling and omniscient, somehow. But I just don't believe in submitting to this higher figure or power, whatever it is." A commitment to God threatens everything we've done on our own. We think God (or the church) will rob us of our fun, our lifestyle, our autonomy, our sense of freedom.

At the same time, we have a gnawing sense that in rejecting faith, we may be discarding a sense of our worth in society and our meaning in the universe. Without a personal God to believe in, the universe is a very cold, scary and impersonal place—and we are just adrift in the universe like little splinters of driftwood on the great wide ocean. The underlying anxiety of Xer existence is the troubling fear that we really are worthless as human beings. We were unwanted and neglected as children. We are marginal and shunted aside by our society. We are achieving nothing of value. We are going nowhere at breakneck speed.

I asked Bill Strauss, "Suppose you are a Thirteener with a direct line to God. If you could ask God to do anything for you, what would it be?"

"I would ask," Strauss replied, "for him to give me some way to feel I'm a part of human progress and part of the improvement of man. I would want him to show me I'm not a backstep."

Yes, it's hard to get Xers to make a commitment. Hard, but not impossible. The keys to bringing an Xer to a place of commitment are these:

☐ Help him or her to understand Christianity as a relationship with a living God, not an organized religion. (Thirteeners are hungry for relationships.)

☐ Emphasize the freedom of the Christian life rather than the rules and doctrines of the Christian religious structure. (For a biblical perspective on our freedom in Christ, see John 8:32, 36; Romans 8:2; Galatians 5:1.)

☐ Emphasize Christian community over Christian institutions and structures. The church as an organization leaves us cold. The church as a healing and giving community, a place of *koinōnia*—belonging and sharing—is exactly what we yearn for.

☐ Emphasize the sense of meaning and purpose that comes with commitment to Christ. We have a place in the family of God. We have a purpose for existing in human society and in the wide universe. We are not adrift in the cosmos; we are on a pathway that has been laid out for us by God himself.

☐ Build trust by unconditionally accepting, loving and caring for the Thirteener. My generation is wary of commitment because of past hurts and betrayal. The ability to trust can only be rebuilt slowly and gradually, but as trust is established commitment becomes easier.

☐ Emphasize the mystery, awe and transcendence of God without resorting to intellectual arguments or philosophical apologetics. Thirteeners are open to, and fascinated by, mysteries that are beyond scientific exploration. Don't think you have to apologize for the supernatural, unfathomable nature of our great Creator God.

☐ Avoid doing or saying anything that would suggest that the Thirteener you are building a relationship with is an "evangelistic project" or a "potential convert." Genuinely focus on making a friend and being a friend. Focus on enjoying that person's company and friendship.

☐ Avoid prematurely pushing a person toward commitment and conversion. Thirteeners need space and freedom to process new ideas and new feelings over a period of time. They need to see that the faith you are sharing with them is a faith that works and which makes a difference in their everyday lives. Give them time to make a free and unhurried commitment to Christ on their own terms, on their own timetable.

☐ Never breach a trust or break a confidence.

☐ Seek ways to "level the playing field" between you and the other person; avoid the "one-up" posture. Make friendships with Xers as mutual as possible.

☐ Never show insensitivity to cultural issues that are important to Xers. Many of those issues should be important to us as well.

A Strange Feeling

As Natalia drove Lindsey home, Lindsey began to feel a vague apprehension. She couldn't put her finger on the source of it.

Natalia talked with Lindsey in an easygoing way—sometimes joking, sometimes serious. She asked about Grant, about how the doctors were doing in locating the cause of his pain. She asked about Lindsey's family background, where she worked, what she did for fun. When Lindsey asked about Emilio, Natalia was open and matter-of-fact, though she sometimes dabbed at her eyes.

"I shouldn't have brought it up," Lindsey said apologetically when she saw Natalia's tears.

"Why not?" said Natalia, smiling, though her eyes glistened. "I love Emilio. I like to talk about him. It's good to talk about him."

It was a strange emotional mix Lindsey felt as they drove. She felt comfortable with Natalia—almost as if they were old friends. Yet there was that gnawing, indefinable sense of unease . . . of apprehension.

Natalia pulled up to the curb in front of Lindsey's apartment building and got out of the car. She walked Lindsey to the door, and as they were going up the walk it suddenly occurred to Lindsey where that vague sense of apprehension came from. She felt a resonance, an echo, from a past experience.

In a flash, Lindsey remembered the time Perry, her manager at the print shop, had invited her to go with his family to a church concert. There had been a lot of music she couldn't relate to, a preacher whose message didn't make any sense to her, and a high-pressure invitation for people to walk down the aisle and be "washed in the blood of the Lamb." She hadn't gone forward. Fact is, she had never felt so awkward and out-of-place in her life. All the way home, Perry had talked to her about becoming a Christian—about her need to "get straight with God." It was horrible, and she had never been so relieved as when she had finally escaped from Perry's car and made it to the safety of her own apartment. That was over a year ago.

Now, here she was, walking back to her apartment alongside another evangelical Christian. Was Natalia's invitation to go to the concert just another evangelistic setup? Was Natalia getting ready to ambush her with Bible verses and the Four Spiritual Laws?

Lindsey paused at the door, turned to Natalia and said, "Well, good night—"

"Lindsey," said Natalia, "I just want you to know, I'm praying for you and Grant. I'm praying that the doctors will find out what's wrong and make him well again."

"I—well, thank you," said Lindsey. She wanted to say more. She felt as though she should say, *And I'm praying for you and Emilio and little*

Oscar, too. But she couldn't say that. Who would she pray to? Instead, she said, "Thanks for the evening. I had a great time."

As she went to bed that night, Lindsey nurtured a warm, cozy little spot inside her soul. Something had happened tonight. She didn't have a name for it. She didn't have words to describe it. But something had happened.

Natalia hadn't pressured her to make a commitment. She hadn't even tried to witness to her. Natalia had just been a friend.

That was the last thought on Lindsey's mind as she drifted off to sleep . . . *a friend* . . .

Down to the Deep River

Billy Joel is not an Xer, but his song "River of Dreams" speaks to people who are feeling adrift in the cosmos. It is a song about a man who has made a journey from the mountains of faith to a river so deep; a man who is searching for something sacred, something taken out of his soul, something undefined, something that has been lost. It is a song that expresses the spiritual longing of Generation X, and these lines should break our hearts:

I hope it doesn't take the rest of my life

Until I find what it is that I've been looking for.

We have what Generation X is searching for. We have the truth that is beyond my generation's ability to imagine or hope for. We have the life-changing story of Jesus. It's the middle of the night and Xers are sleepwalking through life. It's time for us to come down off our mountain of faith and go down to the deep river where people are struggling and drowning and trying to get across.

Reach a hand down into the darkness of the deep river. Grab hold of a struggling soul. Pull someone to shore.

8

All Screwed Up

When my period stopped," said Josie, "I thought I was pregnant. But I took one of those do-it-at-home pregnancy tests, and I wasn't pregnant. So I went to my gynecologist, and she figured out what I was doing to my body."

"How did she figure it out?" asked the psychologist.

"She did some tests and found out my potassium was low and I didn't have enough white blood cells or something. She looked in my mouth and down my throat and said something about my tooth enamel being bad. Then she asked me if I ever had an irregular heartbeat, and I said, 'Yeah, how did you know?' Then she goes, 'Josie, how long have you had bulimia?' That really freaks me. I go, 'Why do you think I have bulimia?' And she goes, 'Just tell me how long you've been bingeing and purging.' I mean, she really has me cornered. I say, 'Oh, about a year, I guess,' and she just stares at me and waits me out. Finally I say, 'Five years. Since I was fifteen.' "

"Did your gynecologist recommend you seek counseling?"

"Yeah. She said I really needed help bad. She said if I keep doing this to myself I'll end up dead. She said bulimics screw up their bodies in horrible ways and often end up in cardiac arrest. Well, that scared me enough to do something about it. If I'd known the doctor could tell I was bulimic just from checking me over, I probably never would have gone. But I'm glad now that I went."

"I'm glad you did too."

She reached up one hand and absent-mindedly twisted a strand of blond hair. "People tell me I look like Madonna," she said. "They don't know that I've spent the last five years puking my guts out to look like this. They don't know how guilty and ashamed I feel all the time. They don't know that once I start eating I can't stop, and that food is the drug I take to kill my pain."

"Tell me about your pain, Josie."

Josie's eyes seemed to focus somewhere off in the distance. "My pain . . ."

No Emotional Center

Forty percent of my peers were children of divorce. Many were among the first major wave of "latchkey kids"—kids who came home from school to empty houses because their parent or parents were at work. They wore a latchkey around their necks so they wouldn't lose it.

Part of the reason so many of us have such an obsession and fascination with TV is that we were raised by TV, even more than by our parents. TV was our after-school friend, our comforter, our role model, our guide to the intricacies of life. We still look at life and wish it could be as simple for us as it was for *The Brady Bunch* and the castaways on *Gilligan's Island.*

Mine is the generation whose Boomer parents lavished praise on children for doing nothing. We were given few responsibilities, few boundaries. We grew up with a sense of entitlement, expecting praise and privileges and resenting those who placed demands and expectations on us. We grew up with a sense of self-esteem that had no firm foundation. We expected to be pampered, to have others do the hard work for us and to pick us up when we incurred the hard consequences of our choices and actions. We never learned self-reliance, and even in adulthood we run to Mom and Dad for help when things get tough.

"When I was still at home," said one young female focus-group participant, "everything was pretty much provided for me. I think that made me a kind of passive person, and I expected things to be easy. Then I got out in the world and had to do things for myself. I found out that the real world is a lot of struggle and a lot of hassle just to survive."

While some of us were being spoiled and pampered, others of us were being abandoned, neglected or abused. Many of us had parents who divorced, who had affairs, who dragged us through a series of unhappy, short-lived marriages or who walked out on us. "I come from a family of divorce, like half my generation," said a young man in one of my focus groups. "I wish my childhood had been happier, but it's something I just need to accept. I hope my generation will be able to make some different choices and that life won't be as unhappy for the next generation." The emotional residue of these dysfunctional family experiences hovers over my generation like a storm cloud: anger, alienation, frustration and low self-esteem.

ABC's *Nightline* with Ted Koppel devoted a Friday-night special segment to the subject of the troubled American family (September 9, 1994). In that segment reporter Chris Bury cited statistics that chart the alarming trends in our society. For example, in 1965 there were ten divorces per year per one thousand marriages. By 1979 that figure had increased to twenty-three divorces per year per one thousand marriages—a 130 percent jump in fourteen years.

In 1970 66 percent of children lived in a traditional two-parent, *Leave It to Beaver*-style family. In 1980 that figure had declined to 57 percent. In 1991, 50 percent. The 1991 statistics were further broken down by race: 56 percent of white children lived in a traditional nuclear family versus 38 percent of Hispanics and 26 percent of blacks. And the trend is continuing.

Experts interviewed in the *Nightline* report cited two primary social causes for these trends: the expansion of women in the work force and the absence of fathers, due to either divorce or out-of-wedlock births. "The Census Bureau believes this trend away from the traditional family is too strong to turn back," Bury concluded. "To a majority of American kids, growing up in the same home with two married parents will soon have little more meaning than something they used to watch on TV."

The same *Nightline* segment also disclosed that in 1970 only 13 percent of children lived in one-parent households versus 30 percent in 1991. That 30 percent figure for 1991 was broken down by race as follows: 19 percent of white kids live in single-parent households versus 49 percent of black children and 31 percent of Hispanic children.

Another alarming trend is the rise of out-of-wedlock births in America. In 1960 the overall illegitimacy rate in America was 5 percent; in 1991 it was a shocking 30 percent. By race, it breaks down as follows:

	white	**black**
1960	2 percent	22 percent
1991	22 percent	68 percent

Bury concludes, "If the numbers continue in this direction, as census experts predict they will, a majority of American children will, for the first time in history, spend several years at least in single mother households. No other trend so dramatically drives the changes taking place in the American family."

We see the effects of these changes in the behavior patterns of Generation X. A larger percentage of my generation finds itself in crisis situations than any previous generation—more addictive behavior, more sexual abuse problems, more depression, more suicide. Whereas postmodernism affects the way my generation thinks, the dysfunctionality of our childhood families affects the way we feel. As a generation, we have lost our emotional center.

Family Secrets

"My brother's suicide was the final horror," said Josie, "out of a life that seemed like a bad dream. After Rex was gone there was nothing left to stay for. So I moved out of my parents' house for good. Long before Rex shot himself I hated my life, I hated my parents. Our family was always so screwed up. Image was real important to my mom and dad, so Rex and I were always taught to put on this front of perfection. But inside our four walls, where no one else saw, we were the family from hell." She laughed a little humorless laugh.

"Tell me about it," said the psychologist.

"My dad was, like, real distant . . . real cold. He worked all the time, and we didn't see him all that much. I remember that whenever he came home I didn't like it. He was like this evil presence, and the whole house had a shadow over it while he was there."

"Was he angry? Violent? Abusive?"

"No. He was just . . . mean . . . nasty in a sneaky sort of way. He wouldn't yell at you or hit you, but he would say things to you that made you feel terrible. Cutting remarks about your looks or your brains or something. He would always find some flaw and point it out. He was harder on Rex, but he did it to me too. It was like he always had to make other people look small . . . feel small. I guess that made him feel bigger or something."

"Your mother—"

"She was weak."

"How do you mean that?"

"Weak. No personality. A nothing. A zero. She was depressed all the time. She never did anything, never contributed anything, never accomplished anything. She would just cry all day, or sit and stare, or sleep . . . I mean, sometimes she'd spend an entire day in bed! She wouldn't get up, wouldn't even get dressed. Why my dad ever married her I'll never know."

"Are your parents still married?"

Josie shrugged. "It's been a few years since I've been home. They could be dead for all I know. And for all I care."

"Tell me one memory of your dad. The first thing that pops into your mind."

"Easy. It was the time I came home early from school. I was, like, eleven or twelve years old, and I got sick at school so I came home before noon. My dad's car was in the driveway, and my mom's car was gone. I don't know where she was, but she was out of the house. I let myself into the house and headed for my room—and then I heard these noises coming from down the hall. I walked down to my parents' bedroom and there was my dad and some other woman. They were doing it right there, on the bed, with the bedroom door open. I guess they were making so much noise they didn't hear me come in. Well, the woman saw me and screamed, and my dad jumped up and slammed the door in my face."

"What did you do?"

"I went back to my bedroom and sat on my bed. I was really shook up. I was trembling. I didn't know hardly anything about sex. I didn't know people did that with each other. A few minutes later my dad came in my room, and he had this silly grin on his face and had this talk with me. 'This is something all men do,' he said. 'But don't ever tell your mom, okay? You don't want to mess up our family, do you? That's a good girl.' He was nicer to me for a while after that, but I knew what was going on. I knew I was keeping a secret that could really blow my family apart. It was really awful, having to carry that secret around with me all the time. I'll never forgive him for that. Never."

The Problems of Families

James Osterhaus, clinical psychologist and author of *Family Ties Don't Have to Bind,* observes that the troubled family life of Generation X has contributed to the problem of evangelizing this generation.

What is the purpose of the family? To protect us, to define us, to model for us what society is all about and to offer us a sense of continuity linking the past to the future. In the family we learn about ourselves as individuals and as parts of a system of relationships. The family is an entire society between four walls. Families teach us who we are through the numberless interactions we have with family members, beginning with Mom and Dad. We learn what feelings and emotions are, and how to express them. We see how relationships work and how people get along with each other in various situations. Families protect and teach us to trust. They teach us the truth.

When the family works properly, when it is functional, the children grow up feeling safe, connected, skilled, confident and equipped to deal with the real world. To be properly functional a family must have healthy, safe boundaries, clear gender roles, a clear demarcation between the generations and a sense of hierarchy—that is, a sense that the parents are authorities who are wise, loving and available to discipline and to lead. A functional family has a repertoire of behaviors and strategies for solving problems and negotiating life changes. There are clear rules, but those rules are also flexible and subject to change when needed. A functional family operates in the present and is not haunted by the past. Communication is open, honest and clear, and allows for the expression of feelings as well as ideas.

What Osterhaus has just described is an ideal functional family. No family lives up to that ideal all the time. But families should be characterized by these qualities on at least a semiconsistent basis. When a family fails to demonstrate the characteristics that make a family functional, then it is said to be dysfunctional. The problems that make families dysfunctional, Osterhaus says, come in two categories.

1. Sins of omission. "This is where Mom and Dad have to work because of economic pressure," says Osterhaus, "or both parents choose to work because of a desire for self-fulfillment. There's a lack of hugs, a lack of affirmation, not enough milk and cookies after school, not enough Kodak moments. Mom and Dad don't intend to hurt their kids, but through their behavior they send the message that the kids are not wanted. Mom and Dad are not there for them."

As children, Thirteeners grew up feeling deprived and cheated. Economic forces dragged Mom out of the house and into the workplace, leaving the children feeling neglected. The new psychology of self-fulfillment turned parents away from primary parental functions and toward personal agendas. Abortion was legalized. Childbirth was discouraged. Thirteeners got the message that they were unwanted children—that they were contraceptive errors, Dad's draft dodge tickets or Mom's welfare ride.

2. Sins of commission. "These are acts of abuse—physical abuse, sexual abuse, verbal abuse, emotional abuse," says Osterhaus.

These acts of abuse can take some very subtle forms—forms that from the outside may not even look like abuse, such as excessive religious legalism. When abused, children respond with unconscious defense mechanisms that help them defend their egos—defense mechanisms such as denial that the abuse took place, repression of anger or other feelings over the abuse, displacing anger onto other people, or compulsive behavior and addictions, which not only numb the pain but also provide a substitute for love.

As these children grew up and entered into relationships, there was a chronic sense of vulnerability and danger, no matter how safe the partner was. (Unfortunately, the most common pattern is for abused people to select abusive people as mates, unconsciously replaying the abusive patterns of childhood.) An entire generation grew up lacking the skills of intimacy, feeling wary in relationships, approaching each other hesitantly, defensively and with little intention of making any lasting commitments.

As one university student told me, "I don't want a relationship. Relationships make everything so much harder."

The Home I Never Had

Barry pulled his Ford Ranger up to the curb in front of the professional building. Josie had just come out of the psychologist's office and was standing on the sidewalk, her arms folded so that she seemed to be hugging herself. She looked unhappy. Barry reached across the seat and opened the door. Josie climbed in and slid across the seat, close to him. On the stereo Soul Asylum was singing,

I'm so homesick but that's not so bad

because I'm homesick for the home I never had.

"How did it go?" asked Barry.

"It was rough," Josie replied. "I hate having to remember that stuff. I don't know if it's doing me any good or not—seeing a shrink, I mean."

"I couldn't do it."

"Couldn't do what?"

"Talk to some stranger about my problems. About my past."

"Could you talk to a friend?"

He looked at her, then back at the road. "Yeah," he said. "Sometime."

Josie looked out the side window. "Sure."

Barry frowned. "What do you mean, 'sure'?"

"I mean," she said, with more than a trace of annoyance in her voice, "that you always say you'll talk to me 'sometime.' Well, now is 'sometime,' isn't it?"

"No," he said. "Now is now. Sometime is . . . sometime later."

"Fine."

"Oh, jeez. Don't do this to me, Josie."

"I just feel like—like you don't trust me. You don't share with me. I've told you all the stuff I told my shrink, but you tell me nothing. This relationship is a one-way street—your way. There's something inside you that's . . . that's like a big, huge, dark part of you. And you won't share that with me. You hold back. If you were open with me about that, then maybe we'd both feel better."

Barry drove on in silence for a couple of minutes.

"Barry?"

"Yeah."

"Forget it."

"Forget what?"

"Forget it that I tried to get you to open up to me. I was wrong. When you're ready to talk, you'll know it, and it'll be okay."

"Thanks."

More silence.

"Josie?"

"Yeah?"

"I think I want to tell you."

"Really?"

"Really."

"I'm listening."

"Not here. Let's go to my place."

The Defining Moment

James Osterhaus sees two trends in family structures that are shaping the lives and molding the souls of Thirteeners.

The family is in transition. I see two trends developing. First, an increasing tendency for families to come apart, an accelerating divorce rate. Not only is divorce more common than it was twenty years ago, but we know much more now than we did then about the psychological effect of divorce on children. We used to think that divorce had only a short-term effect on children—they feel some sadness, some anger, but eventually they get used to the idea and bounce back. Now we know that the old adage "Kids are resilient" was a lot of bilge. The effects of divorce are long-lasting—

in some ways lifelong. For most children of divorce, that event represented the disintegration of the child's entire world and sense of security. It was the defining moment in that person's life.

Second trend: blended families. We break our families apart, then we Scotch-tape them back together again. But blended families don't function exactly like first families. I'm not saying blended families can't become healthy families, but it's harder, it takes a lot of work, and a lot of blended families lack the insight or commitment to carry it off well. *The Brady Bunch* is a nice fantasy, but you don't find it in real life. There are all kinds of issues that children in blended families have to confront: Does my stepparent really have authority over me? To whom should I be loyal? Am I being disloyal to my real dad if I am friends with my stepdad? Where is my real family identity?

These growing trends in our families produce a number of troubling issues in the lives of children—issues that continue to be a problem when they become young adults.

☐ *A diminished sense of safety and security.* Thirteeners feel more vulnerable and insecure than the young adults of previous eras. The family, which should be an enclosure of safety, is often an emotional kickboxing ring. Not only are there insufficient boundaries against external threats, the parents themselves are often the threat. Families today raise children who do not feel safe and secure.

☐ *A diminished sense of individual identify and definition.* "I continually meet people in my office who lack a sense of who they are and how they are defined as individuals," says Osterhaus.

I am treating more people than ever before—particularly more young people—who have character problems, problems such as personality disorders, problems that affect the basic constitution of their identity. We call this category of problems "severe personality disorganization," and it's difficult to treat because it exists at the most primitive level of the individual. It's not a case of treating a person for some problem with a painful memory or a troubled relationship. It's a case of an individual whose personality has been so distorted by past experiences that the disorder and disorganization are integral to who that person has become.

Increasing numbers of people, particularly young people, are finding it hard to say, "I know who I am apart from you, apart from my parents, apart from everyone else in the world. I am in touch with my emotions, I understand my motivations. I have the skills to handle decisions, relationships and problems. I can broker my emotional life effectively." Because fewer and fewer people can authentically make these claims, we find more and more people who, when you come right down to it, don't know who they are.

☐ *A diminished sense of satisfaction in relationships.* My generation has not acquired the skills and sense of commitment to build strong, healthy relationships with other people. We long for those relationships but don't know how to achieve them. The Boomer parents of my generation—parents who divorced or engaged in multiple adultery—didn't set an example of commitment or healthy boundaries in a relationship. Feeling abandoned and betrayed, my peers are wary of getting close to other people. They are afraid of being disappointed again.

"I Could Have Had a Dad . . ."

"My parents were divorced when I was thirteen," said Barry. "My sister and I lived with my mom in the house I grew up in. My dad moved out." Barry stood by the living room window of his second-floor apartment, his back to Josie, looking at the street below.

"Why don't you come sit here by me?" Josie invited, patting the couch cushion next to her.

Barry didn't move. "No. I don't think I could keep talking if I looked you in the eye, okay?"

"Okay."

"When my parents separated and my dad moved out, I just couldn't understand it. No one really explained the divorce to me. I guess they figured I knew what was going on. But I hurt so much. I couldn't believe our family was coming apart. I couldn't believe my dad would actually leave us like that. I thought—" He fell silent.

"What?" Josie prompted. "What did you think?"

"I thought," he responded slowly, "that my dad had quit loving us. I knew he hated my mom, but I thought he had stopped loving me and my sister too. I mean, if he still loved us, he wouldn't have moved out, would he?"

"Did he visit you?"

"Yeah. Actually, he tried to visit my sister and me about every other weekend or so at first. He'd take us out to Six Flags or to a movie or something. He tried real hard to buddy up to us. But I couldn't see that. I didn't understand. All I knew was he had moved out and it was all his fault that our family wasn't a family anymore. I figured he must really hate us or he wouldn't just spend weekends with us, he'd live with us all the time. I did everything I could to make him feel miserable, to get even with him. Once when he came to visit I really cussed him out. I called him every name in the book, right in front of my mom and my sister. Mom started to yell at me for that, but my dad just stood there and, like, absorbed it. He said to my mom, 'Barry's just mad. He'll cool off. Maybe I better not take him this week.' So he didn't take me that weekend. Or the next."

"Did he ever take you for visits again?"

"A few times. Finally he gave up trying to get through to me. That just confirmed to me what I already believed: he didn't love me anymore."

"You don't believe that now, do you?"

"No. I found out he did love me after all."

Josie waited.

Finally Barry spoke again in a voice that was husky with emotion. "It was a couple years ago. I was in my dorm room at college when I got a phone call from my mom. She said, 'Barry, your father died this morning.' "

Josie gasped. "What happened?"

"It was some kinda cancer. I didn't even know he was sick. I hadn't seen him in years. He wrote me a letter a couple weeks before he died, and he gave it to an attorney so I would get it after he was gone. In that letter he explained everything about the divorce. He said he always loved me, but he could never get me to see that. He said, 'When I lost my family, I lost the only thing that ever really mattered to me. I'm sorry. I wish you knew how sorry I am. I wish you knew how much I love you, son.' That really hurts. He told me he was sorry, but I never got to say 'I'm sorry' to him. I never got to tell him goodby."

Evangelism: The Opportunities and Pitfalls

We've seen that the family life of Generation X has, on the whole, been a troubled one. What, then, are the implications of Xer family issues for evangelism? What are the opportunities? What are the pitfalls?

According to James Osterhaus,

> A key inroad to this generation's heart is the problem of *emotional pain.* If we want to reach this generation, we need to acknowledge the pain they have experienced growing up. Some people deny that pain: "What do you mean, you've had pain in your life? You grew up with all these material advantages. You're not hurting, you're just spoiled!" Well, that's wrong. Kids who have experienced the pain of family disintegration have gone through some of the worst emotional times anyone can face. They've had pain growing up, and now they are young adults who hurt inside. Once we acknowledge that pain, we have something to say to them.

The people of my generation feel robbed of a sense of individual identity. As Christians, we can offer them an identity in Christ. For people who feel marginalized, we offer an assurance that they are no longer on the margins. They are at the center of God's plan and the center of God's love.

We can't take it for granted that Thirteeners will understand the terms and metaphors we use when describing the Christian faith—especially terms and metaphors derived from the family. Osterhaus says,

> Thirteeners don't understand the inner workings of relationships, and they can't always relate to our evangelical jargon. We should never assume we are speaking the same language when we talk to an Xer about a "church family," "brothers and sisters in Christ," "Christian love," "vertical and horizontal relationships" and so forth. We need to always be very concrete and clear.

For example, we need to be very careful in talking to Xers about the fatherhood of God. For previous generations God's fatherhood was a comforting, healing truth. But if a person comes from a dysfunctional family, the concept of fatherhood may not be very appealing. Family relationships aren't safe for a lot of Thirteeners. They may have trouble separating the idea of a heavenly Father from the memories of an abusive earthly father. According to Osterhaus,

> For some, a "father" is a mean drunk who roars around the house

and beats up Mom, so a "heavenly Father" must be another parent who hurts us or curses us or lets us down—only on a cosmic scale. For these individuals the friendship of Jesus may be a more appealing concept than the fatherhood of God.

This doesn't mean we should avoid God's fatherhood completely. Rather, we should approach the subject with care and with the investment of time. One way to do so is by building mentoring relationships with Xers. Mentoring can be a powerful tool for evangelism. When a young person is befriended, encouraged and instructed by an older person in a mentoring relationship, a process of reparenting takes place. *Aha!* says the person being mentored (at either a conscious or unconscious level). *So that's what a father or a mother is supposed to be like.* As the mentoring process continues, the younger individual will gradually become more open to biblical metaphors of God's heavenly parenthood, such as Jesus' parable of the loving father and the prodigal son.

Another effective way of dealing with the fatherhood issue is to clearly explain what our heavenly Father is like and use God's true fatherhood as a contrast to the dysfunctional earthly models of fatherhood many Xers have experienced. For example, when speaking at IVCF campus meetings I often use Jesus' story of the loving father and the prodigal son (see Luke 15) as a springboard.

I start by explaining the Pharisees' understanding of God the Father. To them he is righteous, holy, intolerant of imperfection and demanding. "Perhaps," I say, "this is the kind of father you grew up with—demanding, unloving, a perfectionist, a tyrant. But the entire point of Jesus' story of the loving father and the prodigal son is that God the Father is not like earthly fathers.

"Jesus tells a story about a father who did what ordinary fathers in that culture would never do: he ran to meet his son. It was unacceptable for distinguished men to run in public. What's more, fathers in that culture would have humiliated or shamed a son who had done what this son did—not rushed out to welcome him home.

"This father gave his son the best robe—most likely his own—so that people would see the son and know that he had been accepted back.

"He embraced and kissed his son. Fathers in that culture would have demanded that the son fall down and kiss *their* feet—but not this father.

"He gave his son the family ring—the most valuable family heirloom—even after this son had already wasted the rest of his inheritance. Fathers in that culture never would have entrusted such a valuable to a prodigal, wasteful son.

"He gave his son sandals—bare feet were for servants. Fathers in that culture would have treated this young man even worse than a servant—but this father treated him with honor.

"He gave his son a party and killed the prize calf for the meal—and this makes it clear that the father was inviting the entire community to the feast. A family gathering would have only required the killing of a sheep or goat, but this father was displaying his love for everyone around to see.

"You may have never seen such love in a father before. But that's what the love of God the Father is truly like. That's what his character is like."

In one two-week period—in fact, during the time this chapter was being written—I had the privilege of leading fifteen students to Christ using this story as a starting point. Thirteeners are hungry for this kind of ultrafunctional fatherhood after growing up under the pain of their dysfunctional earthly fathers.

A particular concern regarding Xers and conversion is, Once this person comes to Christ, will the conversion stick? Will the new Christian maintain his or her commitment to Christ? There are factors in the makeup of Generation X that spell potential trouble. One factor is the poorly formed Xer identity. In some ways it is not that difficult to encourage such people to convert to Christianity. Osterhaus says,

> They just go along with what they see others doing. They tend to adopt the identity of the group they are with. If they change groups, they're likely to switch identities. Conversion among Xers needs to be seen not as a single event but as a stage in a protracted process—a process whereby individuals learn who they are and what God has made them to be, a process in which they learn to permit the Holy Spirit to penetrate their being. We should be careful with mass evangelism, and we need to follow up any mass-evangelism

campaigns with efforts that emphasize relationships and close-knit
Christian community.

The deprived family history of many Xers has filled them with a deep
longing for belonging—a yearning for the sense of family and community that all people need but not all receive. This sense of community can be found in many biblical Christian churches. Unfortunately,
it can also be found in the cults. And since Xers tend to think emotionally rather than logically, they are less likely to analyze and test
the claims of a cult. Instead they will soak up the "warm fuzzies" that
the cult offers. *I'm loved and accepted here, I feel excited, joyful and purposeful for the first time in my life, so maybe this cult leader really is the savior
of the world!*

It is the sense of community and belonging of the cults that many
twentysomethings find so attractive. The Christian church invented
this kind of community and called it *koinōnia*—and we must recapture
the koinonia community. But our emphasis on community must not
be separated from our emphasis on a relationship with God. Only
through a deep relationship with God can we experience deep relationships with others. Only through a healthy relationship with God
can we experience healthy relationships with others.

If we truly want to convert members of my generation and keep
them in Christian churches and out of the cults, we need to place a
much greater emphasis on a quality of Christian community that really works and really cares. We need to model a functional Christian
family and functional Christian relationships. We need to demonstrate to a love-hungry generation how authentic Christian community works. If our churches become places of unconditional acceptance and love, then my generation will not have to trek to places like
David Koresh's Rancho Apocalypse in search of a place to belong.

Osterhaus says,

We need to be careful how we present the story of Jesus. Looking
at this generation, we recognize that there is an emptiness at the
core of many Thirteeners—an emotional doughnut hole that des-
perately craves to be filled. We see that they are trying to fill it with
other stuff—risky behavior, entertainment, a momentary high. The
danger is that evangelicals are tempted to advertise Jesus as "the
ultimate fill-up" or "the ultimate high." The gospel shouldn't be

packaged as if it were just another temporary high. That would be selling it short. That would be theologically inaccurate—and it is bound to disappoint.

The advertising approach to evangelism is not going to be effective with this generation. This is a wary generation that has been damaged in its ability to trust. We have to earn their trust in order to tell them our story. That takes time. It takes consistency. It takes congruence in word and action over a period of months or years, so that Thirteeners can see the genuineness of our story. They won't accept our story if they don't trust us. They've seen TV evangelists, they've seen religious rip-offs, and they have been burned. We have to be worthy of their trust before we can communicate the gospel with authenticity.

A New Family

"I think about it every day," said Barry. "It's like my whole life is just one big, aching regret. I can never get all those lost years back. I can never go back and have a father again."

"I think, somehow, in some other plane of existence, your dad knows how you feel," Josie said helpfully. "I mean, I don't believe people just vanish when they die. I don't know if there's, like, a heaven or something, but I think your dad must know that you—"

Barry turned about suddenly. His face was wet with tears. "That's a crock, Josie," he said, his voice blunt and savage. "When people die, they die. Nothing survives. I just have to live with that. I just have to live with the fact that I could have had a dad, at least two weekends a month, but I never let him into my life!"

Josie stared back at him, her eyes filling with hurt and with tears. "I can't allow myself to believe that, Barry," she said, her voice rising. "I have to believe that something of that person goes on . . . I have to! Because if nothing survives, then I'll never see Rex again."

Barry bit his lip. "I'm sorry, Josie, I didn't think—"

"No," said Josie, suddenly subdued, "it's okay. I don't know what reality is. What you said is probably true. I mean, people always act like death is a big mystery. Maybe it's no mystery it all. Maybe death really is just the end, just like you said. It's just kind of hard to believe that a person who made jokes and made love and gave joy to other people is suddenly just a bunch of garbage you have to bury in the ground."

"Josie, if you believe in an afterlife I don't want to take that away."

"You didn't. I go back and forth all the time. Sometimes I believe there's no afterlife. But other times I think, *I can't imagine myself not existing. Even if my body died, the part of me that is really me would have to go on thinking and feeling, wouldn't it? There just has to be an afterlife of some kind, doesn't there?* I mean, my mind just flip-flops between these two ideas, and I never quite believe in one or the other one hundred percent."

"Josie, all I know is that people die and you never get them back. You'll never get Rex back, and I'll never have a father. Not in this life anyway."

"I know," Josie replied sadly.

A few moments of silence passed between them.

Then, in a wistful voice, Josie added. "But I can't help feeling that somehow it just might be possible to find, like, a new family."

"What are you talking about?"

"Look, I know this is crazy but—remember that TV show, *The Brady Bunch?* Now, don't laugh at me—"

"I'm not laughing, Josie."

"Well, it was about these two families, and the girls in one family lost their dad and the boys in the other family lost their mom. So these two hurting families came together and made one big happy super-family. And all of a sudden the girls had not only a father again but brothers they never had before. And the boys had sisters and a mother. Everybody belonged there. They came from different families, but they all belonged to each other. I mean, things can happen like that, can't they? I mean, where people who have lost one family can find a new family."

"I dunno."

"I just wish there was some way people like you and me—people who have lost our families or who never really had a family—could, you know, find someplace to belong. Someplace where we could just fit in and be loved."

"It's a nice idea, Josie," said Barry. "But I don't think anything like that exists."

• • • • • • • • • • •

9

How to Reach Us, Part 1: A Faith That Works

Marisa, would you step in here

for a moment? And bring your pad."

That was Mr. Shifflet's voice, and the sound of it always made Marisa's skin crawl and her stomach clench. Shifflet was director of human resources for the large investment securities firm where Marisa had worked for almost a year. Her desk was in the reception area, just a few steps from Mr. Shifflet's office. Two other desks in the reception area belonged to Laurie, the receptionist, and Cassie, the new clerk-typist. They looked up at Marisa when her name was called, then quickly returned to their work.

Marisa stood, took her pad and pencil, and went into Mr. Shifflet's office. He was sitting behind his desk, leaning back, his head cocked appraisingly to one side. He was a big, round, balding, potato-faced man of about forty-five. He looked Marisa up and down, then nodded slightly as if to say, "I approve." The last thing in the world Marisa wanted was that kind of approval from him.

"What can I do for you, Mr. Shifflet?" she asked.

He chuckled, as if she had just made a smutty little double-entendre. She blushed, and hated herself for blushing.

"I need you to take a letter," he said.

"Would you mind dictating it on tape?" she asked. "I was right in the middle of—"

"Now you know I hate talking into those machines. I'd much rather dictate in person."

Just then Cassie stepped in to the office, holding a small cardboard box. "Here are the tapes you wanted, Mr. Shifflet," she said. "Where do you want them?"

Shifflet waved his hand, annoyed at the interruption. "Set them anywhere. And close the door on your way out."

Cassie set the box down on the floor in a corner of the room. Her eyes met Marisa's. Marisa sensed an instant connection—empathy, and perhaps a message: *watch out for him!* Then Cassie left and closed the door.

Marisa winced as the door closed. Now she was alone with Mr. Shifflet. The man was really scary. He had not done anything as overt as fondling her, but he had repeatedly made sexually suggestive comments, as well as some very unwelcome racial remarks about her relationship with T.J.

Shifflet indicated a chair where Marisa could sit. Then he sat back and began dictating. Only a few sentences into the letter, he reached for a cup of coffee that was on his desk. In a chain reaction the coffee cup nudged a dictionary, and the dictionary nudged a desk caddy full of pens, pencils and paper clips that perched on the edge of his desk. The caddy fell to the floor, and the items scattered at Marisa's feet. Instinctively Marisa got up from her chair, bent down on one knee and began picking up the items.

Suddenly she felt overshadowed. She started to get up but bumped into Mr. Shifflet, who had silently come around the desk and was bent over her. She felt his hot breath on her neck and his hands on her body.

"No!" she said sharply. "Get off me, Mr. Shifflet! Get your hands off me!"

But Shifflet didn't get off, and his hands only continued to roam over her body. "If a pretty thing like you will put out for that—that black boyfriend of yours, you'll put out for a white man. Especially a man who can do a lot for you in this company."

"I said get your hands off me!" Though off-balance, Marisa was able to bring her elbow sharply into the man's rib cage.

"Ooof!" he gasped.

Marisa got up and backed away from him. She stumbled over something—the box of tapes Cassie had set on the floor—but quickly regained her balance.

Instantly Mr. Shifflet was squared off in front of her, his doughy face now red and blotchy. "What's the matter with you?" he said, gasping. "Don't you know what I can do for you? Get you raises, bonuses, good performance reviews. And all you have to do is . . . be nice. Can't you be nice, Marisa?"

"Just leave me alone, Mr. Shifflet," said Marisa, struggling to keep her voice from shaking. "This is sexual harassment, and there are laws . . ."

Shifflet's face twisted in a snarl. "You have to prove a charge like that, missy. No one's going to believe you."

There was a knock on the door—but the person at the door didn't wait to be invited. It was Cassie. "Sorry!" she said. "I forgot something!" She walked briskly over to the box of tapes by Marisa's feet.

Shifflet was so surprised that he jumped back out of Cassie's way and didn't even think to scold her for bursting in.

Marisa stared as Cassie retrieved something small and black from the open box. Then, as quickly as she had come, Cassie was on her way out, leaving the office door wide open. Marisa looked at Shifflet, who was slowly regaining his composure.

"We're not through," he said softly—and ominously.

Marisa couldn't speak—and she had to get out. She followed Cassie out of the open door and turned left, toward the ladies' room. She had begun to cry, and any second now she was going to throw up.

Gateways to the Soul

Up to now I have talked about various challenges this generation presents and different ways to meet those challenges in order to reach

Generation X. The remainder of this book will pull together these various threads in order to create a unified evangelistic strategy.

Maybe as you have read about the challenges of communicating the story of Jesus with this generation, you have begun to conclude, *It's hopeless! Thirteeners are a closed, unreachable generation!* Nothing could be further from the truth. Thirteeners are very open to the Christian story right now—if it is presented in an effective and appropriate way. They may be closed to old, outmoded evangelistic methods, but not to the story itself. The Bible speaks directly to the pain of Generation X, and its message is targeted on Xer yearnings and needs—the need for hope, the need for meaning, the need for community, the need for empowerment and a sense of direction in life.

The Christian story unlocks a number of gateways to the soul of Generation X. Some examples:

☐ Xers are alienated. The Christian story brings reconciliation.

☐ Xers feel betrayed. The Christian story brings promise and restores broken trust.

☐ Xers feel vulnerable and insecure. The Christian story brings a sense of safety within a protective, healing community.

☐ Xers lack a defined identity. The Christian story gives them a new identity in Christ.

☐ Xers are have been burned by pathological models of authority. The Christian story reveals an authority that is positive, not pathological.

☐ Xers feel unwanted and unneeded. The Christian story offers them a place of belonging, a place for involvement, a place where their lives can be used in service of a purpose that is larger than themselves.

My research and my personal experience—along with the research and experience of many experts in evangelism, church growth, the pastoral ministry and youth ministry—strongly suggest that the three most effective strategies for evangelizing Generation X are a faith that works, process evangelism and narrative evangelism.

In this chapter we will examine what it means to demonstrate a faith that works through an embodied apologetic. In chapter ten we will examine process evangelism, and narrative evangelism is the theme of chapter eleven.

An Embodied Apologetic

My generation looks at life through social and emotional lenses rather than intellectual lenses. If the Christian story is to have relevance to their lives and their concerns, it must be a story that changes lives and changes society. Our story is such a story. The gospel is not just about "pie in the sky when you die by and by." It is a practical blueprint for a more just and compassionate society.

The Christian story touches on the issue of racial justice and reconciliation. It touches on the issue of poverty, hopelessness and economic justice. It touches on the needs and hurts of people with sexual addictions, sexual disorders and gender confusion, responding both firmly and compassionately to the gay and lesbian community. It confronts exploitation of every kind, including child abuse, spousal abuse, sexual abuse and sexual harassment. It promotes equality and understanding.

The social dimension is an often-overlooked dimension of the gospel, but it is an extremely important dimension. My generation is searching for a gospel that works. Properly and biblically understood, the Christian story does work. It changes lives. It reshapes societies.

What is needed is a new apologetic for a new generation. For the Baby Boomer generation the apologetic of choice was a logically constructed argument as contained in books like *The God Who Is There* and *Evidence That Demands a Verdict*. But my generation demands a different apologetic—an embodied apologetic, a flesh-and-blood, living and breathing argument for God. The old apologetics of previous generations assumed that the barrier to conversion was intellectual and the way to remove that barrier was to answer all cognitive doubts. But Xers live in an age of intellectual ambiguity, when cognitive answers carry considerably less weight. The question my generation asks is not "Can Christians prove what they believe?" but "Can Christians live what they believe?"

"If you step into the pulpit," says Stanley Grenz, "and you say, 'I'm going to give you five reasons to believe in God,' and the reasons you give are all intellectual, evidential and cosmological, you'll have little or no impact. The impact comes when you can say with authenticity, 'I've been knocked around by life, but through the pain of it all I've experienced that God is there.' That's an embodied apologetic, and that counts with Thirteeners."

An embodied apologetic is able to demonstrate tolerance, understanding and openness to other points of view even while asserting its own point of view. It does not seek to make debating points at the expense of other faiths or other communities. "You don't elevate Christianity by showing how bad Islam is," says Grenz. "That won't cut it anymore."

When Thirteeners begin to see Christians practicing Christian tolerance and love while creating biblical solutions to societal problems, they will discover a faith that works. The rest of this chapter will examine some social issues through which the church can make important evangelistic inroads.

Pro Bono

Marisa came out of the ladies' room and paused, looking down the hall toward the reception area, where her desk and her work awaited her return. But to get to her desk she had to pass by Mr. Shifflet's office. She stepped slowly down the hall, dreading the possibility that he would step out of his office and block her path. Her steps quickened and she kept her eyes straight ahead as she passed his door. She seated herself at her desk and tried to think about her work.

She couldn't. All she could think of was him . . . what he had done . . . what he had tried to do. She wanted to pick up the phone and call T.J. at the printing company—but she discarded that idea right away. T.J. would come right over and give Mr. Shifflet a knuckle makeover.

Marisa was still mentally sorting through her options when a shadow fell on the desk in front of her, startling a gasp out of her. She looked up sharply. It was Cassie.

"Come with me," said Cassie. "I'm taking you to lunch."

"But it's only eleven o'clock—"

"That's all right. Let's go."

Feeling dazed, needing someone else to do her decision-making for a while, Marisa stood up from her desk and said, "Okay."

Outside the building, they got into Cassie's car and pulled out of the parking lot. As they drove, Cassie pulled something out of her purse and handed it to Marisa. It was small and black, about the size of a cigarette pack, but heavier. It was a Panasonic RN-105D micro-cassette recorder. Marisa turned it over in her hands, uncomprehending.

"Rewind it a bit, and listen," said Cassie. "Careful! Don't touch the red button. You'll record over it."

Marisa did as Cassie said, and heard her own voice, frantic and tinny-sounding, but very clear: "I said get your hands off me!"

There was a clattering sound, followed by a gasping male voice, "Ooof!"

More thudding, clacking sounds, then the male voice again—his voice. "What's the matter with you? Don't you know what I can do for you? Get you raises, bonuses, good performance reviews. And all you have to do is . . . be nice. Can't you be nice, Marisa?"

Marisa's own voice. "Just leave me alone, Mr. Shifflet! This is sexual harassment, and there are laws . . ."

Then Shifflet's. "You have to prove a charge like that, missy. No one's going to believe you."

Marisa clicked the off button and looked up at Cassie. "What is this about?" she asked tremulously. Twin runnels of tears slid down her cheeks.

"Shifflet said you have to prove a charge of sexual harassment," said Cassie, looking straight ahead as she drove. "There's your proof."

Marisa's face came alight. "That's why you came into the office right after I did! You had that recorder hidden in that box! You knew he would—"

"I thought he might," said Cassie. "And my instincts were right. Did he pull that 'accidentally-spill-the-desk-caddy' trick?"

Marisa gasped. "He did that to you too?"

Cassie nodded. "I have one of these handy little microcassette tapes of my own. And it's very incriminating."

Marisa was quiet for a few moments. "Now what do we do?" she asked at last.

"We talk to a friend of mine," said Cassie. "He's an attorney. I already called him, and he's meeting us at the coffee shop."

Marisa's eyes widened. "But I can't afford an attorney!"

"Relax!" said Cassie. "He's an attorney from my church, and he's willing to take this case on pro bono."

"Pro what?"

"No fee. He'll donate his services. He's very active in discrimination cases, sexual harassment cases, situations where people are victimized by the system. I've already talked to him about my own case. In fact, he's the one who suggested I plant that microcassette recorder. If you're willing to join with me, we can turn the tables on Mr. Shifflet."

Marisa thought about it for a few moments. "I don't know," she said slowly. "I just don't know if I could do that. Get into a lawsuit and all that."

"You don't have to make any decisions now. Wait till you talk with Jerry—that's the attorney. After you know what all your options are, then you can decide."

Ministries to Gays and Lesbians

Scriptures teach plainly that homosexual practice is self-destructive and abhorrent to God. Many Christians never go farther than that and choose to condemn homosexuals as the most unforgivable of sinners. Yet the Scriptures also teach that God loves all sinners, including those who are involved in a pattern of sexual sin. For their own sakes, as well as for the sake of righteousness, God wants to see people delivered from their self-destructive sexual addictions (see John 8).

Since the word *gospel* literally means "good news," a gospel of judgment and condemnation is not a gospel at all. The good news of Jesus Christ is the story of grace and forgiveness, of hope and affirmation toward people who feel abused, ashamed, rejected and hopeless. When the church becomes less militant against gays and more loving toward gays, when it provides support groups instead of hate groups, we will begin to see healing—and we will see gays and lesbians discovering authentic love through Jesus Christ.

When he was pastor of NewSong Church in Walnut, California, Dieter Zander didn't hesitate to preach the full range of what Scripture says about homosexuality. He tried to balance the law of God with the love of God. And he made sure that NewSong embodied the love of God by offering support groups for people who struggled with homosexual tendencies and temptations. "All too often," says Zander, "we condemn people or their actions without offering an answer. As biblical Christians we should take strong stands on a moral and social issues—but our stands should always be accompanied with answers and action."

Racial and Ethnic Reconciliation

Reconciliation is a distinctly Christian concept. Jesus came to reconcile us to God and to each other. He came to found a new and accepting community in which there is "no division into Jew and non-Jew, slave and free, male and female," and in which "all are in a common relationship with Jesus Christ" (Galatians 3:28).

Many Xers feel shut out of the economic system and divided against one another along racial lines because of affirmative action. White Xers who see a less-qualified person get a job because of racial quotas think, *That's not fair! Why do I have to pay a penalty because of racist policies of past generations? I'm not the one who screwed up race relations in this society! Why am I the one who has to sacrifice to fix the problem? How is it fair to discriminate against me in the name of ending discrimination?* This is an issue our society has chosen to resolve legally and bureaucratically rather than relationally. Institutional solutions to relational problems tend to leave a bitter taste in everyone's mouth. This is one more reason Xers are angry with the system. On the whole, my generation isn't angry with other races, but it tends to be very bitter toward a society that creates new inequities in order to remedy old inequities.

Though government can only provide bureaucratic solutions, the church is in a position to provide relational and spiritual solutions to the race problem. IVCF's Jimmy Long shares a story of a relational solution that was used at the University of North Carolina. The issue: Should the university build a black cultural center? If so, where should it be built? The issue was bitterly, angrily debated for many weeks. But a group of Christian students on campus saw the controversy as an opportunity to build relational bridges. The students convened prayer sessions and met individually with both the dean (who was seen by African-American students as the embodiment of an uncaring power structure) and the director of the black cultural center project. Then the two of them met and talked, and a breakthrough was achieved— all because Christians created an environment where reconciliation could take place through prayer and mutual understanding.

A Fair Question

Jerry, the attorney, was young—thirty-five or so—and dark-haired, with an genial, easygoing manner. His smile vanished and his voice became all business, however, when Cassie handed him the micro-cassette recorder. He held the recorder close to his ear so he could hear the dialogue over the ambient conversations and silverware clatter of the coffee shop. After listening for a minute or so, he put the recorder down.

"Everything on this tape is very clear and audible," said Jerry. "And it's powerful stuff. Put that together with Cassie's evidence and I'd say we have everything we need to put this guy out of business."

"I don't know if I could go through a whole court thing," said Marisa. "I'm shaking just thinking about it."

"I prefer not to litigate," said Jerry. "I try to avoid lawsuits wherever possible. There are other ways to make sure Mr. Shifflet can't do this to anyone else—ways that will help you get this behind you and get on with your life."

"Do you think there are other women he's done this to?" asked Marisa.

"Oh yes," Cassie said quickly and knowingly. "There are others. But they are afraid to say anything or do anything. If you're afraid too, Marisa, I'll understand."

"Well, I am scared," said Marisa. "I'm not even sure what I'm scared of, but I know Mr. Shifflet scares me."

"There are risks," said Jerry, "which I will lay out for you in just a moment. No one's going to make you do anything you don't want to. After we've discussed what is involved you can make your own decision."

"Okay," said Marisa. "But before we go any further, there's something I need to know."

"Yes?"

"Why are you doing this?"

"Doing what?"

"Donating your time. Helping Cassie and me without charging a fee. I mean, what's in it for you?"

Jerry nodded. "That's a fair question. And the answer is that I feel a need to give back to God and to others something of what I've received. God has blessed me in so many ways, including allowing me to build a successful law practice. I believe God wants me to use my legal skills to help people who have been mistreated by the system and who may not have the resources to defend themselves.

"I have a special interest in issues of gender inequity and the imbalance of power between men and women because I was raised by a working single mother who was exploited by the system. My mother's boss relied on her skills to get his job done, but he never paid her anything near what she was worth. She saw men she had trained get promoted over her simply because they were men. She never got promotions or raises because—and her boss actually told her this—'we need to give the promotions to men with families'! And here she was, struggling to raise my brother and me on a secretary's salary!

"When I read my Bible I see that Jesus lived in a society where women were treated as second-class citizens, almost as property. Jesus challenged the injustice of that society. He went around trying to elevate the status of women. For example, there's that story about Jesus and the woman at the well in Samaria. Do you know that story?"

Marisa shook her head uncertainly.

"Well, the net-net of it is, Jesus reached out to a woman who was outcast in terms of her gender and her race, and he treated her with respect. That story says a lot to me about gender reconciliation, racial reconciliation and economic reconciliation. I want to be involved in the reconciliation process and in fighting against injustice and exploitation.

"That's kind of a long-winded explanation, but I can see you really want to know where I'm coming from. I hope that helps."

Marisa was silent for several seconds. Then she said, "That helps a lot. I don't know how to thank you for helping Cassie and me with this situation." She paused, and a look of determination came over her features. "So," she said, "tell me what I have to do."

The Environment

Ecology awareness is a big deal with Generation X. Even small gestures can mean a lot. From holding a "Caring for God's Creation" booth at a university Earth Day festival to recycling Communion cups and avoiding ozone-eating Styrofoam coffee cups at the fellowship hour, churches can show a respect for the planet and a sensitivity to Xer environmental concerns.

We all care about the health of our planet, though some of us are more active than others in ecological efforts. Invite input from Xers to help guide your church's environmental policy in areas like recycling and use of single-use items.

Making our churches a little more "green" is a small price to pay to make them more Xer-friendly. But more to the point, I believe our churches should not only "dress up in green" as a way to reach Xers; we should respect and care for the environment because God commanded us to (see Genesis 2:15).

Homelessness

Here is an issue where Christians are widely seen to lack credibility. Many Christians take a "get-a-job" stance toward the homeless or gripe and moan about the "welfare cheats." But when Christians join together to do something tangible about homelessness—turning church classroom space into midweek homeless shelters or serving meals to homeless people at the downtown park—my generation takes notice.

"One of our InterVarsity campus groups," says Jimmy Long, "was involved in a Habitat for Humanity project with a secular group from another college. They were building houses for the homeless. As our Christian group worked alongside the mostly pre-Christian group from the other campus, the students from the other group began to ask, 'Why are you doing this?' The pre-Christians wanted to know what the Christians' motivation was. This gave our group a chance to share the Christian experience and Christian convictions. It was a powerful message to the pre-Christian students: 'We embody what we believe.' "

This doesn't mean that churches (and individual Christians) should strive to be "politically correct" or pass themselves off as something they are not. It doesn't mean that as Christians we even have to have a stated position on some issues. James Osterhaus recalls that when he was on the staff of the Community Presbyterian Church in Danville, California, someone called the church and asked, "What is your position on nuclear weapons?" The secretary responded, "We don't allow them in the sanctuary."

The point is that we don't always need to agree with the political beliefs of Xers, but we should always demonstrate sensitivity to their feelings and empathy with their concerns.

Press EJECT

Mr. Shifflet got a surprise when he arrived at his office on Monday morning. Someone was waiting for him: Nancy Clark, administrative vice president, and Tod Braling, a staff attorney. Braling was perched on a corner of his desk. Clark was sitting in his chair, behind his desk. Neither of them moved to get up when he walked in. A chill went down his spine.

"Hi, Nancy, Tod," he said, smiling nervously.

Braling nodded.

"Shifflet," Clark responded curtly. She usually called him by his first name, Ray. Something was wrong. "I want you to hear something," she continued. "I just want you to know I take no pleasure in this." She reached over to the dictation microcassette recorder on his desk and punched the play button.

Male voice: "What's the matter with you? Don't you know what I can do for you? Get you raises, bonuses, good performance reviews. And all you have to do is . . . be nice. Can't you be nice, Marisa?"

Female voice: "Just leave me alone, Mr. Shifflet! This is sexual harassment, and there are laws . . ."

Male voice: "You have to prove a charge like that, missy. No one's going to believe you."

"Turn it off," said Shifflet, who was very pale and sweating profusely, even though the room was very cold. "There's an explanation."

Nancy Clark punched OFF. "We're listening," she said.

"I . . . I mean . . ."

"Yes?"

"I think I should talk to an attorney."

"This is not a criminal matter," said Tod Braling. "Sexual harassment is a civil matter. You've created a major liability exposure for this company."

"This is very awkward," said Shifflet, tugging at his collar, Rodney Dangerfield-style.

"We all feel awkward about this," said Clark. "But the fact is, I have to ask you to clean out your desk—your own personal effects, that is. I brought a cardboard box for you. You have thirty minutes, and Mr. Braling and I will stay with you until you are finished."

Shifflet's jaw jutted. "Now, that's not fair! You can't do this to me! I'll sue the company!"

"That's your privilege, Mr. Shifflet," said Braling. "But the attorney for the women who have made this complaint has offered to be very reasonable. If they wanted to, those women could sue this company for millions, but all they want is for the company to deal with the problem. If you want to sue the company for wrongful termination, then by all means do so." He reached over to the dictation machine, popped the eject button and took out a microcassette—a copy of the tape Cassie had made. He held up the miniature audiotape between his thumb and forefinger. "Frankly, Mr. Shifflet, I think you're gonna have a tough time winning this one. In fact, you being a family man and all, I wonder if you're even going to want to have something like this played in open court."

Shifflet's shoulders sagged. It was over.

Abortion and Other Politically Divisive Issues

My generation is disgusted and offended by angry Christian attack groups—the pickets and protests, the name-calling, the violence, the bombings, the doctors who have been shot to death. In seeking political power, many Christians have sacrificed their moral authority. Xers can respect and tolerate a wide range of opinions and convictions if they are stated in a respectful, tolerant voice. But we cannot tolerate intolerance.

James Osterhaus, author of *Bonds of Iron,* says,

I'm concerned about the unloving attitude Christians often display when they take a moral and political stand. The most embarrassing thing to me is Christian media spokesmen who are bitter, hostile and adversarial toward the other side. Thirteeners are tired of being screamed at from both sides of these issues. They want to see authentic Christians standing up in love to present their case—not just another political action committee. In Washington, D.C., where I'm from, members of Congress are sick and tired of being

lobbied and pressured by angry Christians. I suspect the baby buster generation is sick and tired of it too.

Mother Teresa spoke on abortion at the 1993 National Prayer Breakfast in Washington, D.C. Christians on both sides of the abortion issue
attended that breakfast, and both sides enthusiastically applauded
Mother Teresa's talk. It was clear even to prochoice Christians that
she spoke with authority and credibility. Why? Not because she
marched on Washington or picketed clinics, but because she has lived
a life that demonstrates compassion. She said, "Don't kill your children. Send them to me, and I will take care of them." Everyone there
knew she meant it.

Instead of angry protests, my generation wants to see practical
answers such as church-sponsored counseling, shelters and homes,
financial assistance, and health care for women with crisis pregnancies and for their babies. When Thirteeners see this kind of love being
demonstrated as a solution to a painful social issue, they will see that
there is authenticity to our story. They may not agree with a Christian
prolife stance, they may continue to embrace different values, but they
will respect our caring, practical solutions—and they will respond to
the love that is demonstrated in those solutions.

"Church People" Who Care

The waitress took their orders, then left Jerry, Cassie, T.J. and Marisa
to continue their conversation.

"Risa," said T.J., "I still say you shoulda told me! I woulda gone in
there an whupped that muthuh's—"

"I know exactly what you would've whupped, Teej," laughed Marisa.
"And believe me, this was a better way to deal with Shifflet."

"Right," said Cassie. "The guy is gone. It's over and we can get on
with our jobs."

"Thanks to friends like you and Jerry," Marisa responded, placing
a hand on Cassie's arm. "You two are incredible. I don't know what
I would have done if you hadn't been there."

"Well," Jerry deadpanned, "not all lawyers are scum-sucking ambu-
lance-chasers."

Marisa laughed.

"Seriously," Jerry added, "God's done so many awesome things in my own life. I figure the best way to pay back the debt is by helping out people who need it."

"Well, I sure needed it," said Marisa, her eyes shining. "I'm just amazed that there are, you know, church people who care about issues like this."

"Oh," said Cassie, "our church is involved in all kinds of issues in the community. We have a conciliation service to help people resolve disputes without going to court. We have ministries that help gays, the homeless, Asian and Caribbean refugees, and women with crisis pregnancies. Our youth groups are involved in tree planting and other environmental programs . . ."

"Another thing you'd find interesting about our church," said Jerry, "is that our pastor is black—and his wife is white. Would you two like to visit sometime?"

T.J. grinned and shrugged. "No way, no church for me, man . . ."

"I'd like to," Marisa said suddenly, "just to see what it's like."

T.J. looked at her in surprise. "Something wrong with you, girl? You always said you think church people are—"

"I know what I said before," Marisa interrupted quickly. "But I like Cassie and Jerry—and who knows? There might be more people like them at church!"

• • • • • • • • • •

10

How to Reach Us, Part 2: Process Evangelism

Here's a list of Twelve Step groups

in the area," said the psychologist. "Only two of them deal with eating disorders. I recommend that first group. It meets at the YWCA. That's close to where you work, isn't it?"

Josie nodded. "Too close. I don't want any of my friends to see me going there. It'd be too hard to explain."

"You mean it would be too embarrassing," said the psychologist. "We agreed you were going to be honest with yourself about your feelings."

Josie laughed. "Okay, okay. Too embarrassing then." She looked at the other listing, then wrinkled her nose. "That one meets in a church."

The psychologist chuckled. "The group at Forest Lakes Community Church is a Christian Twelve Step group for adult children of dysfunctional parents. They have people in that group with a lot of different addictions: eating disorders, alcohol, workaholism . . ."

There was a look of resistance on Josie's face. "I still don't know that I really need to go to one of these meetings. I mean, what do they do in these groups?"

The psychologist leaned back in his chair and fixed a hard gaze on Josie. "They save your life," he said.

A Process of Relationships

Xers are a spiritual class of people. True, they are indifferent to the spirituality of Christianity, which they see as cold and institutional. And they have largely rejected the Eastern-oriented New Age spirituality of their Boomer parents as being too intangible and airy-fairy to be of any earthly use. What, then, is "Xer spirituality"?

The spirituality of my generation is transrational, yet it is concrete in its expression. You probably won't find a typical Xer singing hymns in church or chanting his mantra or channeling spirits. To Xers, getting out and rock-climbing can be a spiritual experience. Or sailboarding. Or cycling. Or sex. Xers tend to believe in transcendent realities, but they also like to pour their energies and put their bodies into a "spiritual experience" of the here and now. Taking risks, playing hard, going to extremes—this is how many Xers define spirituality.

Though largely unaware of what the Bible is all about, Xers are naturally accessible and receptive to a worldview that transcends reason and logic. While the worldview of the Bible is reasonable and logical, it is also transrational. It demands that we accept many things we cannot understand: mysteries, paradoxes, prophecies and unanswered questions. Xers will be receptive to the Bible's transcendant and transrational worldview—if that worldview is presented in terms Xers can relate to. While some barriers exist between the Xer mindset and the Christian faith, many old barriers have been torn down, making our task easier than it was for those who sought to evangelize the Boomer generation.

The Boomers were largely agnostic about the spiritual realm. To evangelize Boomers you often had to first debate the question of whether a spiritual realm even existed. The agnosticism of the Boomers was the last gasp of the Enlightenment and of modernism. Before you could engage a Boomer in a discussion of the existence of God, you first had to agree that the nature of God—spirit—was even possible.

Today, however, we don't need to start by framing the question "Is there a God?" Instead we find ourselves back in the days of the first-century church, when superstition and mythology were on an equal plane with science. In those days the question was not "Is there a God?" but "Which god is God?" And that is the question of the 1990s and beyond. For Generation X the answer to that question is not found in an overwhelming mountain of evidence for the existence of God or the resurrection of Jesus. Xers are not likely to respond with a single-moment-in-time decision for Christ. They are much more likely to respond over a longer period of time—a gradual result of a process of relationships.

In process evangelism, the conversion experience takes place over a longer period than we have tended to expect from our technique-oriented evangelistic strategies of the past. In process evangelism people are convinced of the reality of God's love not by propositional arguments or one-time evangelistic rallies but by a daily, consistent, practical demonstration that Christianity works and that God's love is real. In process evangelism pre-Christian people discover the reality of God and the love of God in the transparency and love of God's people.

Off the Wall

The ball came flying off the back wall like a ricocheting bullet. John Takeda's muscular legs pounded like pistons as he launched himself on an intercept course, racquet-arm extended to the max. As he ran he put everything he had into a hard overhand smash. The racquet caught the ball square in the webbing. The ball rocketed on a perfectly flat trajectory to the side wall, caromed to the back wall and rebounded like a streaking meteor.

John's opponent dove for it, but his racquet was short of the mark by a good six inches. Overbalanced, the young man went over, barrel-rolled on the court and skidded to a stop against the wall.

"Adam!" shouted John, his sneakers making a shrill, echoing squeak as he ran to the fallen man's side. "Hey, Adam! Are you okay?"

From the floor, Adam opened first one eye, then the other. "Game," he said, groaning. "You win. Help me up, dude." John grabbed the fallen man's hand and pulled him to his feet.

"You compete hard, man!" said John admiringly. "But you gotta know when to let 'em go by!"

"Now you tell me!" groaned Adam.

"You up for another game, or you want to head for the showers?"

Adam winced, putting both hands against his back and experimentally flexing his body joints. "The showers, John," he said. "Definitely the showers."

They left the racquet court and passed through the weight room on their way to the showers. "Say, John," said Adam, "I was wondering if we could change our regular Thursday-night blood feud to another night."

"Hey, I've been dishing it out to you on that court every Thursday night for three months," said John. "Why do you want to change?"

"They're switching my Bible study to Thursday nights, and I don't want to miss it."

"Bible study?"

Adam nodded. "Yeah. Bible study."

"Gee," said John. "I dunno. Thursday's about the only night I have free. Man, I didn't know you were one of those 'Bible study' types."

Adam laughed. "What's that mean?"

"You know, religious. Christian. All this time I thought you were just a regular guy."

"I *am* a regular guy."

"You don't seem like a religious guy. I mean, we've been friends for what? Five, six months? You helped Kim and me move to our new apartment. You and Joyce have had us over half a dozen times, and you never once tried to convert us or anything. You and Joyce have just been—you know, friends."

Adam chuckled. "Well, we *are* friends."

"Yeah, I know. It's just—I mean, I'm just surprised to find out that you're . . . The thing is, I'm just real careful. There are so many people coming at you with their agenda. Like, there are the Jehovah's Witnesses who want to put a *Watchtower* in your hand. And there's the Amway guy who wants to talk to you about a 'business opportunity.' And there are the born-againers with a tract in one hand and an offering plate in the other."

"Well, not all Christians are like that."

"Yeah. I guess not."

"So, John, back to racquetball. Thursday night's the only night you have free, huh?"

"Yeah. And you don't want to miss your Bible study, huh?"

"No way!" said Adam. "The people in my Bible study are like my second family. I wouldn't miss it for the world." He paused. "But you know, we could meet here right after work and get in a coupla games before I go to Bible study."

"What about dinner?"

"I'll grab a quick burger at Fat Jack's on the way to the study."

"Hey, that'll work."

"And if you like, you could come with me to the Bible study and get religion. Oh, and be sure and bring your money in case they pass the plate."

John laughed. "Get outta here!"

Process Evangelism—the Biblical Model

How do Thirteeners make a decision to follow Christ? Richard Peace of Fuller Theological Seminary says,

This is an issue that's extremely important to me, the whole question of how conversion takes place. There was always a big difference between the way we have traditionally understood conversion (that is, the example of Paul on the Damascus Road) and the actual experience of people in the church. Studies show that less than twenty percent of Christians have had this dramatic "Pauline" conversion—yet this is the model that guided the development of all of our evangelistic strategies! This was the evangelistic paradigm practiced in America for decades and it framed evangelism in commercial terms. You have your product (the gospel) and you have your customer (the pre-Christian) and your job is to sell this product to that customer. Conversion takes place when you "close the deal."

Most people, however, have come to faith in a different fashion—a way that is just as biblical as Paul's conversion, a way that is called process evangelism. We find process evangelism in the gospels, particularly the Gospel of Mark, where we see Jesus evangelizing the Twelve over a period of years. Mark recounts how the disciples began with an understanding of Jesus as an "above-average teacher." As their relationship grew and their understanding deepened, they started seeing that he was a prophet, then the Messiah, until finally they realized that he was the Son of God.

The process Peace describes is one that Jesus invites us to pattern ourselves after. He entered into the world of the twelve disciples. He identified with their pain and their broken condition; he devoted great amounts of time building his life into their lives; he committed himself to a process of evangelizing, not just an evangelistic event.

Peace concludes:

> This is the biblical model for evangelizing in a postmodern, Baby Buster world, and it is imperative that we rethink our understanding of the evangelism process and the conversion process in light of this biblical model and in light of present-day realities. Baby Busters are very resistant to the "Four Spiritual Laws" approach, which says, "Here is the truth. Agree to it and pray to receive Jesus right now." They won't trust a stranger distributing tracts and witnessing in a chance encounter in a shopping mall. Trust must be earned over a period of time through an investment of involvement and relationship.

In my own experience on university campuses I see increasingly that students come into our InterVarsity groups as nonbelievers—pre-Christians. They stay, make friends, get involved in activities and grow in their understanding of the story of God. After a process of months or years it is clear that they are decisively, obediently following Jesus Christ. They are praying, studying the Bible and witnessing enthusiastically and effectively. But when did they make this decision? Where was the point in the process where they crossed the line from pre-Christian to Christian? They themselves don't know. All they can say for sure is that once they weren't Christians and now they are. They have experienced a gradual transformation through a process of relationships.

My favorite definition of evangelism is that of Lon Allison, director of evangelism for the Evangelical Covenant Church Denomination. "Evangelism," he said, "is cooperating with the Holy Spirit to bring a person one step closer to Christ." This definition clearly suggests a process rather than a point in time. We are responsible for one step at a time. We don't need to feel pressured to share the Four Laws within the first five minutes of meeting someone. It is the Holy Spirit's job to bring about conversion; our job is to make ourselves available as the tools he uses to complete his work. Like a carpenter, God uses one tool for a while, lays that tool down and picks up another. Each tool is a valuable part of the building process, but it is God who is the master builder, not we.

The task of evangelism is complicated by the fact that Xers, being fascinated and saturated by entertainment media, have little time to reflect. In fact many Xers fill their minds with noise and music specifically to escape the pain of reflecting on reality. Yet without honest reflection how can anyone make a commitment of his or her life to Jesus Christ? That's one of the reasons it is difficult to bring Xers to commitment through a point-in-time approach. Xers need time to think and reflect on their own lives, their own issues, their own problems—and process evangelism gives them that time.

Fat Jack's

Thursday night rolled around again. John and Adam met at the racquet club. Adam astonished John with three straight wins. "I don't believe this," said John as he walked Adam out to the parking lot. "You never beat me three straight games. Never!"

"I got lucky."

"You got new sneakers? New racquet? New anything?"

Adam laughed. "I got lucky, that's all! Hey, I've still got forty-five minutes till the Bible study. I was gonna go by Fat Jack's for a burger. You want one too?"

"Sure."

"Let's take my car," said Adam. "I'll bring you back here."

At Fat Jack's they ordered a couple of Wowie Burgers with fries and Cokes. As they sat down, bone-dome boogie-woogie rapper Lucas was on the pay-CD player, performing "Lucas with the Lid Off."

"So—like, what do you do at this Bible study thing?" asked John.

"Different stuff. Usually we read a chunk of the Bible, then we talk about how the stuff in the Bible applies to our everyday lives. Sometimes Damon, the group leader, will show a ten-minute movie clip that ties in with the Bible passage we're reading. Last week we were studying the passage where Jesus raised Lazarus from the dead, and we watched a couple excerpts from that movie with Kiefer Sutherland and Julia Roberts and Kevin Bacon—you know, the one where these medical students would give each other near-death experiences . . ."

"Oh, yeah!" said John. "*Flatliners!* I love that movie! You mean you guys will watch a cool movie like that and then talk about the Bible?"

"Sure. I mean, the movie is about death and survival and whether or not the spirit goes on after the body dies. And the Bible talks a lot about that stuff. It's cool, it's fun . . . but it's also kinda like a support group. We talk about hassles we're going through. And the people in the group take care of each other. I mean, it's a real community."

"A community," John repeated.

"Yeah. Now maybe you can see why I wouldn't miss it."

John looked thoughtful. "Say, Adam . . ."

"Yeah?"

"Do they ever let—new people in the group? I mean, just to check it out?"

The Front Lines: Personal Evangelism

The institutional church has a role to play in evangelizing Generation X, and we will explore that role later in this chapter. But if we are honest we have to recognize that the church is not on the front lines of the spiritual battlefront in this world. The church is an encampment just behind the lines. The front lines are out there, in the "real world," on the campuses, in the neighborhoods, in the offices and behind the storefronts, in the clubs and bars, in the gyms and on the courts and in the streets of our world. To put it in sports terms, the church is where we gather for the huddle, but the real game is out there on the playing field where all the grunting and sweating and bone-crunching takes place. The playing field of the outside world is where we do our evangelism and where the game is won or lost.

My friend NASA scientist Robert Slocum wrote a book called *Ordinary Christians in a High Tech World.* There he differentiates between "the church gathered" and "the church scattered." We need the huddle, we need the church gathered, we need the institutional church, we need the weekly worship service. But when we come out of the huddle, it's time to scatter, to fan out and take our positions on the playing field, to put our shoulders and knees and heads into the game, to grunt and sweat and take our shot. With Jesus as our coach we have to move out, fight for yardage and keep our eyes on the goal.

The key to reaching this generation does not involve putting up a sign in front of the church and inviting people in. Odds are they won't come in. The key to the heart of Generation X is personal evangelism practiced by ordinary laypeople with a heart and a vision for taking the story of Jesus Christ to this generation. If we truly want to reach this generation we have to go where the people are.

Jesus certainly went out where the people were. Philippians 2:5-11 tells us that Jesus identified with us, became one of us and moved into our world in order to serve us and to save us. Throughout the Gospels we see him out on the front lines—on the playing field, shoulder to shoulder and elbow to elbow with the people he came to save. In Mark 2:15-17, Luke 15:1-2 and Luke 19:1-10 we see him eating and talking with the despised people of his society. And in Acts 17:16-34 Paul moves out onto the Areopagus—"Mars Hill"—plants his feet on the turf of Athenian culture and tells the story of Jesus in the marketplace of Greek ideas.

My experience, and the experience of others who are working on the turf of Generation X, indicates that our personal effort to evangelize the people around us should be organized around relationships rather than apologetics. Jimmy Long says,

> I've had conversations with people about apologetics. I may convince them of Jesus' life, death and resurrection—but they still respond, "So what?" This doesn't mean truth is not important. It is. But we have to establish the relationship before they will listen to our truth. Our evangelism must be a balance of relationship and truth. If we emphasize only the truth, they will not stay long enough to listen to our truth. If we emphasize only relationship then we will see people drifting into our community for a while, and we may even win them over for a time, but eventually they will drift away to another community and another "truth." They will view their Christianity as a passing fad as soon as the emotion fades. We will see people coming to Christ and the Christian community through

relationships, but we will see them adhering to faith and experiencing growth through an emphasis on biblical depth and understanding.

Process evangelism can be distilled down to four essential cornerstones.

Cornerstone 1: Authenticity. The Christian must be authentic and committed and must have a deep and intimate relationship with Jesus Christ. The Christian faith must be the core reality of this person's life, not an act. *Authenticity can only be demonstrated over time.*

Cornerstone 2: Caring. The Christian must demonstrate genuine caring and unconditional love for the pre-Christian, regardless of that person's level of belief or lifestyle. This doesn't mean we never confront sin, but we must always demonstrate love and acceptance of the individual, whatever the sin. *True caring is lived out and proved over time.*

Cornerstone 3: Trust. The Christian must demonstrate absolute integrity, truthfulness, loyalty, confidentiality and openness. Only after establishing a deep level of trust will the Christian be able to share how the story of Jesus Christ has intersected with his or her life. *Trust can only be earned over time.*

Cornerstone 4: Transparency. To be transparent is to be real and to allow others to see the reality of our lives through our openness and vulnerability. We admit our mistakes. We confess our sins. We tell the story of our pain and our problems, so that others can see God at work in our lives. *Transparency is most effective when practiced in long-term relationships.*

We have failed in our calling if the pre-Christian ever thinks, *I'm just a target, an evangelistic project for you. You don't want to be my friend. You just want to hang my scalp on your belt.* We have failed if we ever breach a trust or break a confidence with that person. We have failed if we are insensitive to the place the pre-Christian occupies on the spectrum of belief or if we try to push that person into a commitment before he or she is ready.

Dieter Zander recalls,

There was one guy I was building a friendship with who was very gradually progressing in his understanding and acceptance of the Christian faith. One time, over lunch, I said to him, "What's keeping you from Christ?" Well, suddenly this guy who was making progress was made to feel on the spot and a bit foolish. He backed out and made a total retreat from faith. That was a hard lesson, one I'll never forget.

Now, I'm not saying that we should never ask a person where he or she stands with Christ. On the contrary, there must come a time where we speak plainly about Jesus, or evangelism will never take place. The point is that we need to be sure that the relationship is strong enough to withstand this kind of conversation. The other person has to know that we care about him or her as a person, not just as a potential convert.

Adult Children

Josie sat down in the back of the room and placed her hand in Barry's. He looked up at her in surprise. "You're shaking!" he whispered to her.

"You noticed," she whispered back, smiling tensely. "Thanks for coming with me. I—I just don't know what to expect."

"Hey, I was glad to be here with you," he said. "It's a group for 'adult children of dysfunctional parents,' isn't it? Maybe it'll do me some good too."

There were about twenty people in the fellowship hall of Forest Lakes Community Church. The meeting began when the group facilitator—an older man with a face that looked like ten miles of bad road—stood and said, "I see we have a number of new people tonight. We won't ask you to stand and introduce yourselves. You don't have to say a word if you don't want to. Just sit there and soak, 'cause just listening to the rest of us share our experience, strength and hope is gonna do you a lot of good. We promise not to make you uncomfortable.

"Now, we're all people in recovery here, and most of us are Christians. That means the Higher Power we name is Jesus Christ and the God of our understanding is the God of the Bible. You don't have to buy that if you don't want to. We just want you to know where we're coming from. Okay, let's begin by saying the Serenity Prayer together. 'God, grant me the serenity to accept the things I cannot change . . .' "

The Importance of Identification

Even communities that have traditionally been ignored, written off or despised by the church—such as the gay and lesbian community—can be reached with the story of Jesus Christ if we adhere to the four cornerstones of process evangelism. "We have made some inroads into the gay community," says InterVarsity's Jimmy Long.

We have done so not by inviting gays to come to us, but by going into their community and identifying with them. We have attended campus meetings of gay and lesbian groups. Our students have been there and have signed an attendance record that was later published. This was hard. These students had to identify with that community—not by endorsing homosexual behavior but by demonstrating solidarity and empathy with the pain and the fears of the homosexual community. It created a great bonding experience with them that has led to very important dialogues and relationship building.

"The issue of identification is extremely important," says Bob Fryling, IVCF director of campus ministries. He continues,

Our focus should be on connecting with pre-Christians, not on getting them to connect with us. At UCLA the InterVarsity students used to wear T-shirts with Christian slogans and Bible verses. Initially it was thought that this would be a great way to witness. We found out this was not true. The feedback we got showed that by literally wearing our witness on our backs, we were creating distance instead of connection. So we have started a whole different approach: Share activities with your friends. Identify with them.

Of course there has to be a balance in our identification. Even while we attempt to create a bond and a connection with pre-Christians, we should never falsify who we really are. If our faith naturally emerges in a situation, it does so because that is what we authentically are: people of faith.

One of our students, Carol, invited her friends to a pizza night during orientation. At this party they played Scruples. In the course of the game it became obvious from her answers that she was a Christian. Some of the other students challenged Carol about her faith, and she thought she had blown it. But when the question came up, "Who in this room would you most like to be?" everyone said, "Carol!" Authenticity is key.

If the evangelism of choice for today's generation is personal and process-oriented, does that mean that other forms of evangelism are invalid? No! Other forms, such as Billy Graham-style mass evangelism and media evangelism, can still used to reach Generation X—but to be effective they must be linked with a personal, process-oriented approach. This has always been true, even with preceding generations. Many people mistakenly assume that "evangelism" is what takes place in a packed arena when Billy Graham gets up to speak—but for the vast majority of people who respond at the crusade, that single-point-in-time event was just the culmination of a process of being evangelized by the people who brought them to the crusade!

One of the most important functions of an event such as a crusade led by an evangelist such as Billy Graham, Lon Allison or Luis Palau is what it does in the lives of Christians. A crusade forces us to ask ourselves, *Do I have friends I can invite? If not, why not? Am I building relationships with pre-Christians? Am I involved in process evangelism with pre-Christians?* The crusade is not the sum total of evangelism. Properly understood, it is a catalyst for process evangelism. A large crusade can have a powerful impact on Xers, but the crusade experience must be preceded by a long, caring relationship with the person who has brought them to the crusade.

In general, Xers don't like to be conspicuous; they'd rather be part of a crowd than be singled out as individuals. Yet on certain occasions I have given public invitations at InterVarsity meetings on university campuses. "If you have accepted Christ," I would say, "then raise your hand and I'll pray for you . . . Now stand up and be welcomed into the family of God, because you're going to have to stand up for the rest of your life!" And people would clap and they would respond. A public invitation can be an effective avenue, enabling the Holy Spirit to draw a person to a place of commitment, but it must be approached with care and sensitivity. Some suggestions:

☐ Avoid emotional manipulation and tear-jerking pleas.

☐ Avoid "used-car salesman"-style pressure. Xers see through it and are turned off by it.

☐ Avoid sugarcoating the gospel. I usually preface a public invitation by letting people know that becoming a Christian is not a cure-all and that life will continue to be difficult.

☐ Avoid religious-sounding language. Keep your vocabulary matter-of-fact and straight-up. I use terms like *commit* and *follow* rather than "receive Jesus as your personal Savior" or "accept the Lord."

☐ Whenever possible, a public invitation should be preceded by months and months of relationship building.

Process evangelism that proceeds naturally out of real relationships breaks down the walls of distrust and wariness so that our story—our truth—can get through. Through the process of relationship building, pre-Christians can see the reality of our faith as we struggle to apply that faith to the problems and trials of our lives. The visible, tangible evidence of a Christian life being lived out under the pressures and stresses of a user-unfriendly world is the most convincing evidence we can possibly present in support of our story.

Dan Webster, a church-planting expert and former director of youth ministries at Willow Creek Church in Illinois, tells this experience:

I've been playing basketball with some guys on a weekly basis. Joel, one of the guys in our group, has cancer. They operated several years ago, and were fairly successful in getting rid of the cancer. A short time ago, Joel learned that the cancer had returned. Joel is a young man with everything in the world to live for, and his wife just had their fourth little girl.

Another guy in our basketball group is a pre-Christian, who I'll call Stephen. One night the group met together, and Joel was there, as well as Stephen. I said to the group, "Joel's having surgery tomorrow for his cancer. Joel, how are you feeling about that?"

"Well," he said, "I'm pretty scared."

"Tell us about it," I said.

So, Joel told us what he was going through, and we all prayed for him. Stephen was sitting there, taking this all in. You could see the amazement on his face. Later that night Stephen said to one of the guys in the group, "I've never seen men love each other like that before." Stephen is very close to coming to Christ.

Getting into Their World

"There was a time," says Doug Schaupp of IVCF in Los Angeles, "when we could preach at people and they would respond to the gospel. But preaching at people doesn't work too well anymore. We can't just come *at* people. We have to go *with* them. We have to get into their world, just as Jesus came into our world and became one of us so that we could come to him. It's called 'incarnational evangelism,' becoming incarnate or figuratively being born into another person's world. Just as we feel loved by Jesus because of all he went through to identify with us, our pre-Christian friends will feel loved by us as we go out of our way to identify with them."

Schaupp describes a five-step process he uses in his incarnational approach to evangelism:

1. Do what they do.
2. Enjoy and accept them.
3. Affirm what is good in their values.
4. Share the story of Jesus in their terms.
5. Invite them to follow Jesus in a way to which they can relate.

Let's look at each of these steps in turn. Schaupp says,

1. Do what they do. I've seen people evangelized in the course of all kinds of crazy activities. Something happens when Christians and pre-Christians get together for skate-boarding, skiing, going to the movies, listening to music or even something as dorky as trick-or-treating—whatever the pre-Christian likes to do. It's called *bonding,* and bonding is a powerful step of trust-building as the foundation for evangelizing. The traditional approach to evangelism is to invite pre-Christians to do what *we* do—worship, Bible study, conferences. I ask you: which approach sounds more inviting to a pre-Christian—going to church or going to the beach? Eventually, after a real bonding has taken place, you can get them to move toward Christian activities, but you have to move toward them first.

2. Enjoy and accept them. People can sniff out insincerity. If I merely go through the motions of doing what pre-Christians do without giving them my heart, they will probably feel patronized instead of loved. Evangelism is the most effective when it is natural and unprogrammed, when you truly enjoy spending time with and talking to the people you are witnessing to, and when you truly enjoy doing the things they like to do.

3. Affirm what is good in their values. This step can be very difficult for Christians because we have a tendency to be judgmental. Sometimes we fear that such affirmation will cause them to think we agree with all of their values and even their sinful habits. In reality, refusing to affirm what is good in their value system creates distance between the Christian and the pre-Christian. It also ignores the fact that God is already at work in the heart of that pre-Christian, planting biblical leanings and values in that person's mind and drawing that person to himself. Finding something that can be authentically affirmed in a pre-Christian's worldview can be a very powerful witness to pre-Christians.

I once became friends with a "heavy metal dude" named Keith. Whenever he had a spare moment, Keith was jammin' on his electric guitar. First I did what Keith liked to do: I listened to his music and learned to play heavy metal chords on his guitar, though I had no personal interest in heavy metal music prior to befriending Keith. I liked Keith and honestly wanted to find something in his heavy metal world to affirm. So Erin, a Christian frosh in my Bible study, worked with me on an inductive study of a heavy metal song by Metallica, a song about drug addiction called "Master of Puppets." We typed up the lyrics on paper and sat down with Keith and really dug into that song and got a lot out of it.

In thoroughly discussing this song, we were affirming part of Keith's life and value system. We agreed with him that there is some good and some truth in heavy metal music. Keith was blown away—so much so that he was open to coming with us to the Bible study and studying inductively about Jesus. It was a lot less threatening to him because he had already been exposed to the inductive study method on his own heavy metal turf.

4. Share the story of Jesus in their terms. This is the tricky step, the transitional step. You've already done the hard work of building trust and incarnating yourself into their world in the first three steps. But here's where we can easily make a mistake. We often forget which words and terms make sense to pre-Christians, and we slip into our church lingo—which is a turnoff to the unchurched. But if we can stay in the other person's world, while remaining cool and be unshockable, we can have a real influence.

One Christian named Scott was witnessing to a pre-Christian named Jon, when Jon offered him a joint. Instead of freaking out or saying, "Hey, Christians don't smoke dope!" Scott just shared with Jon about a "better high." Well, this is right in the tradition of Jesus' talking to the woman at the well about "living water." Jon just couldn't get Scott's comment out of his mind. He had to find out what this "better high" was all about—and he did!

5. *Invite them to follow Jesus in a way they can relate to.* Again, this is another place Christians often get tripped up. They've gotten into the other person's worldview, and there's a good two-way identification going. It's time to extend an invitation. At this point Christians often blow it in one of two ways. Either they "get religious" and scare the pre-Christian person off, or they never get around to inviting the pre-Christian at all! Yet it's so easy, once that bond is established, once that person knows you care and you understand the way he or she thinks, the way he or she feels! All you have to say is, "Are you up for following Jesus? I know you'd really dig what he's about."

This kind of evangelism is not that hard. You just have to be able to get into another person's world, to understand how that person feels about life and to love that person like Jesus would. That's the kind of evangelism he practiced, and it still works today.

Someone Who Really Knows

The recovery group meeting lasted about an hour. Some people told their stories. Some shared problems and struggles. Some, like Josie and Barry, simply sat and drank it in. At the end of the meeting the group—following some fifty-odd years of recovery group tradition—held hands and said the Lord's Prayer.

Josie gave Barry's hand a squeeze and said, "Could you wait for me just a minute?"

"Sure," he said.

Josie hurried off and zeroed in on a twentysomething woman who had spoken during the meeting. "Excuse me," said Josie, placing a tentative hand on the young woman's sleeve.

The woman turned around and smiled. "Hi," she said. "Is this your first time here?"

"This is my first time anywhere," Josie replied. "My name's Josie, and I just had to tell you . . . when you were talking tonight, you were telling my story." As she said this her eyes glistened, then overflowed.

"My name's Sondra, Josie. Would you like to talk? We could go out for coffee or something."

"I'd like that. But I need to tell my boyfriend." Josie waved Barry over. "Sondra, this is Barry. Barry, Sondra."

"Hi Barry," said Sondra.

"Barry," said Josie, "I hate to leave you, but Sondra and I are going out . . . to talk, okay?"

"Sure," said Barry. "You do what you have to do. Sondra, nice meeting you."

Josie kissed him on the cheek and squeezed his hand. "Thanks."

Barry smiled, then walked away.

Watching him leave, Josie said to Sondra, "Barry's been real supportive. But he doesn't know the worst about me. I need to talk to someone who's been there."

Building an Xer-Friendly Fellowship

Church-planting expert Dan Webster says,

I have met very few Thirteeners who actually hate God. When I meet someone who has an aversion to church, I sometimes ask why. With the exception of the few satanists I've encountered, no one says, "I avoid church because I hate God." Instead, they say, "Church is boring." Or "Christians are hypocrites." So I respond, "Well, gee, I go to church, and that's not my experience. If you could go to a church that was not boring, and where the Christians were not hypocritical, where people talked directly and honestly about life, where you got a chance to see how God intersects with human lives—do you think you might be interested?" Without exception, they all answer, "Yes."

Thirteeners need a place where they can belong so they can figure out their identity—a place to relate to other people so they can hear their story reflected back to them—a place where they're needed so they can have an impact on their world—a place where they can think through their issues and sort through their feelings in a safe environment. Thirteeners truly want a place where they can experience the presence of God and where they can feel connected to him—a place where they can learn and grow and process their doubts about God in an accepting environment.

God is not intimidated by the doubts and issues and styles and language differences of Generation X. Unfortunately, many of us in the church are. The church has been having a lot of difficulty relating to and reaching Xers for Christ—but the problem isn't with Generation X. The problem is us.

How do we solve the problem and make our churches more Xer-friendly? "The approach must be real," replies pastor Dieter Zander.

When Thirteeners walk into a typical church, they are affronted by the rituals and traditions and styles. It is all alien to them. The Thirteener thinks, "This isn't real, this doesn't apply to my issues, my lifestyle, my problems." They see the pastor as an authority figure, as part of the system. There's a barrier there—and that barrier is on our side, not theirs. We have to tear that barrier down. As a pastor, I try to create a reality-based experience. I try to share my own struggles, and that helps the people to trust me and to feel that I identify with their own issues. They come into the church feeling disconnected, and I try to offer them a reality to connect with. I try to offer credibility and authenticity.

Pastors like Zander and Webster have been involved for several years in designing Xer-friendly worship environments. Here are some principles and suggestions they offer from their experience with Xer-oriented churches.

☐ Offer worship services that are creative and targeted on Xer tastes and issues. "Worship is an event that gives credibility to the gospel," says Zander. "If unchurched Thirteeners come to church and say, 'This is cool!' then we've hit it. We want people to come into church and immediately feel a sense of excitement and expectation. We want it to feel like a rock concert. They should feel a bit off-balance, intrigued, curious. They should think, *What's going on here?*"

☐ Offer an "entry-level" experience. Assume your audience is starting at square one in their understanding of the Bible and spiritual issues. Let them ease into spiritual concepts. Help them to feel comfortable and familiar with the church environment. Avoid evangelical jargon and "insider" terminology.

☐ Offer events and experiences that are relevant to the interests and needs of pre-Christian Thirteeners: alternative music, standup comedy, drama, sermons that are spiced with attention-grabbers (video clips, audience participation, computer-generated visuals) and so forth. The innovations and experiences you offer will vary according to the cultural context of your church. Obviously, smaller churches may not be able to pull off a flashy service with drama or Xer-oriented music—and that's okay. Xers are used to the very best the secular world has to offer, so if it can't be done with excellence it shouldn't be attempted. Gear your church's events to the level of its own size, resources and talent pool.

☐ Do everything with sincerity. Xers can spot a marketing gimmick light-years away. Remember: authenticity is more powerful than performance. Xers respond much more enthusiastically to authenticity—say, one earnest, sincere guy playing a guitar—than some mediocre MTV-wannabe band doing bad Christian music.

☐ Generate excitement. Make church feel like a party—a celebration, not a funeral. Make Thirteeners feel like VIPs. Use well-produced drama, comedy and media interludes to make Thirteeners feel at home.

☐ Deal with real issues. Raise the tough issues and questions that Thirteeners struggle with in the real world. Avoid easy answers and superficiality, especially to tough, doubting questions. The speaker should be transparent about his or her own life struggles and problems. This creates credibility and helps Thirteeners identify their own problems.

☐ Surprise 'em. Even shock 'em a bit. Shake 'em up. Make worship fun and stimulating. At the same time, be sure to use good judgment (don't simulate a shooting or terrorist attack, for example). "We try to be unpredictable," says Zander. "My model is the David Letterman show—he's so off the wall! In the middle of my message someone will run up and hand me an outrageous note that I'll read, and this will blindside people, rouse them up and get behind their defenses so the message can get through with greater impact."

☐ Give Thirteeners a place to be anonymous, but don't let them go completely unnoticed. This means you will need to balance these two concerns on an individual basis. "In our experience," says Zander, "it would be a sin to have someone stand up and be publicly recognized. They don't want to be recognized because they're afraid of looking stupid."

If you are a pastor or greeter in your church and see a visitor at worship service, you can quickly gauge the situation this way: Look the individual in the eye. If that person responds by meeting your eye, introduce yourself and shake his or her hand. If that person looks away, let him or her maintain a safety zone of privacy and anonymity. Let that person make the first step.

Mind-Blown

Grant sat in a chair in the aisle in the junior-high auditorium. He was, in fact, the only one sitting in a room full of clapping, singing, swaying people. His cast-covered leg was stretched straight out in front of him. He hated that stupid leg with its fractured femur because he wanted to be on his feet with everybody else. In the front of the auditorium, in front of a backdrop of hundreds of white starpoint lights, an alternative band sent waves of surging sound into the air—a sound that filled not only the ears but the diaphragm and the solar plexus and the pit of the stomach and the heart.

Grant was mind-blown. He'd never seen or heard anything like it. The evening ended with some killer guitar licks and one of those big bam-wham-crash drum-and-cymbal finishes, followed by cheers and hoots from the audience. It was awesome.

And all too soon it was over. As people around them started to move toward the exits, Lindsey helped Grant to his feet and got his crutches under him. "What do they call this?" asked Grant.

"Starstream Concert," Lindsey replied.

"But you said we were going to church. I mean, that's why I didn't want to come. I hate church—but this isn't church!"

"Yes it is."

"No way!"

"That's what I said the first time I came."

"If I'd known it was like this you wouldn't have had to drag me!" Grant walked his crutches around until he was turned in the right direction. Then he started moving with the crowd toward the door. "I can't believe it," he said incredulously. "I just went to church!"

The Generational Thing

An Xer-friendly church does not have to be an Xer-only church. A multigenerational church can use the principles explained above to construct special worship services, experiences and opportunities for this generation without excluding other generations. Or, as in the case of NewSong in California, the church can be constructed with a Baby Buster emphasis, but with a multigenerational dimension. NewSong is a two-thousand-member church, of which roughly 75 percent are Thirteeners. Says Pastor Zander,

NewSong is a multigenerational church, but Thirteeners are the focus. The Boomers are there because they have a heart for Busters and can tolerate loud music. If it's too loud, you're too old. One thing that grates on Baby Buster sensibilities is Boomers with a superior attitude, yet Busters truly want to have healthy peer relationships with the Boomer generation. It's on the shoulders of the Boomers to extend a peer relationship as opposed to a paternal relationship to Busters.

Richard Peace observes:

In many churches we are seeing a generation-skip effect. Baby Busters are better able to relate to their grandparents' generation than to their parents' generation. They don't mind being mentored by someone who is two generations upline from them. And they feel a kind of "grandfatherly" and "grandmotherly" kindness and empathy from the Silent Generation that they don't get from the Boomer Generation. Their feeling is, *I wish my parents treated me the way their parents treated them. These older people are willing and able to help me learn some of the things my parents never taught me.*

Without question, the biggest issue of generational division in churches is music. Good preaching can reach out to young and old alike. But music instantly stratifies a church along generational, cultural and ethnic lines. Older people will not tolerate anything that hurts their ears—anything they consider to be "racket." And Xers will not tolerate boredom.

There is a danger in trying to be all things to all people. Peace says, I think it's tricky to reach both Baby Boomers and Baby Busters in the same church at the same time. Not impossible, but very difficult. Experience leads most churches to create an exclusively Xer-friendly environment. Willow Creek, the premiere Boomer church in America, is building an Xer-oriented church ministry. At first they planned to use the Willow Creek site. But they realized that the church facility just reeked of Boomerism. So they decided to find a warehouse location that the Xers could remake in their own way, with their own style, and have a church environment they could call their own.

Though Boomer and Buster elements seem to be like oil and water—you can shake them up but they don't mix well—a few churches seem to be a successful blend, utilizing great traditional hymns of the church, blending in some of the Boomer choruses and praise songs of the past few decades and supercharging the entire mix with some of the driving vitality of Thirteeners' alternative music forms. "It all depends on the feel of the place," says Dan Webster. "There has to be a permeating attitude of acceptance toward all cultures and all generations. Inclusiveness is attractive to Generation X. It feels politically correct. If you build strong relationships in the church, people will tolerate a lot of diversity."

A Place of Acceptance

"Well, John," said Damon, the small group leader, "before we close in prayer, do you have any questions for the group, or anything you'd like to say?"

"Yeah," said John Takeda. "I have something to say."

The twelve other people in the living room, including John's friend Adam, gave him their full attention.

"I didn't know what to expect when I came here," John continued. "Fact is, I wasn't even thinking of coming here until about a half-hour before I arrived! On the way over I asked Adam if it mattered that I'm not a Christian. He said it didn't make a lick of difference and that I should just be myself. And that's what I did. You let me sit back and listen. You let me ask some questions that, to you, probably seemed pretty bogus. Mostly, you just accepted me—and that's something I really didn't expect.

"You see, I've been hassled by born-againers who wanted to convert me. They didn't seem to care about me as a person. But all of you just seem to—I dunno. It's like you just want to be friends. I've been looking for something like this for a long time—you know, a place where I can just be myself, ask my questions, talk through my doubts and frustrations and still have people accept me and say, 'You're welcome here.' If it's okay with you all, I'd sure like to come back next week—and I'd like to bring my wife, Kim."

"Great!" said Damon, and the others chimed in. John was officially and enthusiastically accepted by the group.

Damon asked Adam to close in prayer. Adam's prayer was brief and contained one line of thanks that John could be with them that evening. Then as a couple of members brought out plates of cookies, Damon said, "Don't forget, everybody—next week we meet at Rick and Millie's. Rick has promised to cook up a meal to show us that vegetarian cuisine is far superior to the dead animals the rest of us eat. And mark your calendars for the first weekend in May. We'll all be up at Kent's cabin at the lake. Kent says there are at least a dozen ways to risk life and limb around the lake."

John leaned over to Adam and whispered, "What is it with you people?"

Adam blinked. "Huh?"

"I mean—you're all supposed to be religious people. But you all seem so—so normal!"

Small Groups: A Place to Feel Included

One of the most effective ways to bring people deeper into the life of the church and deeper into their own faith is small groups. Through small groups a large church is able to be as intimate and caring as any small congregation. Through small groups you can bring people of like affinities together out of a highly diversified multigenerational church. Through small groups you can provide a level of openness, relationship, sharing, empathy and healing that is available in no other way, through no other aspect of church ministry.

To be effective in meeting the needs and concerns of Generation X, small groups should be

☐ highly relational and interactive

☐ more experience-oriented and feelings-oriented than cognitive and teaching-oriented

☐ gatherings of "wounded healers" where Thirteeners can make sense of their pain by sharing it with others and helping others in their own experience of pain

☐ innovative and flexibly structured

Dan Webster tells about the many methods and approaches his church has used:

We've finally stumbled upon what we call "life-experience" small groups. We found that the old model of small groups—sitting around in a circle in somebody's basement—had a high rate of deflection for Xers. It wasn't meeting their needs. We discovered the "life-experience" approach when one educator in our church gathered a hundred Xer students together and asked, "What was your most meaningful educational experience in the last six months?"

Webster found three essential characteristics:

1. The educational event took place outside the context of four walls.

2. The educational event had to do with affective (feelings-oriented or emotionally linked) experience, not cognitive or intellectual experience.

3. The educational event took place in a context of relationships with other people.

For example, we wanted to lead a small group experience on the subject of goals. Our text for study was Jeremiah 29:11 (NKJV)— "For I know the thoughts that I think toward you, says the LORD, thoughts of peace and not of evil, to give you a future and a hope." One of our group leaders worked at a golf course, so he took his group to a lake on the course and said, "We're going to wade in and get fifty balls out of this lake." They got fifty balls out in five minutes. So then they tried it again, this time upping the goal to seventy-five. Then to a hundred.

Afterward they went out to McDonald's and discussed what they had experienced together. "What does this tell you about goal-setting?" he asked.

"What do you mean?"

"Well, we set a goal of fifty golf balls. How was that?"

"Too low."

"What if I'd said five hundred golf balls?"

"Way too high! We would've given up!"

"Do any of you have goals?"

And this launched a fascinating wide-open discussion of real issues, of personal and spiritual goals. After the group talked about setting goals, the leader printed up their goals on a word processor, had them laminated and gave them out so the group members could put them on their mirrors and stay focused on their goals. It was a very powerful experience.

"I Think There's Something I'm Missing . . ."

Propping himself up on one crutch, Grant ladled a heaping portion of thick, steaming beef stew onto the metal tray. Lindsey placed a piece of bread on the tray. Natalia set a paper cup of apple juice on it. The tray passed down the line of servers and was picked up at the end of the table by a woman in sorry, colorless clothes and ragged hair with two smudgy-faced children hanging onto her skirt. The woman took the plate over to a picnic table a few yards away. A couple of servers from the end of the serving line took a couple more plates, one for each child, over to the table.

"The park, the picnic tables, food on tin trays," said Lindsey. "It all kinda reminds me of a family reunion—like a picnic. Only these people can't go home when it's over, 'cause they don't have a home to go to."

"Yeah," said Grant. "This is cool, you know? Being able to do something for other people. I think I've been too wrapped up in myself lately."

"Tell me about it!" chided Lindsey. "Ever since you took that header off your bike and broke your leg, you've been a big 180-pound baby!"

"What?"

"You heard me, Evel Knieval. You're a big baby! 'Oh, Linz, it hurts so bad! Oh, Linz, hold my hand! Oh, Linz, get me a drinkie!' "

"Cut it out! I'm not that bad!"

"Way worse!"

Lindsey and Grant had been involved with the Street Haven Outreach team for the past several weeks after being invited to join by their newfound friend Natalia. Once a week the team came out to the city park and served over four hundred hot meals. Lindsey and Grant were simply accepted into the group and made to feel that they were a fully integrated part of the homeless ministry.

Week by week, Grant and Lindsey began to sense the reality of God in the midst of that team. They sensed God's presence not only during the prayer time at the end of the evening but in everything the team members did together. They were drawn to the sense of joy and fun they found in these young Christians who were so much like themselves, yet with an added, undefinable ingredient. They were drawn by the love and compassion of these people who had found a way to make a difference in the lives of the homeless who congregated at the downtown park. And they were drawn by the courage and character of Natalia herself.

Lindsey and Grant had watched Natalia standing by her dying husband. Sometimes she prayed over him, sometimes she wept softly in a corner while he slept, sometimes she joked and smiled and offered the sunlight of her personality to him as he concluded his brief time on earth. At Emilio's funeral, Lindsey and Grant had heard testimony after testimony from the Christian friends who had known him. They had seen Natalia's calm courage and strength throughout the funeral and in the days that followed. And now, on this night only a week after the death of her husband, they had seen Natalia come out to the park and serve the needs of others, even while her own heart was still breaking.

Grant and Lindsey watched these Christians, worked alongside them in ministry and were amazed. They took it all in, not missing a single detail. They saw Christian community and Christian involvement at work. And slowly, without even realizing it, they were changed.

That night, after serving meals at the park and cleaning up the pots and pans in the church kitchen, the people of the Street Shelter Outreach team gathered in a huddle. They sang songs. They prayed for the people they had served that night. They prayed for other needs in the church. They prayed for Natalia and her little fatherless son, Oscar.

Prayer was a regular part of the team's weekly routine. But something happened on this night that was anything but routine. Someone prayed who had never prayed before.

"God, this is Grant. I'm not sure I belong here with these people. But they make me feel like I belong. And I sure want to belong. I think there's something I'm missing here, and I don't know what it is. I mean, I sure like helping out down at the park, God. That really makes me feel good. But, like, I feel there's more to it than just helping other people. These people on this team all seem to know you, God. But I don't know you. I like helping you out with your work out there in the park, but that's not enough. I want to know you like these people know you, God. Could you show me how to do that?"

There was a long silence after Grant finished praying. Lindsey was leaning back in her chair staring at him, her mouth an O of surprise.

Then one of the team members, a blond surfer type named Al, said, "Like, why don't we talk it over, Grant? I mean, I'll stay here as long as you need."

"You guys have jobs and families and stuff. You need to get home."

"Hey, we're not in that big a hurry. Let's talk."

So they talked.

Involvement: A Way to Feel Useful

Another effective way to bring people deeper into their faith and the life of the church is involvement. Thirteeners need to be needed. They don't want to change the whole world, but they do want to make a difference in their corner of it. To be effective, ministry involvement for Thirteeners should be personalized. Says Dieter Zander,

I tend not to start with the ministry needs of the church. I usually start with the uniqueness of each person, with a spiritual gifts analysis and a Myers-Briggs personality assessment. This helps each individual to determine the kind of contribution he or she can make. I try to help them gauge their own biblical and spiritual passion.

Xers come into the church feeling they can't make a difference, thinking the church doesn't want or need them, believing they have nothing special to offer. I try to help them see that God has made them in a unique way so that they can make a unique difference in their corner of the world. I try to empower them to discover God's vision for their own lives and their own ministries. We encourage them to start ministries to the homeless, recycling ministries, outreach ministries, performance ministries, whatever God inspires them to do. We don't see ourselves as gatekeepers of

God's ministry, but permission givers, encouraging God's creativity. Sure, it gets chaotic at times. You can't be a control addict and function in this environment. But we really see God at work in the lives of our young members.

Jimmy Long, Blue Ridge regional director for IVCF, has noticed that Thirteeners will sometimes get involved in a Christian ministry merely for the sense of community and social interaction. They'll get involved in a homeless ministry or an after-school athletic program for latch-key kids. They'll attend Bible studies and worship services. After a few months or even years, they'll realize that they have become a part of a community of believers—and that they are believers themselves. Many Xer Christians have eased into the kingdom through a gradual process involving a community of relationships and involvement rather than making a point-in-time decision.

It is important to understand that a ministry of involvement for Xers should look very different from a ministry of involvement for Boomers. Generation X is responsive to the challenge of the gospel, but tends to be focused on different aspects of the gospel from those that Boomers respond to. For example, the Great Commission doesn't naturally inspire and mobilize Xers, even though many Baby Boomers—who are task-oriented by nature—are profoundly motivated by Christ's call to the task of evangelism. However, Xers may well be more responsive than Boomers to the Great Commandment of loving God and loving one's neighbor. Thus an Xer church may tend to be less mission-minded and evangelistic than a Boomer church, but it may also tend to be less given to division and political infighting and more caring and nurturing than Boomer churches.

The requirements for an effective ministry of involvement for Xers should include creativity, relationships, low cost, a sense of responsibility and a sense that the ministry is meaningful and purposeful. Above all, involvement can and should be fun. This doesn't mean it should be frivolous, but every time Christians gather together there should be a sense of sacred exuberance and holy excitement. We should never forget that the root derivation of the word *enthusiasm* means "filled with God." When we are truly filled with the Spirit of God we can't help but create an atmosphere of excitement, joy and enthusiasm. Involvement in ministry is a powerful way to help Xers experience the Christian faith and taste true Christian joy.

Warmth for the Soul

Sondra drove Josie to the coffee shop at the Barnes & Noble bookstore. Josie had been there at midday before, when the place bustled. But at almost ten o'clock at night it was as quiet and relaxed as a library. Sondra guided Josie to a corner booth, away from any other people.

"Barry doesn't know about the bulimia," said Josie, sliding into the booth. "I can't tell him about that. He'd hate me if he knew. It's too disgusting."

"Oh, I don't know," said Sondra. "He may be able to handle more truth than you think. A lot of people know about my eating disorder. A lot of good friends. My husband. My mother. They've all stood by me and supported me. But don't feel like you have to tell Barry. If a time ever comes in your relationship when you need to turn yourself inside out and show Barry all the lint in your lining, it'll be okay. You'll know when it's right."

"Yeah."

"You said that when I told my story I told yours as well. You mean my struggle with bulimia?"

"I mean all of it. The bulimia. Your abusive father. Your sister who died of an overdose. I never had a sister, but my brother Rex killed himself with a shotgun."

"Oh, I'm so sorry . . ."

"Thanks," said Josie. "The thing is . . . when you tell your story, you seem to be okay. Not that you're happy about a rotten childhood or losing a sister or barfing to keep your figure—"

Sondra laughed at Josie's straight-up description of bulimia.

"But those things don't seem to be wrecking your life," Josie concluded.

"Are the memories of Rex's death and your painful childhood wrecking your life?"

"Yeah. I can't remember one day of my life when I've been truly happy—truly carefree. I have a lot of anger. And a lot of sadness. And on top of all that, I have this thing I do that I can't control."

"The eating disorder."

"Exactly. It's like nothing in my life is under control—not even my own behavior. I mean, I hate this bingeing and purging, bingeing and purging all the time. But what I want doesn't seem to matter. It's like there's another 'me' buried deep down inside, and it makes me do what it wants me to do, whether I like it or not. It makes me eat a half gallon of ice cream in one sitting, and it makes me put my finger down my throat so it all comes up again. Why can't I control my own life and my own behavior?"

"You've read the Twelve Steps."

"Yeah. But I don't know that I really understand them."

"Step One: 'We admitted we were powerless over alcohol'—or bulimia or whatever our addiction may be—'that our lives had become unmanageable.' I'm sure you can identify with that."

Josie rolled her eyes. "Oh, yes! That's me, all right."

"Step Two: We 'came to believe that a Power greater than ourselves could restore us to sanity.' Do you know what that means?"

Uncertainly, Josie said, "No."

"It means that we can't do it alone. I can't. You can't. No one can. If you want to beat your addiction, your painful memories and your guilt, you've got to reach beyond yourself to a Power greater than yourself."

"God?"

Sondra nodded. "Step Three: We 'made a decision to turn our will and our lives over to the care of God as we understood him.' Josie, you were talking about that hidden part of you that you are powerless to control. Part of that hidden you is probably a psychological thing— the unconscious or subconscious mind or something like that. I'm not a psychologist, so I don't pretend to know about such things. But I think part of that hidden you is also a thing called sin. We all have it in us. I certainly do. And I can't control it—not by myself. The only power I've ever found that can control my impulse to sin is my Higher Power."

"Your what?"

"My Higher Power. Jesus Christ."

Josie rolled her eyes. "I don't want religion."

"Neither do I," said Sondra. "I've got no use for religion. Religion can't save anybody."

"But you just said—"

"I said Jesus Christ, not religion. I'm talking about a relationship with a living Person."

"But how do you know that Jesus is real? How can you prove it?"

"How do you know that your boyfriend is real?"

"Barry? That's ridiculous. I can see him, talk to him, touch him."

"You say you can see Barry?" asked Sondra. "Well, I've seen Jesus at work in my life, with my own eyes. If Jesus wasn't real I wouldn't have survived my bulimia. The doctors told me I had done so much damage to my esophagus, my digestive system, my heart and my immune system that I would probably not last a year if I didn't find some way to stop. Jesus was the way. I relied on him to help me get through each day. I haven't had a bulimic episode in four years—but if Jesus wasn't real, I would be dead now."

"But—"

"You say you can talk to Barry? Well, I talk to God every day—and I listen for his answers. I don't need someone to prove the existence of God to me with scientific proofs. I meet with God every day, face to face. You say you can touch Barry? Well, I can feel God's presence with me, as real as any physical touch. I sense his closeness to me—and to you right now, Josie."

They talked until the coffee shop closed, around midnight. Then Sondra took Josie home.

Josie didn't go to bed right away. Instead she turned the stereo on to soft music, curled up on her sofa, then mentally replayed all she had seen and heard that evening. The things Sondra had told her were like a glowing coal that slowly settled into the pit of her soul, warming her all over.

Could it be true? Could there be a place where you could go for refuge and safety—a place where people knew the worst about you and still loved you—where communication was honest and healthy—where healing could be found? Could there really be a God who loves you and accepts you and wants to have a relationship with you?

It was 5:00 a.m. when she finally fell asleep, her lips curled in a dreamy smile.

11

How to Reach Us, Part 3: Narrative Evangelism

Hey, can somebody gimme a ride

home?" asked Michael, walking across the floor of the shipping room.

"Sorry," said Lindsey. "I took the bus today."

"Hey, I'll give you a lift, man," said T.J., "if you can wait an hour. I gotta finish shrink-wrapping that Shoney's job."

"Thanks, Teej," said Michael, "but I live two miles outta your way."

"Well, you're practically on the way home for me," said Perry. "I'm leaving right now."

Michael hesitated. Perry could read it on his face: Michael was thinking, *Oh, bogus! Now I gotta ride home with the "old man."* Michael shrugged. "Sure," he said without enthusiasm. "Thanks."

"The car's out this way," said Perry.

Michael followed him out to the big white Lincoln Town Car that was parked in the stall next to the loading dock. As Perry tapped the keyless entry system and opened the passenger door for Michael, he felt a twinge of regret. He wished he wasn't driving something so big. Michael slid in and slumped in the front seat, ignoring the seat belt. Perry got in, powered up the car, started the CD player and pulled out of the lot.

As they hit the street, a loud funky guitar laid down a hot, raunchy intro.

"Cool!" said Michael with sudden enthusiasm. "The Stones! I've got this CD too!"

Perry laughed. "I bet I've owned half a dozen copies of this album over the years. I first bought it on vinyl in about sixty-nine or seventy, wore it out, bought another vinyl copy, bought an eight-track copy for my van, lost that one when my van got ripped off, bought one on cassette and that one melted to plastic puddle on the dashboard of my old Honda Civic . . ."

From the stereo speakers Mick Jagger began extolling the dubious virtues of a New York City honky-tonk woman.

"Yeah," said Michael. "I've got all their stuff. Right up to *Voodoo Lounge*. Those old dudes have still got it, huh?"

"Yeah," said Perry, chuckling to himself. "Those old dudes still have it. I remember when I hitchhiked up to Altamont—"

"No way!" Michael perked up suddenly. "You were at Altamont? 'Gimme Shelter'? 'Sympathy for the Devil'? The Hell's Angels, the stabbings and all that stuff?"

Perry grinned. "Yeah, I was there. I missed Woodstock, and I thought Altamont was gonna be kind of a Woodstock West. Boy, was I wrong!"

"Wow! Tell me about it."

"Well, some of what happened is a little hazy. It was quite a few years ago, and I was doing a fair amount of LSD back then."

"*You?*" Michael was astonished. "You were doing drugs?"

"Yeah. My life was a bit different back then than it is today. I'll tell you about it, if you like."

"Yeah." Michael leaned back and looked intently at Perry, waiting to hear his story.

The Narrative Lens

Throughout this book I have frequently referred to "the story of

Jesus" or "the story of God." My use of that term has been conscious and deliberate. In fact, one of the main reasons I've used a fictional narrative is to demonstrate the usefulness of story in getting a point across and to use a literary style that is more typically "Generation X."

The concept of story or narrative gives us a new way of looking at evangelism and a new paradigm for reaching my generation. What we have known for centuries as "the gospel" or "the good news" is, in fact, far more than just a statement of propositional truth. It is far more than a body of doctrines. It is far more than a collection of data leading toward a logical conclusion.

The gospel is a story.

In fact, the gospel is, as Leighton Ford says, "*the* Story with a capital S." In his book *The Power of Story* (Colorado Springs: NavPress, 1994) Ford lays out a strategy for reaching the world—and reaching individuals, one at a time—through the power of narrative evangelism.

This approach to evangelism is ideally suited for reaching the soul of Generation X because it is a "new-old" approach. It is a new approach when compared with other twentieth-century strategies because it has not been actively attempted until recently. It is an old approach because it is the same approach used by Jesus himself and by the early evangelists.

Narrative evangelism offers us an innovative paradigm—a fresh new way of looking at the church's task, the Great Commission. Prior evangelistic approaches in the twentieth century tended to focus on communicating the gospel through either a "program" lens—structures or methods—or a "psychological" lens—focusing on felt needs. Narrative evangelism, however, focuses on a "collision of stories." God's story collides with our story and calls our story into question, forcing us to reconsider the course of our lives and the premises of our worldview. His story forces us to consider a new worldview in which Christ is at the center.

The old strategies tended to focus on a "propositional" approach to evangelism. That is, the evangelist set forth his or her proposition, then buttressed that proposition with evidence and logical arguments. That is the approach of classical apologetics, from Thomas Aquinas to Francis Schaeffer. That is the approach of the Four Spiritual Laws. That approach, however, has been less than fully effective in reaching

Generation X. It is not my intention to demean or disparage this approach, because it has been extremely effective in reaching the generations it was designed to reach. Today, however, the propositional approach yields diminishing returns. A new—or "new-old"—approach is needed.

Enter narrative evangelism.

Leighton Ford (okay—Dad, in case you didn't already know) suggests that narrative evangelism owes its effectiveness as a strategy for reaching Generation X to several factors:

☐ It is biblically authentic. The Bible itself is the story.

☐ It is theologically dynamic and appropriate. Narrative evangelism places God at the center.

☐ It is culturally appropriate. It speaks to Xers who have lost any sense of a "megastory" that encompasses the span of the universe and gives us a sense of our own meaning and purpose in this wide and chaotic universe.

☐ It is an integrated approach. Narrative evangelism calls us not only to tell our story but to live it as well, with integrity and humility.

☐ It is relationally effective. It speaks to the human heart. No one can resist a good story, and a good story communicates truth with more impact and more clarity than any other communication medium.

As our culture increasingly moves away from logic- and proposition-oriented thought forms and deeper into feelings-oriented and trans-rationally oriented thought forms, the only evangelism that speaks the language of the culture is a story-oriented evangelism. Narrative evangelism speaks the language of a media-saturated, story-hungry generation. It gives people a point of connection in their everyday lives, enabling them to see how God has interacted with human history and how he can interact with their own individual lives.

Perry's Story

"Nice place," said Perry, looking around Michael's apartment. It was a spare and functional studio apartment. The stereo and TV were against one wall, a single bed was against another, a comfortable (if secondhand-looking) recliner was against another.

" 'Nice place'?" Michael repeated incredulously. "It's a closet with a kitchen. But it's comfortable enough for me."

"It sure beats the bejunior out of some rat holes I lived in when I was your age."

"No kidding?"

"No kidding."

"Hey, you thirsty? You like microbrew? I've got some Pete's Wicked Ale, if you like."

"No thanks, Michael. I had a lot of trouble with alcohol in my younger days. I stay away from it now. But go ahead and have one yourself if you like."

"Okay." Michael went to the refrigerator, took out a bottle and twisted off the cap. "Go ahead and finish your story. Take that chair."

Perry sat down. "Well, like I was saying, I was living with a girl named Lauren at the time. And I was dealing drugs down by the high school, partying, getting loaded. Lauren was into all that drug-culture stuff too. Well, this one time I scored some acid that was either cut with some other drug or it was cut too pure, or something. Anyway, it was the strangest trip I ever took. I mean, I was touring the outer planets for two whole days. I don't know what I was doing all that time, but it really scared Lauren.

"During that trip I saw things I can't describe. It was like a world of spirits or souls, and it seemed more real than the world we're looking at right now—more real than this room. And I realized that what I was looking at was the spirits of people with all the material stuff stripped away. It was like having some kind of spiritual x-ray vision where I could see right through bodies as if they were invisible, and I could see right into the innermost beings of people. And some of the souls I saw were contented and peaceful and full of joy. And some were in torment and screaming this strange silent scream. And I looked down at myself and within myself, and I realized that I was one of the screaming souls. That was the first time I really understood that I was in spiritual torment. And when I came down from that trip, those images stayed with me and haunted me.

"Before that I had never really thought about God or heaven or hell. After that I was a believer. I don't mean I was a committed Christian. I just mean that I believed in the existence of a spiritual reality; I believed in the existence of God and heaven and hell. But I was convinced heaven was beyond my reach. I thought I had sinned too much. I thought I was headed for hell, and that was that.

"I went into a deep depression for weeks after that trip, and Lauren kind of pulled away from me. I think my black mood really put her off."

"Did you tell her about it?" asked Michael. "About what you saw when you were on LSD?"

"No. And she never asked. I think I scared her so bad she didn't want to know. She knew I'd gone through some kind of darkness, and she didn't want any part of it. It was about that time a friend of hers invited her to some sort of coffeehouse thing. They had a lot of these 'Jesus people' coffeehouses back in those days. Lauren was really attracted to something she found there. She made a decision to live her life for Jesus, and she came back to the little over-the-garage apartment we were living in and tried to tell me about it. All I heard was 'Blah-blah-blah-Jesus, blah-blah-blah-eternal-life, blah-blah-blah.' None of it made any sense to me. I told her if she was going to be a religious fanatic she could pack up her stuff and get out."

"What did she do?"

Perry laughed. "She packed up. She said it was a sin for us to live together like this and she was going to go follow Jesus."

"So, like, was that when you became religious?"

"No. It was another year or so after that before I decided to give Jesus a shot. I lost track of Lauren—never saw her again after that. I spent that whole year in a low-down depression. I used drugs more heavily, I drank a lot, I got in the sack with as many women as I could, and I just got more and more miserable.

"Finally one night I was lying in bed all alone, thinking about death and hell and spending eternity in a big black hole. And the thought of it just about suffocated me. I jumped out of bed and started screaming at God. I said, 'God, if you're there, then let me know it! Either kill me now and get it over with, or save me! I don't want to live like this anymore!' "

"What happened then?"

"Nothing big or dramatic. No flashing lights or thundering voices. I just got this—this sense inside me. It was kind of like a voice. It was as clear and definite as a voice, but I didn't hear it. I *felt* it. The 'voice-that-wasn't-a-voice' said to me, 'I'm here, Perry. I'm right here with you.' And I knew that was Jesus talking to me."

Wide-eyed, Michael swore—then apologized.

"That's okay," said Perry. "I was pretty blown away myself. Anyway, I knew that something big had just happened. I felt . . . overshadowed. Right then, I decided to start living a different kind of life."

"Different how?"

"First, I knew I needed to find some other people who knew Jesus on a firsthand basis. I didn't know it then, but the kind of people I was looking for were Christians. I tried to find Lauren, starting at the Christian coffeehouse where she had found God. They told me she had left the state—moved back to where her parents lived or something. But I stayed on at the coffeehouse, got connected with other Christians and got into a Bible study group. In fact, that's where I met my wife, Heidi.

"Another thing I did right after this change came over me was to totally revise my lifestyle. Nobody had to tell me that doing drugs and getting laid all the time was wrong. I knew I had to change my way of life. The Bible calls that 'repentance,' but I had never read the Bible. Still, I instinctively knew I had to stop doing all that compulsive behavior stuff. And I did."

"Completely? You stopped doing all that stuff for good—just like that?"

"Oh, I relapsed a few times at first, but pretty soon I had my new lifestyle down. The funny thing is that even when I knew I had to stop smoking dope, I didn't stop dealing—at least, not right away."

"*What?*"

"Yeah. I quit using, but kept on dealing for a few days. I had a pretty good-sized stash of drugs on my hands—a couple thousand dollars' worth, street value. I couldn't see letting all that stuff go to waste. I was pretty new at being a Christian, so I didn't have the moral sense to just flush the stuff down the toilet. Instead I went on the street and sold it. But after I sold it I got to feeling kinda guilty, so I took all this drug money, stuffed it in my pockets and went down to the nearest church the next Sunday morning. I unloaded the whole wad in the collection plate."

"No way!"

"Yep. Well, that's my story."

"You know, Perry, I always thought you were—" Michael stopped himself. "Well, anyway, Perry, you're a cool old dude."

Perry smiled. "Michael, that's the nicest thing anyone ever said to me."

The Power of Story

The power of story is the power to infuse the mind with imagery so that it can vicariously undergo the events, experiences and feelings that take place in the story. According to Leighton Ford, story leads to a vision, and that vision produces a character. It doesn't just change a person's mind, as propositional arguments are intended to. It changes a person's outlook, worldview and paradigm.

Story reaches not just the intellect, which is contained in the thin, outermost layer of the human brain—the cerebral cortex. Story reaches to the most deeply buried parts of the human personality, to the emotions, and even to that mysterious, elusive part of us that we know only as the human soul. A powerful story tingles our spine, surprises us with laughter, melts us to tears, moves us to righteous anger, tugs at our heartstrings, rivets our *psychē*, involves our *pneuma*, refashions our worldview, colors and filters our perspective, renegotiates our belief structure, calls into question our assumptions and ultimately leaves us a changed human being.

Narrative evangelism begins with the story of God's interaction with human history and with individual human lives. It is the story of how God sent his Son into the world—and how he invades and revolutionizes an individual human life. Narrative evangelism begins with the story of God—Father, Son and Spirit—as narrated in Scripture, and it is God-centered, trinitarian and biblical from the beginning. It challenges those who hear the story to either reject it or join their own stories to it, to become part of the story of God. It leads to a vision of one's own story as a subplot of a grand and inspiring story—the story of God's interaction with the human race over thousands of years and on into eternity. It is a story with a beginning, a middle and a never-ending end, and the story line of that story is inspiring beyond imagining.

That master storyteller J. R. R. Tolkien, author of *The Hobbit* and The Lord of the Rings, seems to intuitively grasp the power of narrative evangelism. In a fascinating and much-overlooked essay he published in a little book called *Tree and Leaf* (London: Allen & Unwin, 1964), he concludes the literary essay "On Fairy-Stories" with a suggestion that all great fairy tales are really echoes of a powerful, wonderful but absolutely true story: the Christian gospel.

All great fairy tales contain an element that is also contained in the story of Jesus, an element Tolkien calls *eucatastrophe*—a sudden and unexpectedly happy turn of events in the same way that a catastrophe is a sudden and unexpected tragedy (he coins the word by placing the Greek prefix for "good," *eu*, in front of the word for disaster, *catastrophe*). Both a great fairy tale and the Christian gospel produce a feeling of joy, and this joy, he says, "can thus be explained as a sudden glimpse of the underlying reality or truth. It is not only a 'consolation' for the sorrow of this world, but a satisfaction and an answer to that question, 'Is it true?' "

Tolkien goes on to say,

The Gospels contain a fairy-story, or a story of a larger kind that embraces all the essence of fairy-stories. They contain many marvels—peculiarly artistic, beautiful, and moving; "mythical" in their perfect, self-contained significance; and among the marvels is the greatest and most complete conceivable eucatastrophe. But this story has entered History and the primary world. . . . The Birth of Christ is the eucatastrophe of Man's history. The Resurrection is the eucatastrophe of the story of the Incarnation. This story begins and ends in joy. . . . There is no tale ever told that men would rather find was true, and none which so many skeptical men have accepted as true on its own merits.

The Christian story, Tolkien concludes, "is supreme; and it is true. Art has been verified. God is the Lord, of angels, and of men—and of elves. Legend and History have met and fused" (pp. 71-72).

Tolkien has given us a profound and elevated vision of the Christian story. It is a story of joy—of unparalleled "eucatastrophe"—and that story gives us an exalted vision, and that vision produces a character. The vision becomes our motivation. Once we catch a glimpse—and a mere glimpse is the most we can hope to catch—of the sweep and depth and scope and power of our story, and once we begin to grasp the role of our own stories as subplots in that story, then our vision is forever changed. We see people, God, the world and ourselves in a new way: as God sees them. We understand that human history—as chaotic and undirected as it somehow seems—is building and focusing on a climactic moment, the eucatastrophe of all history, when Jesus returns and establishes his kingdom on the earth. That vision becomes our motivation. It transforms our character.

That vision reshapes us into evangelists—people who can't help but tell the story. Seen through a narrative lens, the task of evangelism isn't just about programs and strategies. It is about telling the story, seeing the story and being the story. Narrative evangelists aren't just "preachers." In fact, you don't have to be a "preacher" to tell your story and God's story. Narrative evangelists are simply storytellers, vision bearers and truth modelers.

Everyone can be a narrative evangelist, because everyone has a story to tell.

Something to Think About

Brennan set his empty bottle down on the sidewalk at his feet. Sitting on the front porch next to him, Michael tilted his bottle back and chugged the last few gulps, then wiped his mouth with the back of his hand. "That stuff's good. Snapple, huh? Heard about it. Never tried it before."

Brennan picked up the basketball and spun it on his index finger. "Ready to shoot a few more?" he asked.

"Nah," said Michael. "I got a date tonight. Gotta get home and shower."

"Well, come over anytime. This was cool."

"Yeah. You know, your dad gave me a ride home the other day."

"He mentioned it."

"He told me all about his druggie days. Thumbing his way to rock concerts. Dealing drugs. Stuff like that."

"Oh?"

"Yeah. I always figured your dad was—you know."

"Yeah." Brennan nodded. "I know."

"But he's really kinda cool. He's been around, you know?"

"Yeah."

"That acid trip he had—you know, where he saw all those spirits and stuff? You think he really saw, like, the real spirit world? Or do you think it was just an acid dream?"

Brennan shrugged. "I dunno."

"Me either. But I'll tell you something about your dad, Brennan."

"Yeah?"

"That ol' dude has really given me something to think about. Well, I gotta shove. Later, man."

"Yeah. Later."

Brennan watched with mingled wonder and bewilderment as Michael hopped into his car and roared off in a cloud of blue smoke. That evening at dinner Perry wondered why his son kept looking at him strangely, as if seeing him for the very first time.

The Greatest Story Ever Told

"When I have a real bad problem," one Thirteener told me, "I sit down and write. Maybe I'll write my problem out in my journal like a story. Maybe I'll write a poem. Sometimes I go back and read the things I've written before. After the feelings and the tears are out, after I've had a chance to reflect on the story line of my life, answers seem to turn up."

Stories are intensely important to Generation X. We're not big on descriptions and adjectives. We want the feelings, the action, the story. The novel that pasted that label to our foreheads—Douglas Coupland's *Generation X*—reflects the importance of story in our lives. His Thirteener characters constantly tell stories in their quest for meaning. "Either our lives become stories," says one Coupland character, "or there's just no way to get through them." Our stories give us our identity.

It should come as no surprise, then, that the vehicle of story is a powerful and effective vehicle for reaching Generation X. In fact the story of Jesus Christ seems custom-designed to give Xers a story to identify with—a story to pattern their lives after. Jesus' homelessness and rootlessness, his "illegitimate" birth, his persecution by the system, his premature death—all of these are dimensions of his story that penetrate to the heart of the Xer experience.

Leighton Ford cites Robert W. Jenson, who suggests that the modern world—which was defined by reason—is falling apart. Yet

the postmodern world offers nothing new to replace it. In his arti-
cle "How the World Lost Its Story" (*First Things,* October 1993) Jenson observes that the modern world allowed for individual stories
but demolished the notion of a universal Storyteller or an ultimate
story. As a result, people have lost all hope that there could be a
true story that makes sense of their stories. Jenson affirms the Christian church's "task to tell the biblical narrative to the world in
proclamation and to God in worship." In fact, the task becomes
all the more urgent since we now live in a postmodern world that
has no story. Accordingly, we find ourselves in a world characterized by

☐ the collapse of reason. Nothing new has arisen in the postmodern
world to replace the moral and intellectual capital that was depleted
when the old world order was swept away. With the collapse of modernism we find ourselves in a vast postmodern mission field.

☐ a lost sense of what is real and unreal. The modern world viewed
human life as a "realistic narrative." We have lost the hope that the
narrative of the world makes any sense.

☐ a lost sense that we live in a "narratable world." Life was once
viewed as a true story—a notion derived from the Bible. This is
no longer true. Since there is now no widespread faith in a universal Storyteller (God), the universe can have no story line—no meaning.

☐ loss of ability to see the world as a place of structure and meaning.
Fiction and art tell of events that are impossible outside the context
of the story, and much fiction and art is downright absurdist and
incoherent.

I have visited a number of major art galleries featuring a contemporary form of art called minimalism—art that offers mundane ob-
jects such as chairs, old shoes or a wrapped package as if they were
works by Renoir or Matisse. The statement that such nonsensical art
seeks to make is that everything—even art itself—is meaningless and
without purpose. One minimalist show I visited opened at the National Gallery of Art in Washington, D.C., in June 1994. Shortly before
I went there, an incident occurred that demonstrates the level of
meaninglessness to which our culture has sunk.

The show had just opened, and some of the exhibits were still being installed. A number of patrons and nationally recognized art critics gathered around one exhibit—a tool cart used by a gallery technician who set up new exhibits. The patrons and critics were oohing and ahhing and drawing high-blown philosophical conclusions from the placement of the power drill, the flecks of paint on the shank of the hammer, the seemingly haphazard arrangement of the various screwdrivers. Their mouths snapped shut and their faces turned red when the technician pushed through the crowd, muttered "Excuse me," and wheeled his tool cart away. True story!

Art today is absurd, minimalist and meaningless because it reflects the prevailing postmodern belief that life is absurd, minimalist and meaningless. People have lost faith in a world with a meaningful story line—yet, being human, they still long for a world with a story line. If we tell them our story, that story will lead to a new vision of reality in their lives, and that vision will produce a new character—the character of a Christian. And that Christian is a follower of Jesus Christ, who told the greatest story ever told by the way he lived his life.

"He Makes Us Okay"

"I had heard it all before," said Marisa. "People have quoted John 3:16 to me. They've given me tracts and told me that God loves me and has a wonderful plan for my life. It all rolled right off me."

"Why is that?" I asked.

"Because," she said, "it was just words."

"But it's not just words anymore, is it?"

She smiled. "No. Not anymore."

"Tell me about it," I prompted.

"Well, there are these two Christian people who helped me when I needed it. One of them is Cassie, a friend of mine from work. I had this problem at work—and I mean, it was a big problem. My boss was, like, hitting on me, and I just didn't know where to turn. Well, I didn't even know Cassie at that time—she was fairly new there—and she put her job on the line to help me out."

"What kind of help did she give you?"

"Well, she gave me a lot of encouragement and guidance when I wasn't sure which end was up. And she introduced me to a Christian attorney named Jerry. He's the other Christian I was telling you about.

He gave me free legal help."

"And Cassie and Jerry—"

"They were like God's hands reaching out to me and God's voice saying to me, 'Everything's going to be okay, Marisa. I love you and I'm taking care of you.' I mean, God's invisible, right? But when God lives in people, you can actually see him and feel him through his people. When Christians love you and help you it's like God himself talking to you and touching you."

"So how did you come to make a decision for Jesus Christ?"

"A lot of things led up to it, I guess. I went to church and saw Christians who were very involved in the kinds of things I care about. You know, my boyfriend is black and I'm white, and racial justice is a big thing with me. So's the environment and equal rights for women. I had always thought of Christians as, you know, the Jerry Falwell and Dan Quayle types. I guess people like that mean well, but I just can't get into their agenda, you know?"

"Uh-huh."

"But the real clincher for me was a conversation I had with Cassie over at her apartment. I had been going to church with her for a few weeks, and we were talking about all the things I was seeing and hearing there. She asked me if I had ever thought about Jesus. She said, 'You know, the things Jesus did and said seem like he had you specifically in mind, Marisa.' I was like, 'What?' And she said, 'Yeah,' and she told me this story from the Bible."

"What story was that?"

"About Jesus and this woman from Somalia or someplace."

"Samaria?"

"Yeah. That's it. Anyway, this woman was, like, a real outcast. I mean, the first problem she had was that she was a woman! Women were really held down in that culture, you know? And then she was a woman of the wrong race, and the other people, who were racists and stuff, looked down their noses at her for that. And then she was looked down upon because of who she was running around with. You know, like, she'd been married before and she had all these different men and the guy she was living with wasn't her husband, and people really ragged on her about that.

"So she goes out to the well, and she goes in the heat of the day, not when it's cool like the other women do. She goes when it's hot because she's ashamed and scared of the other women. And here comes Jesus, and he tells her she's okay. He doesn't care about her race or the life she's lived or the men she's been with or even the fact that she's a woman in a male-dominated culture. He makes her feel okay about herself. And Cassie explained that it's not that Jesus says, 'You're okay just the way you are.' Instead he says, 'You're okay because I make you okay.' Because we all have sin in us, you know? But when we have Jesus in our lives, when we decide to let him control the things we say and do, then he makes us okay."

"So after Cassie told you this story about the Samaritan woman—"

"I had to do something about it. I mean, I felt like I was that woman and Jesus was talking to me. It was like he was saying to me, 'Marisa, life's been pretty crappy and you've screwed up a lot, but you're gonna be okay. Because I'm going to be with you from now on.' It's like something inside me said, 'Okay.' You know? I was like, 'Yes!' I just had to say yes to a deal like that. And Cassie prayed for me, and I prayed too. I said, 'Jesus, let's do it. I know I've sinned a lot, but I see what you did for that woman in the Bible and I believe you want to change my life too. Please take over, 'cause I'm tired of running my own life. I haven't been doing such a great job of it, so I'm turning it over to you, okay?' And it was like I felt this voice inside me say, 'Okay, Marisa. It's you and me now.' And I've been walking with Jesus ever since."

"How long has that been?"

"Oh—four, maybe five weeks now."

"What about your boyfriend?"

"T.J.? Well, he's having a hard time adjusting to the new me. I don't feel it's right for us to have, like, an intimate relationship. I mean, not unless we get married. I've begun to feel very strongly about that. I don't know what's next for T.J., because I know he loves me and I've been talking to him about Jesus, but he's just not ready. He comes to church with me sometimes, and he likes a lot of what he sees. But, you know, he's just not ready. I guess it's up to God—and it's up to T.J., of course. I pray for him every day."

The Prescription for Narrative Evangelism

It would be easy to look around at our postmodern world and despair.

After all, this is a generation that has lost all hope of living in a narratable world—a world that makes narrative sense, a world with meaning. How can we communicate our story to a generation that has become filled with cynicism and despair? It would be easy to take that position ourselves—but it would be a big mistake!

The fact is, the very storylessness of this generation is our opportunity! Because not only do we have the story—the gospel itself—but we also offer an alternative community, a narratable world in which human meaning can be discovered and lived out. That narratable world is the church.

This is nothing new. The church of the first century confronted the same circumstances. It too faced both the challenge and the opportunity of providing a place of meaning in a chaotic and meaningless world—and it did so by providing a coherent, cohesive story with a beginning (Genesis, the creation and fall of humanity), a middle (the turbulent history of the Old Testament world), a climax (the life, death and resurrection of Jesus) and a triumphant ending and resolution (Revelation). Within the context of that story, all human pain, suffering, sorrow and struggling suddenly made sense. The early Christians could see the stories of their lives as having a dramatic cohesion within the context of the larger story.

And so it is today.

The evangelistic church that seeks to be relevant and effective in telling its story to a despairing world must first offer itself as a real world in which the gospel story is actively lived. The story must be told in the pages of our individual lives and in our life together in the Christian community. This story is not your story or my story or some invented story. It is God's story, contained in the Bible and expressed to the world through the church.

Leighton Ford calls us to consider these questions as we seek to evangelize my generation:

□ Are we telling the true story? God's story? The story of the Father, Son and Holy Spirit? Or are we merely offering slogans and self-help formulas?

□ When we look at Thirteeners, do we see them through a lens of hope or hopelessness? Do we dare to believe that God is at work in a unique way in this alienated—and in many ways alien—generation?

☐ Do we embody the story? Does our story—the story of how God's story has intersected with our own story—have authenticity? Does it ring true? Do we as Christians embody the covenant love of God the Father? the gracious touch of God the Son? the healing, accepting community and fellowship of God the Spirit?

Those who are out on the leading edge of Xer evangelism report that narrative approaches are yielding significant results in many lives. For example, Tim Conder has seen an enormous response to the "storytelling hour" he has implemented with his youth group. A narrative approach to youth ministry has changed not only the way he teaches but also the way he trains, disciples and does crisis intervention.

Stanley Grenz has also found narrative to be a powerful way of imparting faith. He reports that his preaching is more effective when he can get people into the story—when they are able to vicariously feel and experience the story as if they were participants in it.

During the process of writing this chapter I was engaged in evangelistic meetings at two university campuses. In both cases I used a narrative approach in my talks, focusing on Luke 15, where Jesus tells three stories: the story of the lost sheep, the story of the lost coin and the story of the loving father and the lost son. I pointed out that the intensity of the loss increases with each story. In the first story the shepherd has lost one of his one hundred sheep—a loss of 1/100th of his most prized possessions. In the second story the woman has lost one of her ten silver coins—a loss of 1/10th of her most prized possessions. In the third story the father has lost one of his two sons— a loss of fully one-half of everything he holds most dear.

"What is implied at the end of these three stories," I concluded, "is that there is one more story to tell: yours. And here the ratio is not one out of a hundred, or ten, or two. The ratio is one to one. You are the most important and valuable of all God's creations. His love for you is infinite. He can't bear to lose you. He has sent his Son to earth to seek you out, to find you, to save you and to restore you to himself."

I could see it in their eyes as I spoke: they were connecting to those stories, and to the story of God. They were seeing that their own stories—which until that moment might have seemed insignificant and undirected—were intersected and impacted by the story of God. Suddenly their own stories had significance and meaning. And it was exciting to see the response: out of the seventeen students I met with at Radford University in southwestern Virginia, three made first-time commitments to Christ. And out of the one hundred students I spoke to at Virginia Tech in Blacksburg, Virginia, six made a first-time commitment.

The Narrative Evangelism of Jesus

Look at the teaching of Jesus and you will see that he used an approach that was primarily narrative, not propositional. His sermons tend to be collections of stories—all of them riveting, all of them focused on a clear and specific point, all of them vivid and visually powerful. The truths of Jesus come alive in the stories of Jesus. The Gospel of Mark describes Jesus' narrative evangelism approach this way:

> With many stories like these, he presented his message to them, fitting the stories to their experience and maturity. He was never without a story when he spoke. When he was alone with his disciples, he went over everything, sorting out the tangles, untying the knots. (Mark 4:33-34)

And in the Gospel of Matthew, Jesus gives his own reasons and rationales for his narrative evangelism:

> The disciples came up and asked, "Why do you tell stories?"
>
> He replied, "You've been given insight into God's kingdom. You know how it works. Not everybody has this gift, this insight; it hasn't been given to them. Whenever someone has a ready heart for this, the insights and understandings flow freely. But if there is no readiness, any trace of receptivity soon disappears. That's why I tell stories: to create readiness, to nudge the people toward receptive insight." (Matthew 13:10-13)

Narrative theology arises from the same cultural and historical fabric as Thirteeners themselves. Wounded by the past and hopeless about the future, my generation hungers for a story that will bring cohesion and sense to our chaotic lives. Narrative evangelism provides that story.

But there is a risk.

The danger of narrative lies in the inherent problems of postmodernity: the belief that feelings and experience supersede logic and reason, that relativism supersedes absolutism, that subjective interpretation and application supersede objective truth and verification. A story is a starting point, not a conclusion. In Jesus' hands a story was a powerful tool for illumination and persuasion, but he never stopped with a story. Stories attract us, involve us and tug at our emotions, but Jesus always went on to appeal to the intellect and the will. Yes, stories can make us think as well as feel—and the stories of Jesus are definitely thought-provoking. But thinking is not enough. Feeling is not enough. Jesus always went on to call people to respond, to act and to commit themselves.

Though the teaching of Jesus was primarily narrative, it was not exclusively narrative. Some of his most effective teaching was direct, didactic and propositional. Here are some examples, as rendered by Eugene Peterson's street-level paraphrase of the New Testament, *The Message* (Colorado Springs: NavPress, 1993):

> You're familiar with the old written law, "Love your friend," and its unwritten companion, "Hate your enemy." I'm challenging that. I'm telling you to love your enemies. Let them bring out the best in you, not the worst. When someone gives you a hard time, respond with the energies of prayer, for then you are working out of your true selves, your God-created selves. (Matthew 5:43-45)
>
> Let me give you a new command: Love one another. In the same way I loved you, you love one another. This is how everyone will recognize that you are my disciples—when they see the love you have for each other. (John 13:34-35)

Like Jesus, we have to go beyond stories. We have to state our truth. Stories can carry an enormous cargo of truth and meaning, but stories can't carry it all. If we do not make some propositional statements along with our storytelling, we fall into the trap of postmodernism, which suggests that all meaning resides in the hearer's interpretation of the story. As Christians we take the position that there truly is objective truth, and we will not allow our stories—or our Story with a capital *S*—to be left only to the subjective interpretation of the hearer.

How do we tell our own story to others? Each of us has a unique, one-of-a-kind story, yet evangelist Lon Allison has suggested two "story outlines" covering the two principal ways that people come to Christ. Someone has suggested that Christian conversion takes place either as the budding of a rose or as the sting of a bee. Budding and blooming occurs over a long process. A bee sting happens in an instant. For example, my uncle Billy Graham can tell you the story of the exact moment when he decided for Christ—the date, the place, the time of day, the circumstances, the feelings. His wife, Ruth Bell Graham, can't tell you when she committed her life to Christ. In the same way, my dad can tell you the story of his conversion, but my mom cannot.

What about you? What was your conversion like—the budding of a rose or the sting of a bee? Whichever analogy fits your story, there is a model or pattern that you can use, as developed by Lon Allison.

Model 1: "Bee Sting Conversion." For those who experienced conversion in a single point in time.

☐ Your life before Christ. Describe your family life, your pain, your needs, your searching.

☐ Your introduction to Christ. Describe the person who introduced you to Christ—what was that person like? How were your misconceptions of Christ changed? How did Christ seem to meet your deepest needs?

☐ Your life since Christ. What changes have you experienced as a result? How have you experienced more joy than before? What doubts, struggles and disappointments have you had? Remember: it's important to be honest and transparent.

Model 2: "Budding Rose Conversion." For those who experienced conversion through a process over time.

☐ Encounter with Christ. Describe your early life and how Christ was involved.

☐ Crisis or special encounter with God. Describe how one or more events brought you to a deeper understanding of the gospel and deeper trust in Christ. How did you learn to gradually commit more and more of yourself as a result?

☐ Your life in Christ today. Describe how Christ is making a difference in your life today.

Living the Story

We should also remember that in narrative evangelism our story is not just what we say, it is how we live. We must not only tell our story but also embody it. A story that is well told affects the mind and the emotions of the hearer. A story that is well lived can't help but change lives.

My wife, Carly, tells her story as she listens with compassion to the brokenness around her at school and at work, and as she authentically shares how God has mended the broken places in her own life.

My friend John works in the world of finance—a world that is often riddled with greed and slippery ethics. John tells his story as he demonstrates Christlike integrity and morality in the secular business world.

My friend Linda tells her story to her neighbors as she generously shares her time and her resources with those who have been less fortunate.

My attorney friend Dave tells his story as he stands for justice and righteous principles in legal minefields and battlefields.

My musician friend Richard tells his story as he sings in clubs and bars. Like Jesus, he goes where the "sinners and tax collectors" are, where college students congregate to get wasted, to zone out. He tells his story through his words, his songs and the life he leads—and people listen.

My friend Deb tells her story—not a story of saintly perfection, but of struggle and even confusion. When talking to her friends she frankly admits her doubts but also tells how she holds on to what she knows to be true about Jesus Christ. She is totally straight-up—and her friends respect that, and they listen to her story.

I tell my story by being open and vulnerable about the pain and struggles I've experienced over the death of my brother, about the pressures of growing up as a member of a highly visible Christian family and about the periods of sin and rebelliousness in my life.

We all tell our stories—which are subplots of the great story of Jesus—whenever we give Jesus the credit and the honor for giving us the strength and hope to continue pressing on through life, even though the world has gone bust all around us. My generation hungers for role models who will exemplify what it means to live out an honest, gritty, gutsy faith in a user-unfriendly world. When they hear our story and see us living that story out on a day-by-day basis, they will be amazed. They will be disbelieving and wary at first. They will want to test the authenticity of this story. They will want to know more. But in time they will hear, they will understand, and they will respond.

Xers & Xians

I went with Josie to her recovery
group meetings for a couple weeks," Barry recalls. "Then she asked me to stop coming with her. She said she needed to go it alone so she could speak freely in the meetings. I felt, like, cut out and sidelined—but I respected her feelings and I gave her some space.

"That was about three months ago. Then just a couple weeks ago we went out for coffee. She was really agitated, nervous, you know? I'd never seen her like that. I'm like, 'Man, what's with Josie? Is this bad news, or what?'

"Well, she started talking, and everything she said sounded like the big kiss-off. I thought, 'Whoa! She's breaking up with me!' Then she started talking about this problem she had. An eating disorder, you know? Bulimia. I'd heard about it, of course. Everybody's heard about it. It's one of those Oprah-Donahue-Sally Jessy Raphael topics. But I never knew someone who actually had it. And as Josie kept talking it suddenly hits me: the reason Josie sounds like she's breaking up with me is that she thinks *I'm* going to break up with *her!* She thinks I'm going to be so grossed out by her bulimia that I won't love her anymore.

"So I take her hands in mine and tell her everything's okay. Well, a big change comes over her then—a big sense of relief. And she begins to talk about how this is, like, an answer to her prayers. When she said 'prayers,' I thought, 'Whoa! I never knew Josie was religious!'

"It turns out that Josie has really gotten into church and stuff. She says she found Jesus in her Twelve Step program. Now, I didn't mind having a girlfriend who's bulimic, but I didn't know if I could deal with a girlfriend who's a born-againer. But the more Josie and I talk about it, the more I think everything's okay. She says she still has a lot of unanswered questions, but she says she understands enough to keep on trusting Jesus.

"She hasn't had a bulimic episode now for a couple months. She has a friend in the group—her name is Sondra—and whenever Josie gets to where she thinks she can't handle it without bingeing, she calls Sondra, and Sondra, like, talks her down from the ledge, you know? She supports Josie and prays with her. She's been Josie's lifeline. Josie says, 'Jesus and Sondra keep me sober.' I'd never thought of bingeing on food as getting drunk, but that's the way Josie looks at it. The other day she said, 'I've been sober a month now! Let's celebrate!' So we went over to Screwballs for some standup comedy.

"She's a lot happier now. She doesn't, you know, brood all the time like she used to. She isn't as sarcastic about life as she used to be. She doesn't get into those crying jags as much as she used to. She even smiles. She never used to smile before. I really like her smile.

"Personally I'm not interested in this Jesus stuff. If there was a way to be like Jesus without becoming a born-againer, I might be interested. I meet those Jesus fanatics on the street and at the mall and even in my e-mail box on CompuNet, and they give me the shudders. I just hope Josie doesn't turn into one of those."

My Friends, My Generation
Barry and Josie are composites—fictional characters made up of bits and pieces of real people, glued together with story elements that

actually happened in some cases and that could have happened in others. This entire book has been marbled with fiction in the same way fudge-ripple ice cream is marbled with rich, dark fudge.

Some people mistakenly think that fiction is the opposite of truth—that is, that fiction is a kind of lie. You and I both know better. We know that the true purpose of fiction is not to lie to us but to give us a new and different perspective on the truth through the medium of a story.

The best fiction is that which is made out of bits and pieces of truth. I don't pretend that the fictional dimension of this book constitutes great fiction, but I have tried to build these stories out of truth. Barry and Josie, Lindsey and Grant, T.J. and Marisa, John and Kim, Natalia, Cassie, Jerry, Perry, Brennan and Michael—as this book has taken shape, these people have become real to me because they are so much like real people I know.

Now I'd like to introduce you to some of the real people in my life: my friends, my acquaintances, my peers, my generation. These people are not fictional characters. They are not composites. They are living, breathing examples of the truths and principles I have attempted to present in this book.

Scott and Susie

> Be ready to speak up and tell anyone who asks why you're living the way you are. (1 Peter 3:15)

"Hey, Kevin!"

I was walking through the frozen-food section of Kroger's when I heard my name. I turned and scanned the faces around me. I didn't recognize anyone. Well, maybe someone was calling some other Kevin. I turned around and started walking—then I heard it again.

"Hey you! Kevin Ford! Don't you remember me?"

I turned, and there, just a few yards away, stood a guy with a grin as big as life—but I still didn't have a clue who he was! He walked toward me, stuck out his hand and said, "We haven't seen each other since high school. All-State Wind Ensemble." Then he added slyly, "You played second-chair trumpet, I played first, remember?"

Recognition dawned as I gripped his hand, laughing. "Hey, the way I remember it, you played second chair, I played first!"

"Well—I guess we traded back and forth, didn't we?"

"Scott Edlein! How long has it been? Seven years? Eight?"

"Nine." Scott gestured toward a young woman a few feet away. "Kevin, I want you to meet my wife, Susie."

And that was how I renewed acquaintance with Scott Edlein. For the next few weeks I kept running into Scott at the gym where I worked out. Soon we were playing racquetball and golf together on a semiregular basis. What had been a nodding acquaintance in high school soon became a real friendship. We had Scott and Susie over for dinner a few weeks later. Carly and Susie hit it off right away. We learned that Scott had been working in sales since graduating from the University of North Carolina and that Susie was in her last year of law school, planning to work in litigation with a firm in Atlanta the next year.

The more time I spent with Scott, the more interests I discovered we had in common. Scott and I both majored in speech communications at UNC, though I didn't even know he was attending there at the time. We like the same music and the same sports. In fact, we are both fanatical about NCAA basketball—both of us are from North Carolina, where basketball is sometimes confused with religion! The only place where Scott and I are not in sync is in the area of spirituality.

Once on the golf course Scott and I talked about Christianity. He liked most Christians he had met, but, being Jewish, he was turned off by people who said Jesus is the only way. After finishing the round I had a feeling our conversation had been a little strained. I didn't like that feeling. Scott is a friend, a buddy. I didn't want him to think I saw him as an "evangelistic project." I concluded that maybe I was trying to force something that wasn't really there. Scott and I continued to get together at the gym and on the golf course, but we didn't have another "spiritual" conversation for several months.

One night Susie was out of town, so Carly and I had Scott over for dinner. He put *Swamp Ophelia* by the Indigo Girls on my stereo, and we listened for a while. One of the cuts on that CD is "The Wood Song," which contains the lines

No way construction of this tricky plan

Was built by other than a greater hand

With a love that passes all our understanding.

"What do you think those lines mean?" asked Scott.

"Sounds to me like she's searching for Christ," I said.

"Where do you hear that in the song?"

"She doesn't mention Christ by name, of course, but listen to that one line where she says, 'We get to have some answers when we reach the other side.' You know, Emily Saliers, who wrote and sang 'The Wood Song,' is the daughter of a minister. It sounds like she knows who Jesus Christ is but has not yet been able to make a commitment to him."

Well, Scott and I had an absolutely fascinating discussion that night.

A few weeks later Scott and Susie joined Carly and me on a trip to the mountains. I gave them an early draft of the manuscript for this book and let them read it. You might think it's a little weird, asking friends who make no claim to be Christians to give me feedback on an evangelism book! The fact is, they liked it.

"Your book reminded me of a lot of stuff I hadn't thought about in years," said Susie. "You know, stuff from my Catholic upbringing. I still flash back on a horrible experience I had in confirmation class—a teacher who was absolutely monstrous. It was ten years ago, but it really scarred my mind." As she told us the story she dabbed at her eyes. The memories still stung her.

"I just don't see why it's so important," added Scott, "to believe in one specific God, the God of this group or that sect. I mean, does God really say, 'You Baptists have it right,' or, 'You Presbyterians stumbled pretty close to the truth, but you Muslims, you Jews, you Catholics, you Buddhists got it all screwed up. To hell with you'? Any God worth worshiping has got to be more fair than that. The Protestants believe in one God; so do the Catholics, so do the Jews and the Muslims. Who's to say they don't all worship the same God?"

So we talked about spiritual things for a while; then the conversation veered off in other directions. Someone got out a deck of cards, and we played Spades until midnight. Some weeks later I wrote up the story you are reading right now and showed it to Scott and Susie. They agreed to let me use their story in this book.

To this day neither Scott nor Susie has made a decision for Christ. One day maybe they will. That's not up to me. That's between them and God. If they never become Christians that will not affect our friendship, because our friendship isn't based on whether or not they respond to our gospel. I love them as friends, and that's why I want them to know Jesus Christ. They know what I believe and how much I care about them, but I won't ram my gospel down their throats. My Christian faith doesn't get in the way of our friendship, and I think the reason it doesn't is that both Scott and Susie know that our friendship is real and human—not programmed or scripted to produce a certain result.

I'm not responsible for Scott's spirituality, nor am I responsible for Susie's. The spiritual journey of every human being on the planet is an individual matter, purely between that person and God. My only responsibility is to love God, to love people and to share his love with my friends. If that gives God an opportunity to move into someone's life through a process called "conversion," that's beautiful. But it's not my job to force the issue.

Process evangelism requires that we be willing to say, "I just want to be a friend to others. I will love them unconditionally. If God can use me as a factor in bringing someone to a point of conversion, that's great. If not—well, that's up to God."

Bruce

Anyone united with the Messiah gets a fresh start, is created new.
The old life is gone; a new life burgeons! (2 Corinthians 5:17)
My friend Bruce told me a story from his childhood that summed up what his early years were like. One day when he was about eight his dad told him to clean up his room. Like eight-year-old kids typically do, Bruce decided to have fun first, obey later. Instead of cleaning up his room he went out bike riding. While riding through his neighborhood he rounded a corner and found himself in the path of a car. There was no time to avoid a collision, and hardly even time to realize what was happening.

Bruce doesn't remember being hit by the car. He only remembers waking up in a hospital room with his father towering over him, looking grim and tightlipped. "What happened?" murmured Bruce. "What am I doing here?"

With a glower of irritation on his face, Bruce's father replied, "Why didn't you clean your room like I told you?"

Looking back on that experience, Bruce says he just thought it was normal to get a reprimand instead of concern from his father after being nearly killed by an oncoming car. "I just thought that was how families were supposed to be," he recalls. "Only after comparing notes on family background with other people did I find out that my childhood was what they call 'dysfunctional.'

"I'm not angry about my childhood," Bruce says today.

My life was what it was, and I accept it. I've learned to accept the fact that life in my house was never easy. Dad was never around much—he concentrated on his job. When I was eight years old, he and Mom divorced, and then he left home for good. I didn't realize how much the divorce affected me until years later. But it did affect me, and it affected my whole family. I think there's a direct cause-and-effect relationship between the divorce and the conflict we had growing up and the fact that my brother is a recovering addict and my sister ran away at seventeen, got married and is now divorced.

I had little contact with my dad from then on. I learned to make do and take care of myself and my family. I think the insecurity I experienced as a child motivated me to reach for a fast-track career and a secure income. That's why I opted to go into engineering. While I was in the engineering program at Virginia Tech I looked around and saw a lot of kids with intact families. That's when the reality and the anger I felt toward my dad really sank in. It was more than ten years after the fact, but that's when it hit me.

At one point I wrote my dad a letter telling him how angry I was that he never helped me grow up. He responded with a brief note: "Sorry you feel that way." That really hurt. So on Father's Day I went to a card store and picked out a card that thanked him for all he had done for me and praised him for all his wonderful qualities—you know, "Thanks for being such a great dad!" He didn't have to be a genius to get my sarcasm.

I enjoyed college life. I partied on weekends and studied hard through the week. I had a couple of good friends, including my best friend, Dave, who was a Christian. Though I had grown up going to church and I believed in God, my idea of Christianity was that if I was "good enough" God would accept me when I died. Trouble was, I was never sure if I was "good enough." Dave was a good example to me of how a Christian should live, and I started going to church with him.

In the fall of my sophomore year, Dave sat down with me and explained the gospel to me. I agreed with him point by point, but when he asked if there was anything keeping me from making a decision for Jesus Christ, I said, "Yes, there is." I still felt I had to be "good enough" before I could become a Christian. I was trying to clean myself up so I would be acceptable to God. Later I talked with one of the church elders, and he explained the gospel to me again. I saw that I didn't need to clean myself up—that's what Jesus came to do.

When I look back on my friendship with Dave, two facts stand out. First, Dave was really my friend. I wasn't some evangelistic project to assuage his guilt. He genuinely cared for me. We had the same interests—engineering and racquetball—and we enjoyed hanging out together.

Second, if Dave hadn't verbally shared the gospel with me, I never would have known it. I had grown up in a quasi-religious environment, but I needed to hear the gospel. Otherwise I might have spent my whole life trying to live up to an impossible standard without understanding grace and the meaning of the cross.

Today I'm involved in full-time Christian ministry. Being a Christian gives me a whole new perspective on my family. I no longer look at everything in my family as bad. God has taken away the anger and bitterness I felt. He's helping me rebuild a relationship with my dad.

Not long ago I was working in my dad's shop while I was visiting him. He said he was going inside to take a shower, but he just sorta hung around. He was obviously struggling to say something. Finally, he said, "Bruce, I want you to know I did everything I could to keep you." He broke down in tears—a first for me. For the first time I'm able to see some positive aspects of my family, no matter how dysfunctional it was.

Greg

What came into existence was life, and the Life was Light to live by. The Life-Light blazed out of the darkness; the darkness couldn't put it out. (John 1:4-5)

My friend Greg didn't know where he was going—but he was going fast. "I started using drugs when I was six," he recalls, "and I kept using till I was twenty. I started casually, but soon my whole life was controlled by chemical substances. I lived for the stuff. Drugs were my only friend—my only escape from the pain of being sexually and emotionally abused by my parents."

My mom was a single parent from the time I was five until she remarried when I was ten. She never had much time for me. She dated a lot and tried to keep me in the background. My emotional needs were not a priority with her. The guy she married when I was ten was a sexual abuser. He was always either abusing me or beating me or threatening me. My fear of this guy was continuous—twenty-four hours a day, seven days a week. I never knew what to say or how to act around him because anything could set him off.

I attempted suicide numerous times—the first time when I was eight. By age twenty I had been a guest of every psychiatric institution in the state. I was diagnosed with all sorts of psychiatric problems, and every doctor had his own opinion of what my problem was. None of them ever came up with the diagnosis I now believe to be the truth: I was experiencing normal emotional reactions to a horrible and abnormal existence.

My adolescent and early adult life was painted black, and I was involved in a cult that practiced black arts and necromancy. I got really scared. I thought the drugs and the black forces in my life were going to destroy me. It was really an act of desperation when I went into a Twelve Step program to get clean. Through the Steps I found a Higher Power that loved me and wanted the best for me.

Before I got into recovery I would end up every night on my belly, feeling like the lowest creature in the world. I often asked God to just take my life. But instead he gave me back my life—or he took it for his own use, which is fine with me. I've been drug-free now for seven years.

After several years in recovery I began to want more than an anonymous but loving Higher Power. I wanted someone to have a real relationship with—a God with a name and a face. I took some calculated risks. I moved to Charleston to live with my grandparents and attended a religious college, Charleston Southern. I walked onto campus looking like something out of a Harley-Davidson movie, and I scared a lot of people. I mean, I thought of myself as a spiritual person. I thought the people who had verses on their dorm walls were religious fanatics, not living in the real world. I didn't understand how messed-up I still was, so I had some humbling experiences ahead.

I went through an emotionally devastating romantic relationship, involving sinful and dysfunctional behavior. She broke up with me after three months, and that hurt me a lot. The only thing that brought me peace was reading the Bible. Soon I was putting Bible verses up on my walls too—and then it hit me that the people I had dismissed as "religious fanatics" *were* living in the real world. I had been the one who had been living in a fog of fantasy and unreality. God's Word is reality.

I'm still in process today—still moving forward. I'm off most medications such as antidepressants, though I still take medication for a digestive disorder I have as a result of my emotional history. I'm not in counseling anymore. I've learned to give my emotions and my problems over to Christ. I have a sense of purpose and meaning in life. I know I have a loving Father—God, who has created me in his image. I once had a loaded gun to my head, but now I have Jesus Christ—and that fact gives me hope for healing and hope for the future.

Debbie

Jesus graciously welcomed them and talked to them about the kingdom of God. Those who needed healing, he healed. (Luke 9:11)

I met Debbie the first day I moved into my apartment complex. We talked about the usual generic subjects that day: the weather, where to go grocery shopping, where to find the cheapest video rentals. Nearly every day when I got home from work she was around.

Over the weeks as we got acquainted as neighbors, I picked up bits and pieces of information about her family. I learned that her sister was a drug addict. Her parents had abused her. She lived alone and had a lot of fear about being alone in the world.

Debbie also got to know me. She learned I was involved in full-time Christian ministry, and the walls went up immediately. "I don't want to talk about God," she said. "That's too personal. I really don't have a lot of respect for Christians . . . I mean, you seem okay, but Christians in general are just hypocrites—always asking for money, always pushing their views on other people, stuff like that."

I cooled the religious talk for a while, hoping to allay her fears. Over the next few months her ability to trust gradually grew. So did our friendship as neighbors. She opened up about the pain in her life. Her scars were evident, and she was having trouble coping with her painful emotions and broken memories. She was in therapy, but her therapist didn't seem to be helping much. It seemed like the perfect time, after months of keeping our conversations on a secular level, to talk about God.

But something inside me told me to wait. So I waited. What was I waiting for? I was waiting for her to initiate a conversation about spiritual things.

One day she asked me about my life. I told her about some of the problems and pain I have gone through. I told her about the hurt of losing my brother Sandy to a heart condition. I told her about the pressures I had experienced growing up in a highly visible family, the son of Leighton Ford, the nephew of Billy Graham. She was an avid listener and seemed to ponder everything I told her very carefully.

A few nights later I was going out the door, headed for a church meeting, when Debbie stopped me in the hall. I had a few minutes, so we chatted—just another casual conversation. She was trying to understand what I did for a living. (I was a minister in a church at the time.) She couldn't understand it. Then she asked again what my dad did for a living. I had told her before, but the concept was strange to her.

"What my dad does in his way," I said, "and what I do in my way on campus is to tell people the story of Jesus. We call that the gospel— the good news. It's the story about how God created us to be in a relationship with him. But because of our shortcomings—what we call sin—we've broken that relationship. It's just like a broken relationship in your own family, where one person commits an offense and communication and closeness break down as a result. In order to rebuild that broken relationship, Jesus died on a cross. He's kind of like a bridge between God and us. All we have to do is commit our lives to him and ask him to forgive us, and then he does. He forgives us, and he comes into us to live his life through us. Have you ever asked God to do that in your life?"

She shook her head.

"Well, you may want to think about asking him sometime," I said, trying to be as casual and nonthreatening as I could be while still urging her to give her life to Christ. "Anyway," I concluded, "that's what my dad does—and that's what I do over at the church."

I was surprised to see tears welling up in her eyes. "I've never done that," she said. "I've never asked God to forgive me and to live in my life."

"Well, would you like to pray right now?"

"Yeah," she said, "I would."

So we knelt down and prayed, and Debbie gave her life to Christ.

She still calls about two or three times a year, and she always mentions that night—the night she gave her life to Christ.

John

> This exuberant giving and receiving, this endless knowing and understanding—all this came through Jesus, the Messiah. (John 1:17)

John points to a number of influences along the way that led to his discovery of Jesus Christ. Most of all, he credits the influence of three special friends.

"I grew up in the church," John recalls, "but I was definitely not following Jesus. During junior high I got involved with drugs, especially marijuana and alcohol. Looking back, I would estimate I spent approximately five thousand hours of my life intoxicated. By the time I got to college I was tapering off of drugs and drink, but I'd still party and get wasted from time to time."

> My sophomore year in college I lived on the same floor as three crazy Christians. I mean, these guys were different from the typical Christians I had met before. They were just cool guys who liked to hang out and do the things most guys like to do, except they be-

lieved in Jesus and they kept their lives clean. I liked to skateboard and play guitar, and sometimes these guys would board or jam with me. Our floor liked playing the war game Risk, and these guys entered in too—sometimes leading the way in a path of simulated destruction! I didn't feel like they were trying to convert me. They were just my friends, and when we talked about spiritual things it clearly grew out of a genuine concern for me. I could talk about spiritual things with them because I trusted them.

One time a buddy and I were getting stoned, and one of these Christians, Scott, came by the room. We asked him if he wanted to join in the festivities, but he so, "No, that's all right. I get high on God, dude." He was smiling, friendly, with not a bit of judgment in his voice. He just made a different choice with his life. I remember thinking, *Wow! Can you really get high on God?* I was intrigued, and that's when I decided to check it out and see if Jesus was really God.

I began attending a Bible study on the Gospel of Mark. I credit my three Christian buddies with arousing my curiosity about Jesus. I thought I knew who Jesus was from all my years in the church. Probably there had been loving Christians all around me then, but I just didn't get it. Now I do. The Jesus my friends talked about was totally different from my old notions. I also saw Jesus living in their lives. They often let homeless people stay with them in their dorm rooms. A lot of people think compassion is just flipping a quarter to a guy with a "Will Work for Food" sign, but these guys really cared about people.

I can't point to a single moment of conversion. I spent a year studying the Bible and talking it over with these guys and watching their lives. I went through a slow, gradual process of coming to a place where I could say, "Yeah, I'm following Jesus." Getting high on Jesus is not what I pictured when Scott first used that term. It's not like getting stoned. It's better. It's infinitely better than anything else in the world.

My Own Story

Now I take limitations in stride, and with good cheer, these limitations that cut me down to size—abuse, accidents, opposition, bad breaks. I just let Christ take over! And so the weaker I get, the stronger I become. (2 Corinthians 12:10)

I have a story too. It is a story of many chapters and, God willing, with many chapters still to be written. God has given me the privilege of sharing portions of my story with different people in recent years, including people who have been hurting or broken by grief. He has even used my story as a factor in drawing several people to himself.

One of the most difficult chapters of my life began when I was ten years old. That's when I found out that my older brother, Sandy, had a serious health problem. Just before his fifteenth birthday Sandy was trying out for the junior-high basketball team. After practice he started feeling faint and turned pale. He was immediately rushed to the emergency room of the hospital. They found his pulse was racing at an incredible 360 beats per minute. After several hours they were able to control his heartbeat and save his life. But this was only the beginning for my brother.

As a ten-year-old, I wasn't sure what was happening when they took Sandy to Duke University Medical Center for surgery. All I knew was that something was wrong with Sandy's heart and they were going to fix it. I later learned that the condition he had was called Wolfe-Parkeson-White (WPW) syndrome. The heartbeat, regulated by an electrical pulse, is transmitted via the A-V (atrioventricular) node, which is located on a wall of muscle within the heart. The A-V node keeps the various chambers pulsing in sync with each other. A person with WPW has nerve pathways that bypass this regulator, causing the heart to "misfire" and beat rapidly or erratically.

Sandy recovered quickly from the surgery, and my own concerns for his health receded into the background. I now understand, however, that Sandy was living every moment with a changed perspective and a crystalline awareness of his own mortality. He was elected president of his high-school class, and he was on the track team, where he became one of the outstanding milers in North Carolina. He was well respected by his friends for his commitment to Christ.

After high school Sandy attended the University of North Carolina, where he quickly became a leader in InterVarsity Christian Fellowship and president of the freshman honor society. His junior year he contemplated a run for student body president. Sandy was an outstanding young man in every way: academically, athletically, socially and spiritually. He lived every moment for Christ, cherishing every day of life as an irreplaceable gift from God.

Then one night the nightmare started all over. I had just come back from a Young Life Club at my school and found my parents looking grim. Wiping tears from his eyes, my dad said, "Sandy's had another heart attack. He's in the hospital at Chapel Hill." The doctors had thought Sandy's heart problems were solved with the first surgery when he was fifteen. But Sandy's problem was elusive and fooled the doctors. He was now in more serious trouble than the first time.

The day Sandy underwent his second surgery I was spending the weekend at Windy Gap, a Young Life camp in North Carolina. I assumed this surgery would go as smoothly as the first. So when I received a phone call midway through the surgery, I was stunned. "They're having some problems with Sandy's surgery," I was told. "Please be praying." Tears streaming, I sat down next to the basketball court with a couple of friends and prayed harder than I had ever prayed in my life.

It was around 7:30 that evening when I suddenly felt the strongest sensation deep within me—a feeling that Sandy was speaking to me. "Goodby, Kevin," he said. "I love you." I felt a presence and a loss all at the same time.

Just a few minutes later a car pulled up, and my Uncle Billy got out and walked over to me. "Kevin," he said, "your brother Sandy has gone home to be with the Lord."

I looked him in the eye, searching his face for some ray of hope— some slim possibility that this was a mistake. *Sandy can't be dead,* I thought. *Not Sandy! How can they be sure?*

But Sandy was dead. The world suddenly seemed black and over-shadowed. And I began to cry in big, racking sobs. My brother—my friend—was not in my world anymore.

Uncle Billy took me home. On arriving I found my two best friends, Richard and Charles, waiting for me. They didn't say much or do much. But they were there. Over the next few months and years they walked beside me through my grief. I didn't have the answers to life's problems. I still don't. Sandy had so much potential, so much ability, so much integrity, so much desire to be a man of God. Why did God let him die? To this day I don't know.

But I do know that God was with me in my pain. He was present through the caring and the prayers of Charles and Richard and many other friends and loved ones. As I underwent the most difficult trial I had ever experienced in my young life, I learned that only a relationship with Christ can give us hope in those times of complete darkness and loss.

Skeptics and agnostics sometimes tell me that Christianity is a crutch—and I agree. Wounded people need a crutch. There have certainly been times when I needed a crutch to support me through life because I couldn't get through it alone.

We are all wounded people. We all need a crutch. We all need a Great Physician. We all need healing. Jesus is our physician. He wants to touch us and heal us at our point of need.

Some people argue that our evangelism shouldn't deal with "felt needs," but I strongly disagree. It is our need, our pain and our woundedness that God so often uses to drive us to him. It is precisely our need that reminds us of our fallibility and finiteness and confronts us with the fact that there is Someone beyond ourselves who is worthy of our devotion. When we feel no need of him, our tendency is to go our own self-sufficient way.

We all come to Christ with an understanding of our need for him. I know very few people who simply run to Christ out of an innate desire to glorify him. We all tend to be driven by our needs. Some of us have experienced hurt, grief and despair, so we go to Christ for healing. Others fear hell and punishment, so they go to Christ for refuge. Others are lonely and need to be a part of a community, so they cling Christ and his church for fellowship and belonging.

I've never seen any indication in the New Testament that we shouldn't appeal to the neediness of pre-Christians. Need is the great attention-getter. Need is the great motivator. Need is the great revealer of eternal issues. And this is good news for all of us who want to reach this generation for Jesus Christ, because Generation X is a needy generation. Their need is God's opportunity.

Our Story: Tell It and Live It
In 1994 Douglas Coupland followed his 1991 novel *Generation X* with

a new book, *Life After God* (New York: Pocket Books, 1994). In that book he again articulates the unspoken cry of my generation:

> Now—here is my secret: I tell it to you with an openness of heart that I doubt I shall ever achieve again, so I pray that you are in a quiet room as you hear these words. My secret is that I need God—that I am sick and can no longer make it alone. I need God to help me give, because I no longer seem to be capable of giving; to help me be kind, as I no longer seem capable of kindness; to help me love, as I seem beyond being able to love. (p. 359)

The hunger for God is there, and it gnaws at the vitals of my generation. The people I meet and talk to on campuses and in the marketplace every day want what God has to offer. They want to know the degree of giving, kind, unconditional love that Jesus came to bring us. They are afraid, angry, alienated and depressed, and they are accelerating into a frightening future at warp speed. They are in crisis, obsessed with death and prone to suicide. They are distrustful of authority and wary of the system. They cannot conceive of "true truth." Their past is full of pain, and their future is a brick wall. To them, the world is user-unfriendly, overcomplicated, chaotic and unstructured. Obviously this is a generation with many needs, and each of those needs is an opportunity for God and his story.

But the story must be told well. If it is told via media, it must be told in a sophisticated way with the same fast-paced excitement and electric style that Xers have come to demand of all their media—and it must be accompanied by a real human touch. If it is told by word, we must avoid commercializing and packaging the story. It must flow from our hearts and our experience. If it is told by our lives as an embodied gospel, it must be told with authenticity, caring and seamless integrity.

To a generation torn by division and violence we bring a story of reconciliation and peace. To a generation that hungers for belonging, for justice and for reparenting in a functional family system we bring a story of a new way of life—a new family system in which there is no racist, sexist or economic division and where all are equal and accepted in Jesus Christ. To an empty postmodern generation we bring the story of One who fills the holes in our souls and who opens the door to transcendent, supernatural realities. To a generation that has lost its sense of direction, that has lost its belief in objective truth, that has become drenched in death and mourning, we bring the story of the way, the truth and the life.

To summarize all that we have explored in this book, here are the keys to reaching Generation X:

☐ Move toward the Xer's worldview. Don't just witness but listen, understand and identify.

☐ Demonstrate authentic love to Xers. My generation hungers for— and responds to—loyalty, friendship, caring, acceptance, affirmation, integrity and transparency.

☐ Build trust through unconditional acceptance.

☐ Never breach a trust or break a confidence.

☐ Focus on authentic friendship. Avoid doing or saying anything that suggests that a Thirteener is your "evangelistic project" or a "potential convert."

☐ Demonstrate and embody a faith that works. Be open about your own struggles and issues. Be involved in applying your faith to the issues and problems around you. Let pre-Christians know that your faith is your foundation, not an add-on.

☐ Demonstrate that Christianity is a relationship with a living Person, not just another religion. Xers hunger for relationships; they are wary of organized religion.

☐ Emphasize Christian joy and freedom, not legalism.

☐ Emphasize Christian community rather than cold institutions or structures.

☐ Emphasize the sense of meaning and purpose that a relationship with Christ brings. Emphasize the place of belonging we have as members of the family of God.

☐ Avoid overintellectualizing the gospel. The gospel is not a technical manual or a philosophical treatise. It is a story.

☐ Don't hesitate to underscore the awe and transcendence of God. Xers are open to the mystery of God's singular and supernatural identity.

☐ Become an "embodied apologetic" by demonstrating tolerance and openness. Avoid trying to elevate your faith by criticizing another faith. Instead of debating the fine points of Christianity, focus on simply telling your own story and the Christian story.

☐ Be sensitive to the emotional pain of the Xer experience. If you have a story of pain in your own life, use it as a bridge of connection and understanding. Listen, then speak.

☐ Be patient. Practice process evangelism. The world leaves Xers little time for reflection, so you should give your Xer friends *extra* time for reflection. Avoid prematurely pushing a person toward commitment and conversion. Earn trust. Earn the right to tell your story. Recognize that you may only be one link in a chain of influences used by the Holy Spirit to bring someone closer to Christ.

☐ Be a storyteller. Practice narrative evangelism. Tell your story (with a small *s*) and link that story to God's Story (capital *S*), showing how God's story has collided with yours, and has changed the course of your life.

Finally—and I've saved this for last because I believe it is the most important key of all:

☐ Pray. Evangelism is not the marketing of a product. It is a process of working in partnership with God to achieve his goals in people's lives. If we cover everything we do and say with prayer, then God can use us even with our blunders and mistakes. If we go out in our own strength, following our own will, then even the most magnificent and eloquent performance of evangelism will produce nothing in human lives. In prayer we don't so much bend God's will to ours; rather, we attune our will and our hearts to his. When we pray we talk to God, we listen to God, then we act under the direction of his Spirit. In every generation, from the generation of Jesus to Generation X, prayer is the foundation of effective evangelism.

So pray, and then tell your story. Let this marginalized generation know that while they may be at the outer edges of an unfeeling society, they are at the center of God's love and God's plan. Let them know that Jesus himself identifies with their low estate, their sorrows, their struggles and their pain. Let them know that in their battle against the system, God is on their side.

The Story of Jesus X

X is the twenty-fourth letter of the English alphabet. It comes from the Greek letter *X* (*chi* or *xi*), which was the first letter in the Greek form of the word *Christ*. From the early days of the Christian church until today, the letter *X* has been a shorthand symbol for *Christ*, as in the abbreviation *Xmas* in place of *Christmas*.

The use of X as a symbol for Christ offends some people. They say, " 'Xmas' takes the Christ out of Christmas." I understand that sentiment, but I don't feel that way. I think X is a fitting symbol for Christ. It looks like a cross—the cross of Christ—tilted on edge. It also looks like a man with feet firmly planted and with arms outstretched in a welcoming gesture. It was a symbol the early Christians cherished as an emblem of their Lord.

Near the beginning of this book, I said there was something unpleasant and disturbing about the letter *X* as a label for my generation—and I still think so. It sounds like "Brand X"—like a blankness or a negation. You draw an X over something you want to eliminate. There is nothing attractive in being labeled an "Xer," a faceless member of "Generation X." Though I've used such labels throughout this book for the sake of clarity and convenience, I have hated having to do so. I think "Generation X" is an ugly label. I don't like being tagged an "Xer."

But you can call me an "Xian" all you want. Paint a big red X on my back. That's fine with me. I will wear the X of Christ proudly. Jesus Christ has redeemed an ugly letter—a symbol of negation and annihilation—and has turned it into something beautiful. With the most evil intent imaginable, the system tried to negate and annihilate Jesus Christ by nailing him to an X—a cross of wood. The system thought it could X out his life and X out his message, and that would be the end of him. The system was wrong. More powerful than the terminator, Jesus promised, "I'll be back."

And he did come back!

He is X, the Christ. And we are Xians, followers and imitators and storytellers of the Christ.

My goal and my prayer is that all of us who are within arm's length and speaking distance of an "Xer" will pray, love, reach out, become involved in the process of that person's life and tell the story of Jesus X, the man of the cross. My goal and my prayer is that you and I will see Xers become Xians and that this generation will be won for God. My goal and my prayer is that someday the ugly term "Generation X" can be invested with a new and beautiful meaning: the Generation of Christ.